Bloom's Modern Critical Views

Bloom's Modern Critical Views

MAYA ANGELOU
New Edition

Edited and with an introduction by
Harold Bloom
Sterling Professor of the Humanities
Yale University

BLOOM'S
LITERARY CRITICISM
An imprint of Infobase Publishing

Bloom's Modern Critical Views: Maya Angelou—New Edition

Copyright ©2009 by Infobase Publishing

Introduction ©2009 by Harold Bloom

Bloom's Literary Criticism
An imprint of Infobase Publishing
132 West 31st Street
New York NY 10001

Library of Congress Cataloging-in-Publication Data

Maya Angelou : edited and with an introduction by Harold Bloom.—New ed.
    p. cm.—(Bloom's modern critical views)
Includes bibliographical references and index.
ISBN 978-1-60413-177-2 (hardcover : alk. paper) 1. Angelou, Maya—Criticism and interpretation. 2. Women and literature—United States—History—20th century. 3. African Americans in literature. I. Bloom, Harold.

PS3551.N464Z76 2008
818'.5409—dc22

                                 2008044406

Cover design by Ben Peterson

Printed in the United States of America
Bang BCL 10 9 8 7 6 5 4 3 2 1

This book is printed on acid-free paper.

Contents

Editor's Note

My introduction attempts to locate the universal American appeal of Maya Angelou's autobiographies in our native gnosis.

The essays here reprinted are social, political, and popular-cultural in their orientation. As the dozen essayists share a common stance and program, I will preface them here as a group. They are generous in their insistence on human rights, and justly proud of Maya Angelou as an exemplary autobiographer of the social struggle. Not much given to formal analysis—which is not wholly relevant to Angelou's work—they do explore most of the contours of their author as a benign contribution to our era's espousal of societal equality.

HAROLD BLOOM

Introduction

Maya Angelou is best known for the initial volume, *I Know Why the Caged Bird Sings*, of her still-ongoing autobiography. Her poetry has a large public, but very little critical esteem. It is, in every sense, "popular poetry," and makes no formal or cognitive demands upon the reader.

Angelou's achievement has a complex relation to at least two among the principal antecedents of African American memoirs: the slave narrative and the church sermon. Since she is a spellbinder of a storyteller, other elements in African American tradition, including the blues and the oral eloquence of street ways, also enter into her work. Though Angelou is essentially a secular biographer, her extraordinary and persistent sense of self, one that rises both through and above experience, seems to me to go back to the African American paradigm of what I have called the American Religion. What survived of West African spirituality, after the torments of the Middle Passage from Africa to America, was the gnosis that early black Baptists in America spoke of as "the little me within the big me." Though converted to the slaveowners' ostensible Christianity, they transformed that European faith by a radical "knowing" that the "little me" or most inward self did not stem from the harsh space and time of the white world, but emanated ultimately from their unfallen cosmos that preceded the Creation-Fall of the whites. Angelou's pervasive sense that what is oldest and best in her own spirit derives from a lost, black fullness of being is one of the strongest manifestations in African American literature of this ancient gnosis.

I think that this is part of the secret of Angelou's enormous appeal to American readers, whether white or black, because her remarkable literary voice speaks to something in the universal American "little me within the big me." Most Americans, of whatever race or ethnic origin, share the sense that experience, however terrible, can be endured because their deepest self is beyond experience and so cannot be destroyed. Particularly in her best book, *I Know Why the Caged Bird Sings,* Angelou achieves an almost unique tone that blends intimacy and detachment, a tone indeed of assured serenity that transcends the fearful humiliations and outrages that she suffered as a girl. Hundreds of thousands of readers have found in *Caged Bird* an implicit image of the resurrection of their own innermost self, a fragment of divinity that transcended natural birth, and so can never die.

   As a poet, Angelou seems best at ballads, the most traditional kind of popular poetry. The function of such work is necessarily social rather than aesthetic, particularly in an era totally dominated by visual media. One has to be grateful for the benignity, humor, and whole-heartedness of Angelou's project, even if her autobiographical prose necessarily centers her achievement.

JAMES ROBERT SAUNDERS

Breaking Out of the Cage:
The Autobiographical Writings of Maya Angelou

In his seminal work, *Black Autobiography in America* (1974), Stephen Butterfield establishes the existence of a black autobiographical tradition that
has its roots in the American slave narrative, a genre "so powerful, so con-
vincing a testimony of human resource, intelligence, endurance, and love in
the face of tyranny, that, in a sense, it sets the tone for most subsequent black
American writing." Acknowledging the slave narrative form as an essential
base, Butterfield goes on to specify certain characteristics as being consistent
across the spectrum of slave narratives and on into the twentieth century,
influencing such relatively modern works as Booker T. Washington's *Up
From Slavery* (1901) and Richard Wright's *Black Boy* (1945). There is, in all
of these works, the initial instance of resistance, a denial of the then existing caste system. Of equal importance is the struggle for education, often in
the midst of difficult circumstances. That education is sometimes formal as
in the case of Booker T. Washington who attended Hampton Institute. At
other times, it is informal as with Frederick Douglass who, in his *Narrative
of the Life of Frederick Douglass* (1845), recounts having been secretly tutored
by his slavemaster's wife.

It is, furthermore, Butterfield's contention that a physical movement between geographical regions has been part of that literary tradition, a given in
slave narratives where virtually all of the authors first had to escape southern

Hollins Critic, Volume 28, Number 4 (October 1991): pp. 1–11. Copyright © 1991 The
Hollins Critic.

slavery and then make their way north before being in a position to record the events of their lives. Such geographical movement has been particularly important in the life and autobiographies of the artist Maya Angelou, described by Butterfield as one who "does not submit tamely to the cage. She is repeatedly thrust into situations where she must act on her own initiative to save herself and thereby learns the strength of self-confidence." Butterfield here makes specific reference to Angelou's first autobiographical installment, *I Know Why the Caged Bird Sings* (1970); however, it actually will be several autobiographical volumes later before the confidence Butterfield refers to evolves into its fullest dimensions.

So much of Angelou's first volume shows her to be the tossed-about victim of circumstance. She was born Marguerite Johnson in 1928, in St. Louis, Missouri. However, at the age of three, she finds herself being shuttled, along with her older brother Bailey, to Stamps, Arkansas, where her paternal grandmother takes up the task of raising her through her formative years. As though it is not enough that she is the offspring of a shattered marriage, she has to live those early years under the tenets of segregation. In *Caged Bird,* the author comments "Stamps, Arkansas, was Chitlin' Switch, Georgia; Hang 'Em High, Alabama; Don't Let the Sun Set on You Here, Nigger, Mississippi; or any other name just as descriptive." The future writer resides in a place where, as critic Myra McMurry has noted, "the caged condition affects almost everyone in her world."

This first autobiography provides detailed testimony to the daily insults visited upon members of Angelou's extended family as well as neighboring blacks who work hard picking cotton, never to get ahead or even see beyond their debilitating financial situations. While her grandmother is indeed the proud owner of a local general store, even that matriarch suffers insults delivered by young, poor white girls who insist on addressing her by her first name, Annie. That grandmother is further outraged when a dentist, to whom she had lent money when he was in danger of losing his practice, now refuses to examine her granddaughter and adamantly proclaims, "I'd rather stick my hand in a dog's mouth than in a nigger's."

After Marguerite and Bailey have lived in Stamps several years, their father appears one day, giving them the impression that he will take them back with him to California. In actuality, he is merely picking them up for deposit with their mother, Vivian Baxter, who was, at the time, still residing in St. Louis. Whether Angelou was seven years old, as she has maintained in some interviews, or eight, as she provides in the autobiography, she is raped (by her mother's boyfriend) and, as a consequence, lapses into a prolonged silence.

Vivian Baxter had never been very good at parental nurturing, so it is accordingly deemed best that the victimized daughter be returned to the grandmother, who is sensitive enough not to force her grandchild to talk.

The silence continues for several years until a teacher, Mrs. Flowers, introduces the young girl to an assortment of literary classics, including the works of Charles Dickens. This educational encounter proves to be a vital turning point, reminding us of an important aspect of American slave narratives. In *Caged Bird*, Angelou explains the sensation of listening to Mrs. Flowers as she read from *A Tale of Two Cities* (1859): "I heard poetry for the first time in my life. . . . Her voice slid in and curved down through and over the words. She was nearly singing." It is Mrs. Flowers who is finally able to get Marguerite to talk, having her read from works that in themselves are demanding recitation. The therapy is so effective that it must have carried over into the writer's own poetic career, in the production of such "oral" poems as "Still I Rise" and "Phenomenal Woman." Lines from the former poem include:

> You may trod me in the very dirt
> But still, like dust, I'll rise. . . .
>
> Did you want to see me broken?
> Bowed head and lowered eyes?
> Shoulders falling down like teardrops,
> Weakened by my soulful cries.
>
> Does my haughtiness offend you?
> Don't you take it awful hard
> 'Cause I laugh like I've got gold mines
> Diggin' in my own back yard.

The following lines make up the other poem's conclusion:

> Now you understand
> Just why my head's not bowed.
> I don't shout or jump about
> Or have to talk real loud.
> When you see me passing
> It ought to make you proud. . . .
> 'Cause I'm a woman
> Phenomenally.
> Phenomenal woman,
> That's me.

Both of those samples are taken from Angelou's third book of poems, *And Still I Rise* (1978), which in general conveys a sense of extreme self-assurance.

However, that is not the condition in which we find Marguerite at the conclusion of *Caged Bird*. Quite the contrary; at the end of this volume, she is sixteen years old and mired in the difficulties of a teenage pregnancy. Having journeyed to California to be finally with her mother, Marguerite had had insecurities about approaching womanhood, thinking it necessary to hurry and get a boyfriend. "A boyfriend," she envisions, "would clarify my position to the world and, even more important, to myself." But a problem is presented: "Understandably the boys of my age and social group were captivated by the yellow- or light-brown-skinned girls, with hairy legs and smooth little lips, and whose hair 'hung down like horses' manes.'" Unfortunately, Marguerite is dark-skinned and six feet tall in a world where the standard of beauty is strict.

So Marguerite must settle for whatever she can get: for instance a one-night stand that, as she puts it, "I not only didn't enjoy . . . but my normalcy was still a question." The movement of the young artist in pursuit of adulthood has become a quite prickly affair with limitations seeming to outweigh the possibilities. It was only fitting that the author should employ a Paul Laurence Dunbar poem as the source for her first volume's title:

Sympathy

I know what the caged bird feels, alas!
    When the sun is bright on the upland slopes;
When the wind stirs soft through the springing grass,
And the river flows like a stream of glass;
When the first bird sings and the first bud opens,
    And the faint perfume from its chalice steals—
I know what the caged bird feels!

I know why the caged bird beats his wing
    Till its blood is red on the cruel bars;
For he must fly back to his perch and cling
When he fain would be on the bough a-swing;
    And a pain still throbs in the old, old scars
And they pulse again with a keener sting—
I know why he beats his wing!

I know why the caged bird sings, ah me,
    When his wing is bruised and his bosom sore,—
When he beats his bars and he would be free;
It is not a carol of joy or glee,
But a prayer that he sends from his heart's deep core,
    But a plea, that upward to Heaven he flings—
I know why the caged bird sings!

Dunbar's caged bird is a brilliantly wrought metaphor, representing human beings locked away from life's wonders.

Angelou is one who has experienced the cage, yet in *Gather Together in My Name* (1974), her second autobiographical installment, we are shown how an individual can be involved in many experiences and still be severely limited. In a 1983 interview, she explained the book's title: "*Gather Together in My Name,* though it does have a biblical origin, comes from the fact I saw so many adults lying to so many young people, lying in their teeth, saying, 'You know, when I was young, I never would have done . . . Why I couldn't . . . I shouldn't . . .' Lying. Young people know when you're lying; so I thought for all those parents and non-parents alike who have lied about their past, I will tell it." And tell it she does. Recapitulating events that took place over a three-year period leading up to her nineteenth birthday, she portrays what it was like having to scratch for every penny, holding jobs such as short-order cook, nightclub waitress and dancer, prostitute, and madam in charge of her own house of prostitution.

We watch aghast as Angelou takes her "first great slide down into the slimy world," volunteering to be a prostitute for a married man, Louis Tolbrook, who is old enough to be her father. Tolbrook is involved with organized crime, owes money to the mob, and, in desperation, helps Marguerite reach this rationalization: "There are married women who are more whorish than a street prostitute because they have sold their bodies for marriage licenses, and there are some women who sleep with men for money who have great integrity because they are doing it for a purpose." In another context, different from Marguerite's situation, we might have been willing to examine that statement more closely for its possible feminist merit. But we detect Tolbrook's manipulation and realize all too well that at the heart of her remark is the same sort of desperation that earlier had led to her teenage pregnancy.

While Marguerite is indeed in the process of developing an independent personality, she nevertheless is obsessed by her yearning for "a man, any man, to give me a June Allyson screen-role life with sunken living room, and cashmere-sweater sets, and I, for one, obviously would have done anything to get that life." She further imagines, "We would live quietly in a pretty little house and I'd have another child, a girl, and the two children (whom he'd love equally) would climb over his knees and I would make three-layer caramel cakes in my electric kitchen until they went off to college." The author, on occasion, has made the comment that she probably would have been a committed housewife had a reasonable opportunity presented itself. As fate would have it, though, the future writer will continue to add on to what is already a myriad of experience.

In *Singin' and Swingin' and Gettin' Merry Like Christmas* (1976), the saga advances with Angelou recalling yet another string of jobs she has had to hold in order to survive. At one point, she says, "My salary from the little real estate office and the dress shop downtown barely paid rent and my son's baby-sitter." Notwithstanding financial difficulty, she refuses to go on welfare, preferring instead simply to move. One such move is from San Diego to San Francisco. The author speaks fondly of her visits to a record shop where she had listened to the music of John Lee Hooker and Charlie Parker. Then we witness a surprise, as she herself characterizes it, when the proprietor of that record store befriends her:

> All my life, my body had been in successful rebellion against my finer nature. I was too tall and raw-skinny. My large extroverted teeth protruded in an excitement to be seen, and I, attempting to thwart their success, rarely smiled. Although I lathered Dixie Peach in my hair, the thick black mass crinkled and kinked and resisted the smothering pomade to burst free around my head like a cloud of angry bees. No, in support of truth, I had to admit Louise Cox was not friendly to me because of my beauty.

The artist, as a young woman, still operates under the assumption that she does not appeal physically to black men. So when a white woman seeks out her friendship, she is impelled to wonder why?

Louise Cox plunges beneath the surface, beyond the superficiality of physical features, and what she finds in turn is a woman of character. She subsequently offers Marguerite a job that will enable her to quit her other two jobs and spend more time with her five-year-old son. Angelou assesses her association with that employer as "my first introduction to an amiable black-white relationship." Previously, the writer had been taught to regard whites with keen suspicion.

Events become even more complex when she meets and is wooed by a white man, Tosh Angelos, who professes Greek origin and has recently "been discharged from the Navy and found a job in an electrical appliance shop." He actually courts her through her son, Clyde, taking him on cable cars to Fisherman's Wharf and the zoo. Marguerite and Tosh marry, and as she prepares for a life of domesticity, she loses her hard won independence. Angelos is dictatorial, forcing her to quit work, quit the church, and then one day he returns home and matter-of-factly states, "I think I'm just tired of being married." Not wanting to appear frivolous, the author has been reluctant to say how many times she has been married. But one can calculate, pretty easily, that this first marriage lasted no longer than three years.

Once again on her own, Marguerite falls back on her industriousness. She finds work at a local bar as a dancer where she must wear a costume that "made stripping absolutely unnecessary." Many a weaker person would have given in to depression, but she maintains a positive perspective, declaring, "Once more adventure had claimed me as its own, and the least I could do was show bravery in my strut and courage in the way I accepted the challenge." From that local bar she moves on to the Purple Onion, one of the most popular nightclubs on the entire West Coast. It is here that she is encouraged to replace the "s" in her last name with a "u". She will now also need an exotic first name. That is when she remembered, "My brother has always called me Maya. For 'Marguerite.' He used to call me 'My sister,' then he called me 'My,' and finally, 'Maya'." Marguerite Johnson Angelos becomes Maya Angelou, and shortly thereafter she has more job offers than she is able to accommodate. Her six-month contract at the Purple Onion prevents her from joining the cast of New Faces of 1953. Then when the Purple Onion contract does expire, she must choose between either starring alongside Pearl Bailey in the Broadway production of *House of Flowers* or joining the cast of *Porgy and Bess,* featuring such gifted luminaries as Cab Calloway, Leontyne Price, and William Warfield.

She decides on the touring company of *Porgy and Bess,* and her performances in numerous countries add a wealth of experiences. In Venice, members of the cast are "hailed in the streets like conquering heroes and given free rides on the canals by gondoliers, who sang strains from *Porgy and Bess.*" In Paris, the show is held over for months. In Rome, Angelou becomes friends with the fabled Bricktop, a black entertainer from Chicago who, over a period of several decades, had become a living legend on the European continent. The title of this third autobiography is most appropriate, as the author intimated in her 1983 interview:

> *Singin' and Swingin' and Gettin' Merry Like Christmas* comes from a time in the twenties and thirties when black people used to have rent parties. On Saturday night from around nine when they'd give these parties, through the next morning when they would go to church and have the Sunday meal, until early Sunday evening was the time when everyone was encouraged to sing and swing and get merry like Christmas so one would have some fuel with which to live the rest of the week.

Rent parties were especially popular in the 1920s, during the height of the Harlem Renaissance when, if rent money was short, tenants cooked a big meal, played records, and charged anywhere from ten to twenty-five cents for admission. People helped other people survive financial hardships. *Porgy and Bess* helped accomplish a similar two-fold mission. The entertainers earned a living and simultaneously enjoyed promulgating their distinctive black culture.

However, all is not going well back at home. Clyde, a budding nine-year-old who has been shuttled back and forth much more than is normal, has been missing his mother to the point where he has been having physical side effects. The writer maintains, "He had developed a severe rash that resisted every medical treatment." Thus the dutiful mother serves notice that she soon will be leaving the troupe. She picks up an additional job, singing at Bricktop's for awhile, lands another job teaching at the Rome Opera House, and is able in a month to earn what she needs to pay her way back to the United States. When she arrives back, in an emotional encounter, she promises her young son that she will never leave again, never, that is, unless she takes him with her.

It is at the beginning of her next autobiographical volume, *The Heart of a Woman* (1981), that Angelou regretfully confides, "In his nine years of schooling, we had lived in five areas of San Francisco, three townships in Los Angeles, New York City, Hawaii and Cleveland, Ohio. I followed the jobs, and against the advice of a pompous school psychologist, I had taken Guy along." Perhaps mimicking his mother, Clyde has changed his name to Guy, claiming that the former name sounds too mushy. In actuality, he himself is struggling for identity in the midst of a world that becomes increasingly inhabited by a multitude of celebrities, including the likes of Billie Holiday and Abbey Lincoln. Having ventured, by now, into the literary arena (particularly the Harlem Writers Guild), Angelou adds other acquaintances of note, including Paule Marshall and James Baldwin. By the year 1959, the multitalented artist has been asked to replace Bayard Rustin as northern coordinator of the Martin Luther King-led Southern Christian Leadership Conference (SCLC). Angelou's friendship circle of notables has expanded dramatically and continues to grow as she broadens her horizons to include even more employment fields.

Drama was the vehicle whereby Angelou had gotten involved in SCLC work. Both she and aspiring actor-comedian Godfrey Cambridge had worked diligently to produce a play, the proceeds of which were to go to that civil rights organization. Upon completion of that work, she immediately engages herself in related pursuits, eventually landing a role in Jean Genet's play, *The Blacks*. As members of the cast are being introduced to each other, we are awestricken at the Who's Who of black entertainers:

> Godfrey Cambridge is Diouf. Roscoe Lee Brown is Archibald. James Earl Jones is Village. Cicely Tyson is Virtue. Jay Riley is the Governor. Raymond St. Jacques is the Judge. Cynthia Belgrave is Adelaide. Maya Angelou Make is the White Queen. Helen Martin is Felicity, or the Black Queen. Lou Gossett is Newport News. Lex Monson is the Missionary. Abbey Lincoln is Snow and Charles Gordone is the Valet.

Among other things, it will be evident that the artist has acquired a new surname. Her political involvements have led her to meet the exiled South African freedom fighter, Vusumzi Make. Concluding that he must be "the ideal man," she struggles once again to be a housewife. While Vusumzi and Guy are enjoying themselves talking, our heroine:

> tried to overhear their interesting conversations, but generally I was too busy with household chores to take the time. . . . I washed, scrubbed, mopped, dusted and waxed thoroughly every other day. Vus was particular. He checked on my progress. Sometimes he would pull the sofa away from the wall to see if possibly I had missed a layer of dust.

We had seen the author in similar predicaments before in earlier autobiographical installments.

A poem by Georgia Douglas Johnson is the source for this volume's title:

The Heart of a Woman

The heart of a woman goes forth with the dawn,
As a lone bird, soft winging, so restlessly on
Afar o'er life's turrets and vales does it roam
In the wake of those echoes the heart calls home.

The heart of a woman falls back with the night,
And enters some alien cage in its plight,
And tries to forget it has dreamed of the stars
While it breaks, breaks, breaks on the sheltering bars.

As with Dunbar's poem, "Sympathy," there is the haunting metaphor of a fluttering caged bird. However, the significance of Johnson's poem, for Angelou, is somewhat different. Having traversed, since the events of *Caged Bird*, over more of "life's turrets and vales," the author is in search of a home. Believing, at the beginning of their relationship, that she has found it with Make, she in actuality has returned to the cage, an increasingly "alien cage" in which she is ultimately tormented, remembering all the promise that her life once held.

Angelou was certainly prepared to make the sacrifice if it took that to ensure her family's stability. But Vusumzi's level of commitment is at the very least questionable. At a diplomatic party in New York, "he was dancing with the little sexy woman, holding her too close, gazing too deeply in her eyes." At other times, Angelou discovers the telltale lipstick and perfume. Vusumzi insists, "My dear, there are no other women. You are the only love in my world." He is a talented liar, but inept at handling his own financial affairs. At one point, they face eviction, and after they are forced to move to Cairo, Egypt, Angelou decides to seek a job, finding work as an associate editor of the *Arab Observer*.

When Vusumzi discovers her accomplishment, he is livid and calls her to task: "You took a job without consulting me? Are you a man?" His tirade continues while she is sitting quietly, "watching him, listening and thinking." She arrives at the conclusion that she is no longer in love, and he becomes "a fat man, standing over me, scolding." The relationship, for all intent and purposes, has ended, but the author is vindicated, her integrity intact.

During the years 1961 and 1962, Angelou continues working with the *Arab Observer*. Guy has turned seventeen, graduated from high school, and plans to attend the University of Ghana. Angelou, the proud mother, will escort her son to college and, from there, pursue a job offer from Liberia's Department of Information. But as has so often been the case in her life, she will have to remain flexible. She is forestalled, never making it to Liberia, and instead finds work as an administrative assistant at her son's university.

In a 1975 interview, the author said:

> I never felt I belonged anywhere until I went to Ghana. Then parts of me relaxed that I didn't even know I had. My soul relaxed. Of course, I could never write that line. Too purple. But that's how I felt.

Of course, in recent years the color purple has come to symbolize the often-times precarious situation of being a black woman in America. It is, in fact, rather interesting that Angelou used the color quite a few years before Alice Walker's phenomenal bestseller, *The Color Purple* (1982), had appeared.

What does it mean for one's soul to be relaxed? The character Shug, in Walker's novel, proclaims, "I think it pisses God off if you walk by the color purple in a field somewhere and don't notice it." In giving that advice, Shug had been trying to help Celie attain self-consciousness. Celie is not totally unlike Angelou, who even in her latest volume, *All God's Children Need Traveling Shoes* (1986), is still engaged in the vital process of self-discovery. But what makes Ghana different is that here she looks physically like almost everyone else. She will not have to worry about discrimination based on color.

We had already come to expect a great deal from this quintessential master of survival, and are not disappointed when she informs us how two of her acquaintances, both Americans with graduate degrees, are only able to obtain office-support jobs while she, with only a high school diploma, is able to work creatively with the Ghanian Broadcasting Corporation. Opportunities again start to abound. She freelances for the *Ghanian Times,* edits for the

African Review, and parlays her university job into a means whereby she can perform in such plays as the highly acclaimed *Mother Courage,* which winds up being put on at the Ghanian National Theatre. We are not even surprised when an Ahanta chief offers Angelou work comparable to what she is already doing, but at twice her present salary—with the added incentives of a car and bungalow.

At times, *Traveling Shoes* suggests a certain mysticism. On one occasion, some Ghanian citizens insist she is their relative. In another instance, she is mistaken for a member of a village that was destroyed long before she had even arrived in the country. And then there is the unexplainable episode at a bridge between the cities of Keta and Accra. Riding in a car, returning from Keta, Angelou suddenly shouts, "Stop, stop the car. Stop the car." The enormity of the situation is made clear as the writer reveals, "the possibility of riding across that bridge so terrified me that had the driver refused to stop, I would have jumped from the still-moving car." We wonder what could be the problem. She has already described the bridge as "sturdy and graceful," making us aware there is no present danger. However, what we will learn later is that bridges in Ghana used to be so poorly constructed that "people in conveyances of any kind lost their lives, so a century ago passengers in palanquins used to stop and get down in order to walk across." In those days, "only people on foot could hope to reach the other side." Is there some sort of spiritual connection between how Ghanians generations ago responded to having to cross the bridge and Angelou's hysterical reaction? Or is her inclination to walk just a coincidence?

Whichever was the case, of this we can be sure: Angelou has developed strong ties with this continent, and her insights are thereby enhanced. She visualizes, for example, the horror of slavery:

> Children passed tied together by ropes and chains, tears abashed, stumbling in dull exhaustion, then women, hair uncombed, bodies gritted with sand, and sagging in defeat. Men, muscles without memory, minds dimmed, plodding, leaving bloodied footprints in the dirt. . . . None of them cried, or yelled, or bellowed. No moans came from them. They lived in a mute territory, dead to feeling and protest.

She further reflects, "These were the legions, sold by sisters, stolen by brothers, bought by strangers, enslaved by the greedy and betrayed by history." Tortured by the thought that Africans themselves were involved in the conspiracy, she consequently accepts that she is "no more moral than the commercial bandits upon whom I heaped every crime from slavery to

Hiroshima." The artist who was about to make Ghana her home, now must concede that her search has not ended.

In August, 1963, as Americans are preparing for the historic march on Washington, she becomes even more ambivalent about where she is living. She and other black Americans stand outside of their Embassy, and she resolves they "had only begun to realize in Africa that the Stars and Stripes was our flag and our only flag." Emotional seeds have been laid for the return to her country.

No sooner is Angelou back in the United States than she takes up her work with fervor. Continuing with her writing, she also begins narrating documentaries, one a ten-part television series about the extent to which Africanisms have influenced American culture. In demand as a performer and lecturer, she has visited numerous colleges and universities. Furthermore, she has been nominated for such prestigious prizes as the National Book Award, the Pulitzer, the Emmy, and the Tony. She has come to be recognized now as the "phenomenal woman" of that earlier mentioned poem; her honorary doctorates defy a brief listing.

Still, Angelou would be the first to say her quest is incomplete. In a 1982 interview, she admonished:

> "We have allowed ourselves too much laxity in the use of our brains. The brain will do anything . . . we can do the most wonderful things. We can do almost anything."

The writer has faith in humankind's vast potential while yet acknowledging her own frailty. Even in recent years she has experienced insecurity, musing, "Sometimes I think I'm too old or too fat. Or wish I was prettier." As we listen to those ponderings, we respect her brutal honesty, the same honesty prompting her to accept a distinguished professorship at a southern university amidst the clamor of those who wondered why she would return to this region. She returned to come home, her real home, the only place—with its eerie combination of atrocity and retribution—where a once-caged bird is, at last, free.

WORKS CITED

I Know Why the Caged Bird Sings.
Just Give Me a Cool Drink of Water 'Fore I Diiie.
Gather Together in My Name.
The Heart of a Woman.
And Still I Rise.
I Shall Not Be Moved.
Poems.

Singin' and Swingin' and Gettin' Merry Like Christmas.
Now Sheba Sings Her Song.

Books by Maya Angelou

I Know Why the Caged Bird Sings. New York: Random House, 1969.
Just Give Me a Cool Drink of Water 'Fore I Diiie. New York: Random House, 1971.
Gather Together in My Name. New York: Random House, 1974.
Oh Pray My Wings Are Gonna Fit Me Well. New York: Random House, 1975.
Singin' and Swingin' and Gettin' Merry Like Christmas. New York: Random House, 1976.
And Still I Rise. New York: Random House, 1976.
The Heart of a Woman. New York: Random House, 1981.
All God's Children Need Traveling Shoes. New York: Random House, 1986.
The Aristocrat. Newton, Iowa: Tamazunshale Press, 1986.
Mrs. Flowers: A Moment of Friendship. Minneapolis: Redpath Press, 1986.
Poems. New York: Bantam, 1986.
Now Sheba Sings Her Song. New York: Dutton/Dial, 1987.
I Shall Not Be Moved. New York: Random House, 1990.

PIERRE A. WALKER

Racial Protest, Identity, Words, and Form in Maya Angelou's I Know Why the Caged Bird Sings

Maya Angelou has told in interviews how Robert Loomis, her eventual Random House editor, goaded her into writing autobiography, teasing her with the challenge of writing literary autobiography. Considering herself a poet and playwright, she had repeatedly refused Loomis's requests that she write an autobiography until he told her that it was just as well: "He . . . said that to write an autobiography—as literature—is almost impossible. I said right then I'd do it'" ("Maya Angelou," with Hitt 211). Angelou often admits that she cannot resist a challenge; however, it was not the challenge of writing autobiography per se that Angelou could not resist (and that led to the 1970 publication of I Know Why the Caged Bird Sings), but the challenge implied in Loomis's remark about the difficulty of writing autobiography "as literature."[1]

Angelou does not elaborate on how she distinguishes literary autobiography from any other kind of autobiography, and of course, for a poststructuralist, the challenge to write literary rather than "ordinary" autobiography is meaningless because there is no difference between the two (see Eagleton 201). For a formalist aesthetic, however, the distinctive qualities and characteristics of literary or poetic language as opposed to ordinary language are central operative concerns (see Brooks 729–731, Shklovsky 12, Fish 68–69). Cleanth Brooks's belief that "the parts of a poem are related to each other

College Literature, Volume 22, Number 3 (October 1995): pp. 91–108. Copyright © 1995 West Chester University.

organically, and related to the total theme indirectly" (730) was a primary tenet of interpretation for American New Critics, ultimately related to their determination to distinguish literary from ordinary language. Poststructuralism in its most vehemently anti-formalist manifestations usually belittles Brooks's beliefs in organic unity and in the uniqueness of literary language, but criticisms of formalism, and of "literature" as a distinct and privileged category, so typical of much poststructuralist theorizing, become specially problematic in relation to African-American literature.

Many African-American texts were written to create a particular political impact. As a result, one can hardly ignore either the political conditions in which the slave narratives and Richard Wright's early works, for example, were composed or the political impact their authors (and editors and publishers, at least of the slave narratives) intended them to have. Even African-American texts that are not obviously part of a protest tradition are received in a political context, as is clear from the tendency in much critical commentary on Zora Neale Hurston to demonstrate an elusive element of protest in her novels.

So important is the political to the experience of African-American literature that it comes as no surprise that the increasing incorporation of the African-American literary tradition into mainstream academic literary studies since 1980 coincides exactly with the increasingly greater significance of the political in the prevailing critical paradigm: what better for a political literary criticism to address than an overtly political literature?

The problem is that African-American literature has, on more than one occasion, relied on confirming its status as literature to accomplish its political aims. Since slavery relied on a belief that those enslaved were not really human beings, slave narrators responded by writing books that emphasized the fact that they themselves were humans who deserved to be treated as such. Since emancipation, African-American authors have used the same strategy to fight the belief in racial hierarchies that relegated them to second-class citizen status. One way to do this was to produce "high art," which was supposed to be one of the achievements of the highest orders of human civilization. African-American poetry provides many examples of this strategy: Claude McKay's and Countee Cullen's reliance on traditional, European poetic forms and James Weldon Johnson's "O Black and Unknown Bards." Cullen's "Yet Do I Marvel," for instance, relies on recognizable English "literary" features: Shakespearean sonnet form, rhyme, meter, references to Greek mythology, and the posing of a theological question as old as the Book of Job and as familiar as William Blake's "The Tyger."

Thus for a critical style to dismiss the closely related categories of form and of literature is to relegate to obscurity an important tradition of African-American literature and an important political tool of the struggle in the

United States of Americans of African descent. This is clearly true in respect to *Caged Bird*, which displays the kind of literary unity that would please Brooks, but to the significant political end of demonstrating how to fight racism. Angelou wrote *Caged Bird* in the late 1960s, at the height of the New Criticism, and therefore in order for it to be the literary autobiography Loomis referred to, Angelou's book had to display features considered at the time typical of literature, such as organic unity. This is a political gesture, since in creating a text that satisfies contemporary criteria of "high art," Angelou underscores one of the book's central themes: how undeservedly its protagonist was relegated to second-class citizenship in her early years. To ignore form in discussing Angelou's book, therefore, would mean ignoring a critical dimension of its important political work.

Because scholarly discussions of Angelou's autobiographical works have only appeared in any significant number in the last fifteen years, *Caged Bird* and her other books have avoided—or, depending on one's view, been spared—the kind of formal analysis typically associated with New Criticism or Structuralism.[2] Scholarly critics of *Caged Bird*, often influenced by feminist and African-American studies, have focused on such issues as whether the story of Angelou's young protagonist is personal or universal, or on race, gender, identity, displacement, or a combination of these. In relation to these issues, they discuss important episodes like the scene with the "powhitetrash" girls, young Maya's rape and subsequent muteness, her experience with Mrs. Flowers, the graduation, the visit to the dentist, Maya's month living in a junkyard, or her struggle to become a San Francisco street-car conductor.[3] What they do not do is analyze these episodes as Angelou constructed them—often juxtaposing disparate incidents within an episode—and arranged and organized them, often undermining the chronology of her childhood story and juxtaposing the events of one chapter with the events of preceding and following ones so that they too comment on each other. The critics do not explore how Angelou, who has never denied the principle of selection in the writing of autobiography,[4] shaped the material of her childhood and adolescent life story in *Caged Bird* to present Maya's first sixteen years, much as a bildungsroman would, as a progressive process of affirming identity, learning about words, and resisting racism.[5] What scholars have focused on in *Caged Bird* does merit attention, but an attention to the formal strategies Angelou uses to emphasize what the book expresses about identity and race reveals a sequence of lessons about resisting racist oppression, a sequence that leads Maya progressively from helpless rage and indignation to forms of subtle resistance, and finally to outright and active protest.

The progression from rage and indignation to subtle resistance to active protest gives *Caged Bird* a thematic unity that stands in contrast to the otherwise episodic quality of the narrative. To claim thematic unity is to argue that form and content work together, an assertion that is an anathema to much current literary theory. However, the formal in *Caged Bird* is the vehicle of the political, and not analyzing this text formally can limit one's appreciation of how it intervenes in the political. Critics should not focus on the political at the expense of the formal but instead should see the political and the formal as inextricably related. Indeed, some of the most well-received works on American literature in the last decade offer compelling demonstrations of such a symbiosis of form and content. Jane Tompkins' *Sensational Designs* and Walter Benn Michaels's *The Gold Standard and the Logic of Naturalism,* for instance, are exemplary instances of new historicism or cultural criticism, but they nevertheless integrate virtuosic close formal analyses of literary texts into their overall projects.[6]

Caged Bird's commentators have discussed how episodic the book is, but these episodes are crafted much like short stories, and their arrangement throughout the book does not always follow strict chronology.[7] Nothing requires an autobiography to be chronological, but an expectation of chronology on the reader's part is normal in a text that begins, as *Caged Bird* does, with earliest memories. Nevertheless, one of the most important early episodes in *Caged Bird* comes much earlier in the book than it actually did in Angelou's life: the scene where the "powhitetrash" girls taunt Maya's grandmother takes up the book's fifth chapter, but it occurred when Maya "was around ten years old" (23), two years after Mr. Freeman rapes her (which occurs in the twelfth chapter).

Situating the episode early in the book makes sense in the context of the previous chapters: the third chapter ends with Angelou describing her anger at the "used-to-be-sheriff" who warmed her family of an impending Klan ride (14–15), and the fourth chapter ends with her meditation on her early inability to perceive white people as human (20–21). The scene with the "powhitetrash" girls follows this (24–27), indicating how non-human white people can be. But if that was all that motivated the organization of her episodes, Angelou could as easily have followed the meditation on white people's non-humanity with the episode where young Maya breaks the china of her white employer, Mrs. Cullinan. What really organizes chapters three through five is that Angelou presents the futility of indignation and the utility of subtle resistance as ways of responding to racism. The scene with the ex-sheriff comes at the beginning of this sequence and only leaves Maya humiliated and angry:

> If on Judgment Day I were summoned by St. Peter to give testimony to the used-to-be sheriff's act of kindness, I would be unable to say anything in his behalf. His confidence that my uncle and every other Black man who heard of the Klan's coming ride

would scurry under their houses to hide in chicken droppings was too humiliating to hear. (14)

The scene with the "powhitetrash" girls causes Maya to react with the same helpless anger and humiliation, but through the response of her grandmother Henderson (whom she calls Momma) to the girl's rudeness and crudity, Maya learns there can be a better and more effective way to respond.

At first, Maya's reaction to the "powhitetrash" girls is like her reaction to the used-to-be sheriff: rage, indignation, humiliation, helplessness. When the girls ape her grandmother's posture, Maya weeps, thinks of getting her uncle's rifle, and wants to throw lye and pepper on them and to scream at them "that they were dirty, scummy peckerwoods" (24–25). When they leave and Momma politely calls good-bye to them, Maya's rage peaks:

> I burst. A firecracker July-the-Fourth burst. How could Momma call them Miz? The mean nasty things. Why couldn't she have come inside the sweet, cool store when we saw them breasting the hill? What did she prove? And then if they were dirty, mean and impudent, why did Momma have to call them Miz? (26)

But once the girls leave, young Maya realizes that her grandmother has achieved something: "Something had happened out there, which I couldn't completely understand . . . Whatever the contest had been out front, I knew Momma had won" (26–27). Angelou claims that her ten-year-old self could not fully understand what had happened, though she did understand that there had been a contest of wills and that her grandmother had won it.

The young girl can be only vaguely conscious of how to comprehend the nature of the contest, but her next act and the organization of the whole chapter indicate nonetheless how readers should comprehend it. Angelou's description of the "powhitetrash" girls emphasizes their dirtiness. They are "grimy, snotty-nosed girls" (23), and "The dirt of [their] cotton dresses continued on their legs, feet, arms and faces to make them all of a piece" (25). In contrast to this, Maya's household is a model of cleanliness. The first thing Momma tells Maya after the "powhitetrash" girls have left is to wash her face (26). This seems appropriate because of how much Maya had been crying, but its real significance is apparent when considered in the context of the chapter's beginning and of what Maya does at the end of the chapter. The chapter begins: "'Thou shall not be dirty', and 'Thou shall not be impudent' were the two commandments of Grandmother Henderson upon which hung our total salvation," and the two subsequent paragraphs recount the ends to which Momma went to ensure her grandchildren's cleanliness (21). At first glance, this would appear to have nothing to do with the pain and humiliation of racism. But what the entire chapter demonstrates and what the ten-year-old Maya vaguely understands is that cleanliness, racism, and her grandmother's "victory" over the "powhitetrash" girls have everything to do with each other. Maya would seem to have understood this—even though the adult Angelou claims she did not—for once she has washed her face, without being told to do so, she rakes the trampled front yard into a pattern that her grandmother calls "right pretty" (27).[8]

Maya and Momma demonstrate that, unlike the white trash girls, they are neither dirty nor impudent. This is where the victory lies. Part of it consists of Momma's resisting the white girls' attempts to goad her into descending to their level of impudence. But another part of the victory lies in maintaining personal dignity through the symbolic importance of cleanliness and politeness. The victory will not of itself bring about the downfall of segregation (which is perhaps why some critics see Grandmother Henderson as ultimately helpless against racist oppression [see Kent 76, and Neubauer 118]), but it does allow Momma and Maya to be proud of themselves. By demonstrating their own cleanliness and politeness, Maya and her grandmother establish their family's respectability in the face of racism and subtly throw the attempt to degrade them back on their oppressor. Furthermore, there is a more effective strategy for reacting to racism and segregation than rage and indignation, a strategy of subtle resistance, what Dolly McPherson calls "the dignified course of silent endurance" (33). Later episodes demonstrate the limitations of subtle resistance, but one should not underestimate its powers: without risking harm to life, liberty, or property, Momma is able to preserve her human dignity in the face of the white girls' attempts to belittle her. It may be all that she can do in the segregated South at the time, but it is something. What is more, as Angelou subsequently shows, it serves as a basis from which Maya can later move to actively protesting and combating racism.

An important feature of the chapter is that Angelou organizes it like a short story. It begins where it ends, with cleanliness and raking the yard bracketing the scene with the white trash girls, and it leaves the reader to work out the relationship between the confrontation with the girls and the cleaning of the yard. Because of this organization, the chapter becomes more than just a narration of bigoted behavior and Momma's and Maya's responses to it: "Such experiences," says McPherson, "are recorded not simply as historical events, but as symbolic revelations of Angelou's inner world" (49). The "powhitetrash" chapter takes on the additional dimension of a lesson in the utility of endowing everyday activities such as washing, raking a yard, or minding one's manners with symbolic value as a way of resisting bigotry. Making every minute of the day a symbolic means of fighting segregation in turn means that segregation is not a helpless and hopeless situation.

Angelou organizes the fifteenth chapter, the one about Mrs. Flowers, in a similarly tight fashion, interrelating the themes of racial pride, identity, and the power of words that run throughout. The positive effect that the attention of the elegant Mrs. Flowers has on the insecurity and identity crisis of young Maya is obvious.[9] By helping Maya to begin to have some self-confidence, Mrs. Flowers contributes to the young girl's affirmation of her identity: "I was liked, and what a difference it made. I was respected . . . for just being Marguerite Johnson . . . she had made tea cookies for me and read to me from her favorite book" (85). Such respect and affection from an older person Maya admired surely had an important positive effect on a young girl suffering from the guilt and self-loathing that resulted from being raped by her mother's boyfriend. It is no wonder Angelou feels that Mrs. Flowers "threw me my first life line" (77).

While the Mrs. Flowers chapter seems, at first glance, not to have much to do with the politics of racism, this important step in Maya's sense of identity has everything to do with race. Since she had been twice sent away by her parents to live with her grandmother, it is no surprise that Maya had an insecurity and identity problem. In the opening pages of the book, Maya suffered from a strong case of racial self-hatred, fantasizing that she was "really white," with "light-blue eyes" and "long and blond" hair (2). At that point, Maya entirely separates her sense of self from her sense of race, and this is part of her identity crisis, since she refuses to accept being who she is and hankers after a foreign identity that is a compound of received ideas of white feminine beauty. By the end of the book, the opposite is the case. When the white secretary of the San Francisco street-car company repeatedly frustrates her attempts for a job interview, Maya is at first tempted not to take it personally: "The incident was a recurring dream, concocted years before by stupid whites . . . I went further than forgiving the clerk, I accepted her as a fellow victim of the same puppeteer." But then Maya decides that the rebuffs, which have everything to do with her race, also have everything to do with her personally, and this is because her personal identity and her racial identity cannot be entirely separated: "The whole charade we had played out in that crummy waiting room had directly to do with me, Black, and her, white" (227). Attaining the street-car conductor's job becomes not only a victory for civil rights, as a result, but also a personal victory for Maya's sense of self. One of the crucial transition points in this evolution over the course of the entire book from the total separation of self-image and race to the connection of the two comes in the Mrs. Flowers chapter, for not only does Mrs. Flowers make Maya feel liked and respected, but "she made me proud to be Negro, just by being herself" (79).[10] This is the first statement of black racial pride in the book, but others appear later: Joe Louis's victory, which "proved that we were the strongest people in the world" (115), and Maya's conclusion at the end of the graduation scene that "I was a proud member of the wonderful, beautiful Negro race" (156).

The Mrs. Flowers chapter emphasizes black racial pride by combining two apparently disparate episodes on the basis of their thematic affinity, much as the "powhitetrash" chapter did. Here the affinity is not cleanliness but the power of words, a theme central to African-American autobiography, from the slave narratives to Richard Wright's *Black Boy* and beyond. The importance of the power of words, in themselves and in poetry, and by implication, the importance of literature run throughout *Caged Bird*,[11] especially after the rape, when Maya fears that her lie at Mr. Freeman's trial caused his death. *Black Boy* demonstrates the negative power of words each time Wright is abused for not saying the right thing,[12] yet the book concludes on a positive note when Wright realizes that he can harness the power of words to his own artistic and political ends. Much the same thing happens in *Caged Bird*. Maya refuses to speak because she fears the potentially fatal power of words, but throughout the second half of the book she acknowledges that the imagination can harness the power of words to great ends. One of the high points in this realization comes at the end of the graduation scene, when the audience, having been insulted by a white guest speaker, lifts its morale by singing James Weldon Johnson's "Lift Ev'ry Voice and Sing" (155). Maya realizes that she "had never heard it before. Never heard the words, despite the thousands of times I had sung them," and this leads her to appreciate the African-American poetic tradition as she never had before (and Angelou expresses that appreciation with an allusion to another Johnson poem): "Oh, Black known and unknown poets, how often have your auctioned pains sustained us? Who will compute the lonely nights made less lonely by your songs, or by the empty pots made less tragic by your tales?" (156). Because Johnson's words, like Angelou's story, are gathered "from the stuff of the black experience, with its suffering and its survival," to use Keneth Kinnamon's words, the singing of "Lift Ev'ry Voice and Sing" at the end of the graduation episode "is a paradigm of Angelou's own artistic endeavor in *I Know Why the Caged Bird Sings*" (132–133).

Mrs. Flowers lays the groundwork for this later appreciation of the power of the poetic word by explicitly stating the lesson of the positive power of words in her conversation with the ten-year-old Maya (her message is further emphasized because the main point of her invitation and attention to the mute girl is to convince her to use words again). "[B]ear in mind," Mrs. Flowers tells Maya, "language is man's way of communicating with his fellow man and it is language alone that separates him from the lower animals. . . . Words mean more than what is set down on paper. It takes the human voice to infuse them with the shades of deeper meaning" (82). Mrs. Flowers's speech and her reading from Dickens themselves make Maya appreciate poetry—"I heard poetry for the first time in my life" (84), she says about Mrs. Flowers's reading—and the spoken word, but Angelou arranges the entire chapter to emphasize the power of words. The chapter begins with a description of Mrs. Flowers and her elegant command of standard English, which contrasts in their conversations with Momma's heavy dialect, much to Maya's shame: "Shame made me want to hide my face. . . . Momma left out the verb. Why not ask, 'How are you, Mrs. Flowers?' . . . 'Brother and Sister Wilcox is sho'ly the meanest—' 'Is,' Momma? 'Is'? Oh, please, not 'is,' Momma, for two or more" (78–79). As a result, Angelou has focused the chapter on the importance of words and their pronunciation, even in its very first pages, before Maya enters Mrs. Flowers's house.

The chapter's end, after Maya returns from her visit, also emphasizes the importance of words, this time in contrast to the way white people use words. When Maya tells her brother, "By the way, Bailey, Mrs. Flowers sent you some tea cookies—," Momma threatens to beat her granddaughter (85). The crime is that since "Jesus was the Way, the Truth and the Light," saying "by the way" was, in Momma's view, blasphemous (86). This episode would seem thematically unrelated to the rest of the chapter and only an example of Momma's domestic theocracy were it not for the chapter's final sentence: "When Bailey tried to interpret the words with: 'Whitefolks use "by the way" to mean while we're on the subject,' Momma reminded us that 'whitefolks' mouths were most in general loose and their words were an abomination before Christ'" (86–87). While the "by the way" episode concludes the chapter, *Black Boy* fashion, with an example of the awful power of words, this final sentence concludes both the episode and chapter just as the emphasis on cleanliness concluded the "powhitetrash" chapter: through their greater attention to details, the Henderson/Johnson clan shows itself to be superior to whites, and instead of showing Momma to be abusive and tyrannic, the "by the way" episode anticipates the affirmation later in the book of the strength blacks find in the careful—even poetic—use of words, just as Mrs. Flowers does in her reading and in her speech about words.

The internal organization of chapters, as in the "powhitetrash" and Mrs. Flowers chapters, into thematic units that would make Cleanth Brooks proud is but one of the effects Angelou uses in *Caged Bird*. Equally effective is the way Angelou juxtaposes chapters. For example, she follows the Mrs. Flowers chapter, with its lessons on the power of words and on identity, with the chapter (the sixteenth) where Maya breaks Mrs. Cullinan's dishes because the white employer neglects to take a single but important word—Maya's name—and Maya's identity seriously. This chapter comments, then, on the previous one by showing Maya acting on the basis of what she has learned in the previous chapter about the importance of words and about affirming identity. Maya's smashing of the dishes is also an important stage in the progression of strategies for responding to racial oppression from helpless

indignation, to subtle resistance, to active protest. No longer helplessly an-
gered and humiliated, as she was by the former sheriff and the white girls
taunting her grandmother, Maya shows in the Mrs. Cullinan chapter that she
has internalized the lesson of the "powhitetrash" episode and can figure out,
with her brother's advice, a way to resist her white employer's demeaning of
her that is subtle and yet allows her to feel herself the victor of an unspoken
confrontation. After Mrs. Cullinan insists on calling her Mary instead of
Margaret (which best approximates her real name, Marguerite), Maya realizes that she can neither correct her employer nor simply quit the job. Like
her grandmother with the rude white girls, Maya cannot openly confront her
oppressor, nor can she allow the situation to continue. Instead she breaks Mrs.
Cullinan's favorite dishes and walks out, exulting as Mrs. Cullinan tells her
guests, "Her name's Margaret, goddamn it, her name's Margaret!" (93).[13]

Angelou follows this chapter with a series of three chapters, the seventeenth through the nineteenth, each of which depicts subtle black resistance to white oppression. However, while the sixteenth chapter ends with
Maya exulting at the efficacy of her resistance of Mrs. Cullinan, these chapters increasingly express the limitations of subtle resistance. The seventeenth
chapter tells of Maya's and Bailey's viewing movies starring Kay Francis, who
resembles their mother, and describes how Maya turns the stereotypical depiction of black people in Hollywood movies back onto the unknowing white
members of the audience. As the whites snicker at the Stepin Fetchit-like
black chauffeur in one Kay Francis comedy, Maya turns the joke on them:

> I laughed too, but not at the hateful jokes. . . . I laughed because,
> except that she was white, the big movie star looked just like my
> mother. Except that she lived in a big mansion with a thousand
> servants, she lived just like my mother. And it was funny to think
> of the whitefolks' not knowing that the woman they were adoring
> could be my mother's twin, except that she was white and my
> mother was prettier. Much prettier. (99–100)

This passage works very much like Momma's victory over the white trash
girls: the whites' taunts are turned back on them, though the whites may not
know it. Nonetheless, this permits the black person to feel superior instead of
humiliated while avoiding the kind of open confrontation that could lead to
violence. What is problematic about the seventeenth chapter is that, as in the
eighteenth and nineteenth chapters, the end of the chapter casts a shadow on
the success achieved in the moment of subtle resistance by describing Bailey's
very different reaction to the movie: it makes him sullen, and on their way
home, he terrifies Maya by running in front of an oncoming train (100).

In the eighteenth and nineteenth chapters, which tell of the revival meeting and the Joe Louis fight, a black community is able to feel superior to whites. Both chapters, though, end ambiguously, with a reminder that the feeling of superiority is transitory and fragile. At the revival, the congregation thrills to a sermon that subtly accuses whites of lacking charity while reminding the congregation of the ultimate reward for their true charity. The congregation leaves the revival feeling, "It was better to be meek and lowly, spat upon and abused for this little time than to spend eternity frying in the fires of hell" (110–111). Again, the oppressed are able to feel superior without risking the violence of an open confrontation. The final two paragraphs of the chapter, however, compare the gospel music at the revival with the "ragged sound" of the "barrelhouse blues" coming from the honky-tonk run by "Miss Grace, the good-time woman" (111). Like the parishioners at the revival, the customers of the suitably named Miss Grace "had forsaken their own distress for a little while." However,

> Reality began its tedious crawl back into their reasoning. After all, they were needy and hungry and despised and dispossessed, and sinners the world over were in the driver's seat. How long, merciful Father? How long? . . . All asked the same questions. How long, oh God? How long? (111)

Whereas the "powhitetrash" and Mrs. Cullinan chapters ended on a note of victory, this chapter ends on one that rings more of defeat. This is because the book moves through the three strategies for responding to white racist oppression—helpless indignation, subtle resistance, and active protest—and at this point is preparing the transition from the limited victories of subtle resistance to the outright victory of active protest.

The next chapter, the nineteenth, which describes the community at the store listening to a Joe Louis match, follows the same pattern as the revival chapter. Louis's victory provides his fans a stirring moment of racial pride and exaltation: "Champion of the world. A Black boy. Some Black mother's son. He was the strongest man in the world. People drank Coca-Colas like ambrosia and ate candy bars like Christmas" (114). But while Louis's victory allows his black fans to feel themselves stronger and superior to their white oppressors, there are limits to how far the black community can rejoice in its superiority. The chapter ends by mentioning that those who lived far out of town spent the night with friends in town because, "It wouldn't do for a Black man and his family to be caught on a lonely country road on a night when Joe Louis had proved that we were the strongest people in the world" (115).

Because chapters eighteen and nineteen explore the limits to subtle, but passive, resistance, the book has to go on to present other possible ways of responding to white oppression. The climactic response, one that consists of active resistance and outright protest, is Maya's persisting and breaking the color line of the San Francisco street-car company, described in the thirty-fourth chapter. Since *Caged Bird* was written in the late sixties, at the height of the black power movement, and at a time that was still debating the value of Martin Luther King's belief in non-violent protest, it is no surprise that this act of protest is the climactic moment of resistance to white oppression in the book, a moment that says: Momma's type of resistance was fine in its time and place, but now it is time for some real action.[14] There are at least three other episodes in the second half of *Caged Bird*, however, which explore the line between subtle but passive resistance and active, open protest: the graduation scene (chapter twenty-three), the dentist scene (chapter twenty-four), and the story Daddy Clidell's friend, Red Leg, tells of double-crossing a white con man (chapter twenty-nine).

Falling as they do between the Joe Louis chapter and the San Francisco street-car company chapter, these three episodes chart the transition from subtle resistance to active protest. The graduation scene for the most part follows the early, entirely positive examples of subtle resistance in *Caged Bird*. The only difference is that the resistance is no longer so subtle and that it specifically takes the form of poetry, which in itself valorizes the African-American literary tradition as a source for resisting white racist oppression. Otherwise, the graduation chapter conforms to the pattern established by the "powhitetrash" and Mrs. Cullinan chapters: first, there is the insult by the white person, when the speaker tells the black audience of all the improvements which the white school will receive—improvements that far surpass the few scheduled for the black school (151). There is Maya's first response of humiliation and anger: "Then I wished that Gabriel Prosser and Nat Turner had killed all whitefolks in their beds" (152), shared now by the community: "[T]he proud graduating class of 1940 had dropped their heads" (152). Then there is the action on the part of a member of the black community—Henry Reed's improvised leading the audience in "Lift Ev'ry Voice and Sing" (155)—that at the same time avoids an irreversible confrontation with the white oppressor and permits the black community to feel its dignity and superiority: "We were on top again. As always, again. We survived" (156).

The primary difference in the graduation chapter is that because the audience sings together, the resistance is a community action. The resistance is still not exactly an outright protest and it still avoids open confrontation, since the white insulter has left and does not hear the singing. Otherwise, the scene resembles a civil rights protest two decades later. The graduation also serves as an introduction for the dentist chapter, which is similar to the graduation chapter because of the way it highlights literature as a possible source for resisting racist oppression, and which is the crucial transitional chapter from subtle resistance to active protest because it opens the door to the eventuality of open confrontation by presenting the closest instance in the book of a black person in Stamps openly confronting a racist white.

The insult in the dentist chapter occurs when Stamps's white and only dentist—to whom Maya's grandmother had lent money, interest-free and as a favor—refuses to treat Maya's excruciating toothache, telling Maya and Momma, "[M]y policy is I'd rather stick my hand in a dog's mouth than in a nigger's" (160). From this point on, though, the chapter ceases to follow the pattern of the previous examples of resistance. Instead, Momma leaves Maya in the alley behind the dentist's office, and in a passage printed in italics, enters the office transformed into a superwoman, and threatens to run the now-trembling dentist out of town. Readers quickly perceive that this passage is italicized because it is Maya's fantasy, but they do have to read a few sentences of the fantasy before realizing it. The chapter ends, after Maya and Momma travel to the black dentist in Texarkana, with Angelou's explanation of what really happened inside the white dentist's office—Momma collected interest on her loan to the dentist, which pays the bus fare to Texarkana—and Angelou's remark: "I preferred, much preferred, my version" (164).

The fantasy scene bears attention because it is the only one like it in *Caged Bird*. It is the only italicized passage in the book and the only one that confuses the reader—even if only for a moment—over what is real and what is fantasy. Some critics have argued that this passage serves the purpose of underlining how limited Momma's ability to fight racism is,[15] and it is true that in a better world, Momma would have been able to exact proper and courteous care from a dentist who was beholden to her. This reading, however, does not account for either the uniqueness of the presentation of the passage or the very real pride Maya feels for her grandmother as they ride the bus between Stamps and Texarkana: "I was so proud of being her granddaughter and sure that some of her magic must have come down to me" (162–163). On the one hand, the italicized passage does highlight the contrast between what Maya wishes her grandmother could do to a racist with what little she can do, thus again demonstrating the limitations of subtle resistance as an overall strategy for responding to racist oppression. On the other hand, the fantasy passage anticipates the kind of outright confrontations between oppressed black and racist oppressor that occurred when Maya broke the street-car company's color line and in the civil rights movement. Although it is only a fantasy, it is the first instance in *Caged Bird* of a black person openly confronting a racist white, and thus is the first hint that such confrontation is a possibility.

The fact that the fantasy passage is an act of imagination is also significant, since it hints that imagination and storytelling can be forms of resisting racism. It is natural to read the fantasy passage in this way because of its placement immediately after the apostrophe to "Black known and unknown poets" at the end of the graduation chapter (156). Because of this passage praising black poets, we are all the more inclined to see the imagined, italicized, fantasy passage five pages later as itself an instance of poetry. For one, the apostrophe includes in the category of "poets" anyone who uses the power of the word— "include preachers, musicians and blues singers" (156). Thus, anyone who uses language to describe pain and suffering and their causes (i. e., blues singers) belongs in the category of poets. According to this definition, the author of *I Know Why the Caged Bird Sings* is a blues singer, and therefore a poet, too, since telling why the caged bird sings is an instance of describing pain and suffering and their causes, an instance of the blues. Loosely defined, poetry is also an act of imagination, and thus the italicized fantasy passage in the dentist chapter is poetic, since it is an act of imagination. In fact, it is the first instance of Maya being a poet, and thus the first step towards the far more monumental act of writing *I Know Why the Caged Bird Sings* itself. Poetry, in all its forms, can be an act of resistance. The graduation chapter has already made that clear, but the dentist chapter makes it clear that the victim of racial oppression can herself become a poet and use her poetry as a form of resistance. Maya had begun to learn the positive power of poetry and of words in the Mrs. Flowers chapter. Now she begins the process of harnessing the power of words to positive effect, a process that concludes with the composition almost thirty years later of the very book in hand.

The final instance of not-quite-outright resistance is the scam Red Leg tells (in chapter twenty-nine) of pulling on a white con man. This episode is not the open, active protest of Maya's integration of the street-cars, since it does not involve a direct confrontation with the white racist, but it is closer to it than any of the previous examples of resistance because the white person ends up knowing that he has been had at his own game. The inclusion of the episode is at first glance irrelevant to the heroine's personal development, but Angelou's comments at the end of the chapter make clear how the passage fits with the rest of the book. For one, Angelou remarks that, "It wasn't possible for me to regard [Red Leg and his accomplice] as criminals or be anything but proud of their achievements" (190). The reason for her pride is that these black con artists are achieving revenge for wrongs incurred against the entire race: "'We are the victims of the world's most comprehensive robbery. Life demands a balance. It's all right if we do a little robbing now'" (190–191). The scam is, therefore, another example of fighting back against white domination and racist oppression, an example that, like the others, meets with the author's approval.

The scam artist chapter ends, like so many other chapters, with a paragraph that appears to have little to do with what precedes. It tells of how Maya and her black schoolmates learned to use Standard English and dialect in their appropriate settings. This short paragraph certainly belongs to the commentary running throughout the book on appreciating the significance and power of words: "We were alert to the gap separating the written word from the colloquial" (191). It also serves to emphasize the superior ability of blacks to adapt to and get the best of circumstances and situations: "My education and that of my Black associates were quite different from the education of our white schoolmates. In the classroom we all learned past participles, but in the streets and in our homes the Blacks learned to drop s's from plurals and suffixes from past-tense verbs" (191). Angelou shows here the superior adaptability of her black schoolmates (and that Maya has come a long way from her scorn of her grandmother's use of dialect): the blacks learn all the whites do and more. This lesson is entirely appropriate to the con artist chapter, since what the stories about pulling scams demonstrate is the black version of heroism, which is to make the most of what little one has—in other words, adaptability: "[I]n the Black American ghettos the hero is that man who is offered only the crumbs from his country's table but by ingenuity and courage is able to take for himself a Lucullan feast" (190).

Within strictly legal confines, such an ability is the essence of the American myth of success, and undoubtedly, at least part of the appeal of *Caged Bird* is that it corresponds both to this definition of black heroism and to the outline of a typical success story.[16] The product of a broken family, raped at age eight, Angelou was offered at first "only the crumbs" from her "country's table." She suffers from an inferiority complex, an identity crisis, and the humiliation of racist insults. By the end of the book, however, she no longer feels inferior, knows who she is, and knows that she can respond to racism in ways that preserve her dignity and her life, liberty, and property, and she knows—and demonstrates in addition through the very existence of the book itself—that she can respond by using the power of words. It may be impossible to convince a poststructuralist that there is something uniquely literary about Angelou's autobiography, but certainly part of what this autobiography is about is the power and utility of literature and its own genesis and existence as a protest against racism. One serves Angelou and *Caged Bird* better by emphasizing how form and political content work together. As Elizabeth Fox-Genovese says in respect to the general tradition of autobiographies by African-American women:

> The theoretical challenge lies in bringing sophisticated skills to the service of a politically informed reading of texts. To read well, to read fully, is inescapably to read politically, but to foreground the politics, as if these could somehow be distinguished from the reading itself, is to render the reading suspect. (67)

To neglect many of the formal ways *Caged Bird* expresses its points about identity, words, and race is to ignore the extent to which Angelou successfully met Loomis's challenge, an important aspect of her artistic accomplishment, and the potential utility of this text in literary classrooms, especially those that emphasize combining formal and ideologically-based approaches to analyzing literature.

Notes

1. Angelou tells the story of how she came to write *I Know Why the Caged Bird Sings* in several interviews collected by Jeffrey M. Elliot (80, 151–152, 211). She admits having an inability to "resist a challenge" ("Westways" 80) in her 1983 interview with Claudia Tate ("Maya Angelou" 151–152), and in at least two interviews, she discusses James Baldwin's possible role in helping Loomis use her attraction to a challenge as a ploy to get her to agree to write an autobiography ("Westways" 80, "Maya Angelou", with Tate 151).

2. A search in the MLA computerized data bank reveals forty-four items on Angelou, with the oldest dating back to 1973, three years after the publication of *I Know Why the Caged Bird Sings*. Twenty-eight of these forty-four items have appeared since 1985, and only nine appeared before 1980 (and of these, two are interviews, one is bibliographic information, and one is a portion of a dissertation). There are different possibilities for interpreting these facts: on the one hand, it may be that scholarly critics have been slow to "catch up" to Angelou, slow to treat her work—and thus to recognize it—as literature worthy of their attention; on the other hand, it may be that the scholarly status of Angelou's work has risen in concert with poststructuralism's rise and has done so because poststructuralism has made it possible to appreciate Angelou's work in new ways.

3. For the significance of identity in *Caged Bird*, see Butterfield (203), Schmidt (25–27), McPherson (16, 18, 121), and Arensberg (275, 278–280, 288–290). On displacement, see Neubauer (117–119, 126–127) and Bloom (296–297). For a consideration of the personal vs. the universal, see McPherson (45–46), Cudjoe (10), O'Neale (26), McMurry (109), and Kinnamon, who stresses the importance of community in *Caged Bird* (123–133). On the "powhitetrash" scene, see Butterfield (210–212), McPherson (31–33), and McMurry (108). For an extensive consideration of the rape, see Froula (634–636). For the effect of the rape on Maya and her relationship with Mrs. Flowers, see Lionnet (147–152). For the graduation, see Butterfield (207), McMurry (109–110), Arensberg (283), and Cudjoe (14). For the visit to the dentist, see Braxton (302–304) and Neubauer (118–119). For the month in the junkyard, see Gilbert (41) and Lionnet (156–157).

4. See Angelou's interviews with Tate ("Maya Angelou" 152) and with Neubauer ("Interview" 288–289). In an interview included in McPherson's *Order Out of Chaos*, Angelou mentions a number of incidents she omitted—some consciously, some unconsciously—from *Caged Bird* (138–140, 145–147, 157–158). O'Neale, who writes that Angelou's "narrative was held together by controlled techniques of artistic fiction" (26) and that her books are "arranged in loosely structured plot sequences which are skillfully controlled" (32), does not discuss these techniques or arrangements in any detail.

5. Angelou creates enough potential confusion about her protagonist's identity by having her called different names by different people—Ritie, Maya, Marguerite, Margaret, Mary, Sister. For the sake of consistency, I use the name "Maya" to refer to the protagonist of *Caged Bird* and the name "Angelou" to refer to its author.

6. Michaels's book is published in Stephen Greenblatt's series, "The New Historicism: Studies in Cultural Poetics," and Tompkins' book, whose subtitle is *The Cultural Work of American Fiction, 1790–1860,* emphasizes reading literature in its historical context. Tompkins' chapter, "Sentimental Power: *Uncle Tom's Cabin* and the Politics of Literary History," and Michaels' chapter on McTeague strike me as brilliant close literary analysis.

7. Schmidt (25) and McPherson (26) comment on the episodic quality of *Caged Bird*. Schmidt is the one commentator on *Caged Bird* to mention that "each reminiscence forms a unit" (25). An indication of how episodic *Caged Bird* is is how readily selections from it have lent themselves to being anthologized.

8. McMurry argues insightfully that Maya "is using the design [she rakes in the front yard] to organize feelings she could not otherwise order or express, just as Momma has used the song to organize her thoughts and feelings beyond the range of the children's taunts. She triumphs not only in spite of her restrictions, but because of them. It is because, as a Black woman, she must maintain the role of respect toward the white children that she discovers another vehicle for the true emotions" (108). Kinnamon, arguing that "Angelou's purpose is to portray cleanliness as a bonding ritual in black culture" (127), contrasts the importance of washing in the "powhitetrash" chapter with the scene in *Black Boy* where Richard Wright tells of his grandmother's washing him.

9. See Bloom, who points to Mrs. Flowers as "a perceptive mother-substitute" (293). Sexual identity is central to the book's last two chapters, in which Angelou tells of Maya's concerns about her sexual identity and the birth of her son. For discussions of these last two chapters, see Smith (373–374), Buss (103–104), Schmidt (26–27), McPherson (53–55), Arensberg (290–291), Butterfield (213), Lionnet (135–136), Demetrakopoulos (198–199), and MacKethan (60).

10. By being herself, Mrs. Flowers made Maya proud of her racial background, "proud to be Negro," but the real lesson Maya needs to learn is double: by being herself, Maya herself can be "proud to be Negro" and by being "proud to be Negro," Maya can be herself. Thus the language of the phrase implies the link between being "proud to be Negro" and being oneself.

11. See MacKethan, who emphasizes "verbal humor as a survival strategy" in *Caged Bird*. Cudjoe, arguing that "speech and language became instruments of liberation in Afro-American thought," reads *Caged Bird* in the context of this important theme (10–11).

12. Examples of this abuse occur when Wright tells his grandmother to kiss his ass, when he nonchalantly answers his uncle's question about the time of day, or when a drunken white man bashes him in the face for forgetting to say "sir" (40–44, 149–153, 173–174).

13. Thanks to my colleague, Mark Richardson, for pointing out that in Sergei Eisenstein's *Potemkin* the sailors rebelled against their officers by smashing dishes and for implying that dish smashing as an act of rebellion may be a literary trope.

14. Angelou has spoken in at least two interviews of the importance of protest in her work ("Zelo Interviews Maya Angelou" 167; "The Maya Character" 198).

15. See, for example, Neubauer (118). Mary Jane Lupton also feels that in the dentist episode "the grandmother has been defeated and humiliated, her only reward a mere ten dollars in interest for a loan she had made to the dentist" (261).

16. On May 29, 1994, twenty-four years after *Caged Bird*'s initial publication, the paperback edition was in its sixty-seventh week on the *New York Times Book Review* list of paperback best sellers.

WORKS CITED

Angelou, Maya. "An Interview with Maya Angelou." With Carol E. Neubauer. *The Massachusetts Review: A Quarterly of Literature, the Arts, and Public Affairs* 28 (1987): 286–292.

————. *I Know Why the Caged Bird Sings.* New York: Bantam, 1971.

————. "Maya Angelou." With Claudia Tate. Elliot 146–156.

————. "Maya Angelou." With Greg Hitt. Elliot 205–213.

————. "The Maya Character." With Jackie Kay. Elliot 194–200.

————. "Westways Women: Life is for Living." With Judith Rich. Elliot 77–85.

————. "Zelo Interviews Maya Angelou." With Russell Harris. Elliot 165–172.

Arensberg, Liliane K. "Death as Metaphor of Self in *I Know Why the Caged Bird Sings*." *College Language Association Journal* 20 (1976): 273–291.

Bloom, Lynn Z. "Heritages: Dimensions of Mother-Daughter Relationships in Women's Autobiographies." *The Lost Tradition: Mothers and Daughters in Literature.* Ed. Cathy N. Davidson and E. M. Broner. New York: Ungar, 1980. 291–303.

Braxton, Joanne M. "Ancestral Presence: The Outraged Mother Figure in Contemporary Afra-American Writing." *Wild Women in the Whirlwind: Afra-American Culture and the Contemporary Literary Renaissance.* Ed. Joanne M. Braxton and Andrée Nicola McLaughlin. New Brunswick, N.J.: Rutgers University Press, 1990. 299–315.

Brooks, Cleanth. "Irony as a Principle of Structure." 1948; rev. 1951. *Literary Opinion in America: Essays Illustrating the Status, Methods, and Problem of Criticism in the United States in the Twentieth Century.* Ed. Morton Dauwen Zabel. Rev. ed. New York: Harper, 1951. 729–741.

Buss, Helen M. "Reading for the Doubled Discourse of American Women's Autobiography." *A/B: Auto/Biography Studies* 6 (1991): 95–108.

Butterfield, Stephen. *Black Autobiography in America.* Amherst: University of Massachusetts Press, 1974.

Cudjoe, Selwyn R. "Maya Angelou and the Autobiographical Statement." *Black Women Writers (1950–1980): A Critical Evaluation.* Ed. Mari Evans. Garden City: Doubleday-Anchor, 1984. 6–24.

Cullen, Countee. "Yet Do I Marvel." *The Black Poets.* Ed. Dudley Randall. New York: Bantam, 1971. 100.

Demetrakopoulos, Stephanie A. "The Metaphysics of Matrilinearism in Women's Autobiography: Studies of Mead's *Blackberry Winter,* Hellman's *Pentimento,* Angelou's *I Know Why the Caged Bird Sings,* and Kingston's *The Woman Warrior*." *Women's Autobiography: Essays in Criticism.* Ed. Estelle C. Jelinek. Bloomington: Indiana University Press, 1980. 180–205.

Eagleton, Terry. *Literary Theory: An Introduction.* Minneapolis: University of Minnesota Press, 1983.

Elliot, Jeffrey M., ed. *Conversations with Maya Angelou.* Jackson: University Press of Mississippi, 1989.

Fish, Stanley. *Is There a Text in This Class? The Authority of Interpretive Communities.* Cambridge: Harvard University Press, 1980.

Fox-Genovese, Elizabeth. "My Statue, My Self: Autobiographical Writings of Afro-American Women." *The Private Self: Theory and Practice of Women's Autobiographical Writings.* Ed. Shari Benstock. Chapel Hill: University North Carolina Press, 1988. 63–89.

Froula, Christine. "The Daughter's Seduction: Sexual Violence and Literary History." *Signs: Journal of Women in Culture and Society* 11 (1986): 621–644.

Johnson, James Weldon. "O Black and Unknown Bards." *The Black Poets.* Ed. Dudley Randall. New York: Bantam, 1971. 42–43.

Kent, George E. "Maya Angelou's *I Know Why the Caged Bird Sings* and Black Autobiographical Tradition." *Kansas Quarterly* 7 (1975): 72–78.

Kinnamon, Keneth. "Call and Response: Intertextuality in Two Autobiographical Works by Richard Wright and Maya Angelou." *Belief vs. Theory in Black American Literary Criticism.* Ed. Joe Weixlmann and Chester J. Fontenot. Greenwood: Penkevill, 1986. 121–134.

Lionnet, Francoise. *Autobiographical Voices: Race, Gender, Self-Portraiture.* Ithaca: Cornell University Press, 1989.

Lupton, Mary Jane. "Singing the Black Mother: Maya Angelou and Autobiographical Continuity." *Black American Literature Forum* 24 (1990): 257–276.

MacKethan, Lucinda H. "Mother Wit: Humor in Afro-American Women's Autobiography." *Studies in American Humor* 4 (1985): 51–61.

McMurry, Myra K. "Role-Playing as Art in Maya Angelou's *Caged Bird.*" *South Atlantic Bulletin* 41 (1976): 106–111.

McPherson, Dolly A. *Order Out of Chaos: The Autobiographical Works of Maya Angelou.* New York: Peter Lang, 1990.

Michaels, Walter Benn. *The Gold Standard and the Logic of Naturalism: American Literature at the Turn of the Century.* Berkeley: University of California Press, 1987.

Neubauer, Carol E. "Maya Angelou: Self and a Song of Freedom in the Southern Tradition." *Southern Women Writers: The New Generation.* Ed. Tonette Bond Inge. Tuscaloosa: University of Alabama Press, 1990. 114–142.

O'Neale, Sondra. "Reconstruction of the Composite Self: New Images of Black Women in Maya Angelou's Continuing Autobiography." *Black Women Writers (1950–1980): A Critical Evaluation.* Ed. Mari Evans. Garden City: Doubleday-Anchor, 1984. 25–36.

Schmidt, Jan Zlotnik. "The Other: A Study of the Persona in Several Contemporary Women's Autobiographies." *The CEA Critic* 43:1 (1980): 24–31.

Shklovsky, Victor. "Art as Technique." *Russian Formalist Criticism: Four Essays.* Ed. Lee T. Lemon and Marion J. Reis. Lincoln: University of Nebraska Press, 1965. 3–24.

Smith, Sidonie Ann. "The Song of a *Caged Bird:* Maya Angelou's Quest after Self-Acceptance." *Southern Humanities Review* 7 (1973): 365–375.

Tompkins, Jane P. *Sensational Designs: The Cultural Work of American Fiction, 1790–1860.* New York: Oxford University Press, 1985.

Wright, Richard. *Black Boy (American Hunger). Later Works: Black Boy (American Hunger); The Outsider.* New York: Library of America, 1991.

CLARA JUNCKER & EDWARD SANFORD

Only Necessary Baggage:
Maya Angelou's Life Journeys

Any academic familiar with the conference circuit will know the importance of traveling light. The thing to remember is not to overextend credit
cards and suitcases with books we may not read, suits we cannot wear, and
liquor we will drink. Maya Angelou's *Wouldn't Take Nothing For My Journey
Now* (1993), however, would fit quite nicely into an overhead compartment
bag.[1] A slim volume of essays originally written for *Essence* magazine, Angelou's latest work offers a theory of life travel and movement that communicates to readers across the globe the insights she herself has gained on/off the
road. She points out, for example, that itineraries are subject to change:

> Each of us has the right and the responsibility to assess the roads
> which lie ahead, and those over which we have traveled, and if the
> future road looms ominous or unpromising, and the roads back
> uninviting, then we need to gather our resolve and, carrying only
> the necessary baggage, step off that road into another direction.
> If the new choice is also unpalatable, without embarrassment, we
> must be ready to change that as well. (24)

But Angelou never leaves behind the sense of community that informs her work and defines her self. A seasoned traveller, she stresses the

Xavier Review, Volume 16, Number 2 (1996): pp. 12–23. Copyright © 1996 Clara Juncker.

inter of international and interactive, an "in-between space" that, in Homi K. Bhabha's phrase, "may elude the politics of polarity" and allow us "to emerge as the others of our selves" (38). Angelou's communal approach to writing and living accordingly represents a theoretical and political choice. For one thing, by elasticizing self-other schisms, Angelou provides women of African descent, historically "the other of the other," with a chance to speak (Smith 34). She joins, moreover, a narrative circle of women writers who, as Sidonie Smith notes about Harriet Jacobs, "eschews the representation of herself as the isolato, self-contained in her rebellion, figuring herself instead as dependent always on the support of family and friends . . ." (50). With *Wouldn't Take Nothing* Angelou dramatizes, in fact, the dialogic pattern characteristic of African American women writers. Even within the genre of autobiography, usually associated with individual experience and achievement, she calls out and responds to other selves, other experiences, and other spaces than those she has herself occupied.

Despite the "we-ness" (Smith 68) of her narrating voice, Angelou looms large in the text as in the life it represents. Six feet tall and six decades old, she is, frankly, all over the place. This traveling, elusive, yet ever-present "diasporan subject," to use Smith's term for Hurston, wanders in and outside identities, simultaneously critical and appreciative. Continuously mobile, this subject is also, as Smith writes, "intimately tied to community as the other tongue crosses over its tongue endlessly and the other tongue speaks" (124).

Angelou's (language of) mobility takes a good deal of courage, for a woman (writer/traveler). In "On the Road Again: Metaphors of Travel in Cultural Criticism," Janet Wolf suggests a relationship between masculinity and travel metaphors, not simply because access to the road is gender-specific and unproblematic mobility accordingly a deception (235). The "already-gendered language of mobility," she argues, pushes aside women participating in cultural theory, or any other theoretical project. The metaphors of travel and movement, frequently employed in efforts to destabilize "discourses of power," thus work conservatively in terms of gender.

Fearlessly, Angelou nonetheless employs an imagery of movement throughout *Wouldn't Take Nothing for My Journey Now*. In "Passport to Understanding," she extends the title metaphor of the life journey; travel becomes a vehicle for appreciating cultural and national difference: "I encourage travel to as many destinations as possible for the sake of education as well as pleasure" (11). Travel functions, in short, as a metaphor of affinity and tolerance: "perhaps travel cannot prevent bigotry, but by demonstrating that all peoples cry, laugh, eat, worry, and die, it can introduce the idea that if we try to understand each other, we may even become friends" (12). Another chapter heading, "Extending the Boundaries," carries the language of travel into the realm of sexuality and race. In "Voices of Respect," the language of movement serves to communicate Angelou's views on child-rearing in the African American community: "If we persist in self-disrespect and then ask our children to respect themselves, it is as if we break all their bones and then insist that they win Olympic gold medals for the hundred-yard dash" (103).

By depicting herself and others in motion, Angelou reappropriates, as Wolf recommends (235), the metaphors of travel for her own purposes. *Wouldn't Take Nothing* might, for one thing, be read as theory, without the usual signals of abstract language, academic style, use of citations and so forth. In the words of Carol Boyce Davies, the mode in which "women of color theorize themselves often remain outside the boundaries of the academic context, or 'elsewhere.'" Angelou's work thus demonstrates Edward Said's notion of "travelling theory," according to which a theory might move from its original position and function to other use(r)s (Davies 18, 44). Also in various interviews does Angelou theorize about concepts such as identity, mobility, and place. "There is always movement . . . nothing ceases," she states in discussing with Russell Harris the relation of African Americans to the dominant culture. Asked by Harris if she thinks of North Carolina as home, Angelou responds: "This is a home. . . . Life offers us tickets to places which we have not knowingly asked for. (Then it makes us pay the fare.)" (*Conversations* 169).

Angelou reinvents the discourse of travel by rearranging the concept of home, the site that frames the concept of travel. To her, home involves a series of locations, much as bell hooks describes what has traditionally been a place of conflict and repression for (African American) women:

> The very meaning of home changes with the experience of decolonization, of radicalization. At times home is nowhere. At times one knows only extreme estrangement and alienation. Then home is no longer just one place. It is locations. Home is that place which enables and promotes varied and everchanging perspectives, a place where one discovers new ways of seeing reality, frontiers of difference. (qtd. Davies 49).

Home, in other words, can be a site of beginnings, of unpredictability (cp. Bhabha 62).

Angelou further usurps travel as metaphor and mode of existence by relating ideas of identity and motion to the homeland, to Africa. Though she stresses the importance of reading Aristotle, Plato, Pascal, she emphasizes particularly what the African folk tale may teach us on movement:

> One must worry over ideas that if I come forward how far do we have to go before we meet? And when we meet will I go through you and you go through me and continue until we meet someone

else? This is an African concept. Do we stay once we meet or do I actually go right through you and pass through you and continue on that road (*Conversations* 172).

Furthermore, like the editors of collections such as *Charting the Journey: Writings by Black and Third World Women*, she uses the frameworks of home and exile to map where she is going and where she has been.

The African American female persona traveling across the pages of Angelou's works is not, however, the nomad of postmodern feminist theory but rather what Davies labels a migratory subject, "moving to specific places and for specific reasons" (37). Angelou as author-function shares the fluidity and flexibility of the nomadic subject, as when she argues for life as adventure, even art. We must, she writes, "remember that we are created creative and can invent new scenarios as frequently as they are needed" (*Wouldn't Take Nothing* 66). In shifting between the local and the global, between Winston-Salem, say, and the diaspora, Angelou further links postmodern subjectivity. Yet Angelou remains firmly in control of her journey, at least discursively. Her almost sententious style indicates her sense of purpose and positions her simultaneously "elsewhere" and "somewhere."

What constitutes a journey in Angelou's usage further removes her from the travellers Janet Wolf identifies. In *Wouldn't Take Nothing*, Angelou describes what Deleuze calls "trips in intensity" or journeys *in situ* (149). Typical of the genre of autobiography, she charts the distance travelled from a younger version of the self to the moment of writing. At forty-one, for example, she began, as she writes, "a performance which now, more than twenty years later, can cause me to seriously consider changing my name and my country of residence" (110). Moreover, she distinguishes herself from her communities by subscribing to what Davies calls the "visitor theory" approach, "a kind of *critical relationality* in which various theoretical positions are interrogated for their specific applicability to Black women's experiences and textualities and negotiated within a particular inquiry with a necessary eclecticism." Angelou, in other words, goes "a piece of the way" (46) with the characters and positions she introduces in her writings, but ultimately chooses her individual path. The result is in Smith's phrase a "mobility of voice," a "self-multiplication" (120–121) that places Angelou in an intriguing relation to the communities she identifies.

The definition of community is in itself elusive. Variously defined as "an appeal to a collective praxis," "the commonality of our differences" (Scott 42), it depends, as Homi Bhabha reminds us, on "what's being said and who's saying what, who's representing who?" "I have trouble," he admits in *The Location of Culture*, "with thinking all these things as monolithic fixed categories" (3). Angelou, however, gets around the problems of usurping other voices and perspectives by locating herself in a variety of contexts. By choosing the form of autobiography or autobiographical essay, she abandons, as Karla Holloway in *Codes of Conduct*, the division between private and public domains and insists on the perspective of an African American woman (cp. Lindberg-Seyersted 75). "Her history," Holloway argues, "overwhelmingly [encourages] her to hold in tandem all of the components of her identity" (10–11). Angelou's writings, then, remain centered in the history and lives of African Americans. She inscribes, after all, the usage of many of her people in the title of her collection. "Wouldn't take nothing," she says, signaling with the double negative from where and to whom she is primarily traveling. Though Angelou explicitly addresses herself to an international readership, the superaddressee of her life story, to use Bakhtin's term, remains the people of African descent for whom her experiences may have a special resonance.

As Angelou reminds Rosa Guy in a discussion of their student activist days in Harlem, "[we were] really, always talking about Africa. Always . . ." (*Conversations* 229). Africa, real and "imagined" (Davies 20), thus unites the Pan African or diasporic community with whom Angelou primarily identifies. She grounds, for example, her conception of an everpresent spirit in the African religious belief "that all things are inhabited by spirits which must be appeased and to which one can appeal" (33). In describing her clothes at twenty-one in "Getups," she describes, in fact, the color scheme and combinations of African fabrics, for example in Ghana:

> I bought for myself beautiful reds and oranges, and greens and pinks, and teals and turquoise. I chose azure dresses and blouses and sweaters. And quite often I wore them in mixtures which bring surprise to say the least, to the eyes of people who could not avoid noticing me. (53)

A former Ghana resident and the producer of a TV series on African traditions in American life, Angelou subtly takes off on her life journey from the African continent.

She situates her autobiography in the African American community that historically resulted from this passage. She emphasizes, to be sure, the African roots of terms used in slave communities such as "brother," "sister," "aunt" and "uncle," terms that in Africa hold a special meaning. Ama Ata Aidoo writes in *Our Sister Killjoy* about the name of Sissie:

> it is just a beautiful way they call 'Sister' by people who like you very much. Especially if there are not many girl babies in the family . . . one of the very few ways where an original concept from our old ways has been given expression successfully in English. (28)

Angelou argues, however, that among African American slaves the use of kinship terms became even more powerful, because "they pridefully possessed a quality which modified the barbarism" of life in bondage (101).

Other essays of *Wouldn't Take Nothing* establish a link between a present social context and past history particularly poignant to African Americans. In "Further New Directions" the sixteen-year old Maya, just fired from a job, is crying in a upstairs room, only to be met by her mother's radiant indulgence: "'Fired? Fired?' She laughed. 'What the hell is that? Nothing. Tomorrow you'll go looking for another job. That's all'" (80). Angelou's international readership might think of eighties unemployment or nineties short-term jobs. African American readers, however, might focus specifically on the subtext involving systemic discrimination from *Dred Scott, Plessy vs. Fergusson* and beyond, and the strategy for survival and self-respect Angelou promotes with the vignette.

Most explicitly, Angelou as narrator communicates her membership of the African American community through the first and second person plural pronoun. "We have used these terms [of kinship]," she writes in 'Voices of Respect,' "to help us survive slavery, its aftermath, and today's crisis of revived racism." In other statements, however, Angelou discreetly withdraws into third person and preliminary subjects to allow for other readers and experiences to join in: "When African Americans choose to speak sweetly to each other, not only do the voices fall in register, but there is an unconscious increase in music between the speakers" (102).

With this gesture, Angelou establishes a community of writer and audience that contributes to the wide circulation of her works. She includes, for example, a series of anecdotes in *Wouldn't Take Nothing* that minimizes the distance between writers and readers (Allan 137), among them her martini-based attempts at getting and holding the attention of a group of male journalists of African descent, who remain oblivious to her accomplishments in a variety of areas: house-keeping, publishing, sex, clothing, and more. This incident in "Extending the Boundaries," referring to her determination to disregard race and nationality in her choice of future partners, illustrates as well the performative dimension of Angelou's prose. Her career as a performer spills into the pages of *Wouldn't Take Nothing* not only in "Sensual Encouragement," which describes her experience as a dancer, but also in the (self)dramatization of the work. Angelou fills, in a sense, her text with bodies, who enact the life lessons she shares with her readership. As Paul Gilroy explains, the performance of "expressive cultures" seeks to establish connections between the performer and the audience through "*dialogic* rituals so that spectators acquire the active role of which are sometimes cathartic and which may symbolize or even create a community" (qtd.

Bhabha 30). Moreover, as Susan Griffin notes, the essay form itself stimulates dialogue and communication, overtly or covertly (Joeres 155–156).

Angelou identifies as well with a community of writers, predominantly but not exclusively of African American women. "I'm impressed," she states in *Conversations*, "by Toni Morrison a great deal. . . . I'm impressed by the growth of Rosa Guy. I'm impressed by Ann Petry. I'm impressed by the work of Joan Didion. . . . I would walk fifty blocks in high heels to buy the works of any of these writers" (156). Also William Shakespeare, Paul Laurence Dunbar, James Weldon Johnson and James Baldwin belong to this community, which, however rooted in African American experiences and cultures, transcends gender, time, and race.

The courage Angelou stresses as the unifying characteristic of these writers would apply as well to her community of women. She places first in *Wouldn't Take Nothing* the essay "In All Ways a Woman" to signal the importance of this community, and the many calls for courage it faces. "Being a woman is hard work," she states. "Not without joy or even ecstasy, but still relentless, unending work" (6). At times she sounds like a feminist, as when she notes that "in a time and world where males hold sway and control, the pressure upon women to yield their rights-of-way is tremendous" (6). She encourages women to cultivate a sense of humor and an eye for absurdity, qualities that might come in handy in what she implicitly considers a gender war: "Women should be tough, tender, laugh as much as possible, and live long lives. The struggle for equality continues unabated, and the woman warrior who is armed with wit and courage will be among the first to celebrate victory" (7). Angelou moves, however, from this oppositional positioning of women into a more womanist realm, where playfulness and abandonment might liberate women from "becoming a mirror image of those men who value power above life" (7).

Annie Henderson and Vivian Baxter, Angelou's grandmother and mother, combine warrior courage with humor and wit. Both dare to leave the beaten roads and, as Angelou writes about her grandmother, "cut herself a brand-new path" (24). Finding no possibility of being hired at the Stamps cotton gin or lumber mill, she made the factories work for her, by setting up a lunch stall. Vivian Baxter, too, "practiced stepping off the expected road and cutting herself a brand-new path any time the desire arose" (80). Angelou's repetitions strengthen the bonds of biology and personality uniting the figureheads of her community of women. She goes out of her way, moreover, to include others, for example by addressing directly her (female) readers: "Seek the fashion which truly fits and befits you . . . be so much yourself that the clothes you choose increase your naturalness and grace" (57).

Interestingly, Angelou avoids the first person plural in discussing the feminine. She remains an "I," and readers "you," and thus asserts the individual within the communal, as in her advice on style. Writing simultaneously inside and outside the group, she escapes the fixity she finds claustrophobic. Yet womanist loyalties permeate Angelou's texts. As she says in *Conversations*, she dedicates *Now Sheba Sings the Song* to "all my brown, black, beige, yellow, red and white sisters" and attempts with this collection of poetry "to herald the various kinds of beauty of women, some plain, some young, and of all colours" (190). She wishes for radicals, she tells Jackie Kay in 1987, "to remain human and not take on the trappings of the opposition and become dehumanized"; she praises African American women for the gift of sharing and humanity they have managed to retain (197).

Angelou's notions of community demonstrate this gift. Ultimately, she includes all of humanity, as she communicates with a poem at the end of an essay on subtle racism: "We seek success in Finland, / are born and die in Maine. / In minor ways we differ, / in major we're the same." Her repetitions of the lines "We are more alike, my friends / than we are unalike" (125) invite all readers to enter into her global perspective, her direct address suggesting friendship and coexistence, ultimately based in religion: "We are a community of children of God, whether we admit it or not, whether we call it God or the Creator or the Source or Nature. We're a community" (*Conversations* 143). Her oscillations between sameness and difference creates "a multiple *dialogic of differences*," which, in Smith's formulation, "operates to both accommodate and diffuse identification between narrator and reader" (52). In her discussion of community bonds, Angelou remains simultaneously grounded and in flight.

From this traveling perspective, Angelou stresses the importance of alliances. She is concerned with divisions within the African American community and in her writings lavishes first/second person plural pronouns upon discussions of this issue: "We need to examine what the absence of those qualities [morality and piety] has done to our communal spirit, and we must learn how to retrieve from the dust heap of nonuse and return them to a vigorous role in our lives" (70). In other words, she tries to heal the gap between street kids and their parents, between lower class and middle class African Americans, between residents of inner cities and the suburbs, and between men and women of African descent.

These divisions healed, African Americans would challenge the dominant definition of nation and establish instead a diasporic community across traditional political borders. In discussing with Rosa Guy the "casual indifference" of young African Americans to their history, Angelou emphasizes that their future is linked with, say, Nicaragua or the Middle East (*Conversations* 234). Interestingly, Angelou turns immediately afterwards in this 1988 interview to the topic of women of color, implicitly supporting the contention of feminist scholars that "nation" is a masculine, Eurocentric concept. As Davies argues, "the need to understand transnationally the various resistances to Eurocentric domination and to create an 'elsewhere' is embedded in the diaspora formulation." She goes on to quote Michael Hanchard:

> Embedded in the tale of the diaspora is a symbolic revolt against the nation-state, and for this reason the diaspora holds a dual significance. It suggests a transnational dimension to black identity, for it is a human necklace strung together by a thread known as the slave trade, a thread with little regard for national boundaries. (Davies 40)

Angelou returns, in fact, to the shared, often painful history of various ethnic groups out of her belief that human beings are more alike than unalike (or at least that the fates of everybody are intertwined). As she puts it in *Conversations:* "black Americans have been here since the year 1619, and this is as much our country as anybody else's, save the Native Americans. We will all live together or not at all" (158). To all human beings, she argues, community functions as a support system that enables us to survive and endure: "Living is so difficult at best. Even if you have a good job and a family, it's difficult to stand up and oppose gravity and go about the business of your responsibilities" (*Conversations* 144).

Travel and writing help Angelou establish the community bonds that make possible this going about our business. These activities become reconnection, a literal and symbolic way of healing differences in the process of acknowledging them. Carol Boyce Davies explains:

> Because we were/are products of separations and dislocations and dis-memberings, people of African descent in the Americas historically have sought reconnection. From the "flying back" stories which originated in slavery . . . this need to reconnect and re-member . . . has been a central impulse in the structuring of Black thought. (17)

Moving towards her readership, Angelou brings about the confluence Eudora Welty describes in the closing pages of *One Writer's Beginnings*. For both Angelou and Welty, writing, travel, and memory become indistinguishable as they seek the communal. As Welty puts it at the end of her autobiography, "the memory is a living thing—it too is in transit. But during its moment, all that is remembered joins, and lives—the old and the young, the past and the present, the living and the dead" (104).

By crossing boundaries, *Wouldn't Take Nothing* shifts the categories and the canons that have traditionally defined African American women's writings. Movement, and writing, thus bring about a new, more fluid identity, much like Angelou describes herself in "A Day Away": "If I am living in a city, I wander streets, window-shop, or gaze at buildings. I enter and leave public parks, libraries, the lobbies of skyscrapers, and movie houses. I stay in no place for very long" (138). The subjectivity of *Wouldn't Take Nothing* accordingly moves towards the "affinity" politics Donna Haraway associates with the cyborg and Sidonie Smith with late-twentieth-century autobiography (Smith 181 f). Individual/communal, grounded/in motion, the narrator of *Wouldn't Take Nothing* resists, escapes, and writes.

Throughout her writings, from wherever she positions herself, Angelou returns to the importance of racial and global alliances. As she states in *Conversations,* "we will survive together or we will die together; it is imperative that we make alliances, sincere alliances" (198). Though Angelou continually travels to other perspectives and other backgrounds than her own, she brings, so to speak, her readers and her various communities with her on her journeys. She started out in the South during a period of rigid segregation and discrimination and may, in the "now" of her title, be going business class. The ground changes behind and beneath her, but Angelou remains embedded within African/African American history and culture. She makes room, nonetheless, for all of us, and fits us nicely into the luggage she defines as necessary. That her suitcase may get a "heavy" label is another matter entirely.

NOTE

1. References to *Wouldn't Take Nothing for My Journey Now* will appear parenthetically in the text.

WORKS CITED

Allan, Tuzyline Jita. "A Voice of Our Own: Implications of Impersonality in the Essays of Virginia Woolf and Alice Walker." In Joeres and Mittman. 131–147.

Aidoo, Ama Ata. *Our Sister Killroy.* Essex: Longman, 1977.

Angelou, Maya. *Wouldn't Take Nothing for My Journey Now.* 1993. New York: Bantam, 1994.

Bhabha, Homi K. *The Location of Culture.* London: Routledge, 1994.

Davies, Carol Boyce. *Black Women, Writing and Identity: Migrations of the Subject.* London: Routledge, 1994.

Deleuze, Giles. "Nomad Thought." In *The New Nietzche.* Ed. David B. Allison. New York: Dell, 1977. 142–149.

Elliot, Jeffrey M. *Conversations with Maya Angelou.* Jackson: University Press of Mississippi, 1989.

Grewal, Shabna, Jackie Kay, et al. *Charting the Journey: Writings by Black and Third World Women.* London: Sheba Feminist Publishers, 1988.

Holloway, Karla. *Codes of Conduct: Race, Ethics, and the Color of Our Character.* New Brunswick, NJ: Rutgers University Press, 1995.

Joeres, Ruth-Ellen Boetcher. "The Passionate Essay: Radical Feminist Essayists." In Joeres
and Mittman. 151–171.

———, and Elizabeth Mittman, ed. *The Politics of the Essay: Feminist Perspectives*. Indianapolis:
Indiana University Press, 1994.

Lindberg-Seyersted, Brita. *Black and Female: Essays on Writings by Black Women in the
Diaspora*. Oslo: Scandinavian University Press, 1994.

Scott, Joan Wallach. "The Campaign against Political Correctness." In *PC Wars: Politics and
Theory in the Academy*. Ed. Jeffrey Williams. New York: Routledge, 1995. 22–43.

Smith, Sidonie. *Subjectivity, Identity, and the Body: Women's Autobiographical Practices in the
Twentieth Century*. Bloomington: Indiana University Press, 1993.

Welty, Eudora. *One Writer's Beginnings*. Cambridge, Mass.: Harvard University Press, 1984.

Wolf, Janet. "On the Road Again: Metaphors of Travel in Cultural Criticism." *Cultural
Studies* 7.2 (May 1993): 224–239.

MARION M. TANGUM &
MARJORIE SMELSTOR

Hurston's and Angelou's Visual Art:
The Distancing Vision and the Beckoning Gaze

"Where is me? Ah don't see me."

—*Their Eyes Were Watching God*

"What you lookin' at me for? I didn't come to stay. . . ."

—*I Know Why the Caged Bird Sings*

Integrating another fine art into a literary text, so that one artistic medium comments upon and provides an infrastructure for the literary, is, of course, a valued technique of American literature, particularly of African American literature. Slaves like Frederick Douglass who wrote narratives, as well as W. E. B. DuBois and Richard Wright, have all contributed to a rich tradition of the appropriation of other genres to create literary texts, a tradition that is legacy for other twentieth century writers to call upon.

Two of those more recent writers, Zora Neale Hurston and Maya Angelou, have built upon this tradition in a way that is new, creating verbal art that is thoroughly visual in technique. In two works of Hurston and Angelou, respectively, *Their Eyes Were Watching God* (1937) and *I Know Why the Caged Bird Sings* (1969), each of which has defied classification to any single genre, the constructs of visual art become sometimes the text's subject, sometimes its

Southern Literary Journal, Volume 31, Issue 1 (Fall 1998): pp. 80–97. Copyright © 1998 University of North Carolina Press.

49

strategy, in ways that significantly alter the reader's participation in the text. We may question, as Janie does in our epigraph from *Their Eyes,* "Where is me? Ah don't see me" (21). The answer lies at times in the interconnectedness of reader, narrator, and character, through the intimacy of a beckoning, almost mesmerizing, "gaze," but then it lies in the position we assume as viewer, as subjects become distant—for viewing only: as the narratives compel us to remember, "What you lookin' at me for? I didn't come to stay."[1]

The ebb and flow of intersubjectivity that is at the center of *Their Eyes* and *Caged Bird* is created in both by a tension between, respectively, their author's artistic vision and their persona's or character's subjective "gaze." Through visual artistic techniques applied to language, Hurston and Angelou alternately hold the reader outside the text, offering a vision of aesthetics at work, and then, abruptly, through the starkly personal and riveting gaze of their characters or personae, compel the reader to enter—to experience personally—their works' reality.

This study's examination of the workings of the visual into the literary in both of these texts offers insights into how each author effects the reader's participation; and the comparison of the two furthers our understanding of the intertextuality of the two books, as we explore in the conclusion of this study.

Margaret Olin's argument that two distinct arts, documentary and photography, become not only blurred but merged in *Let Us Now Praise Famous Men* (1941) provides the impetus for this study. In the case of its authors, James Agee and Walker Evans, merged genres result in a text that is transformed into a new type of art defined not by any similarities between the genres but, instead, by their differences: "When one regards the book as art, its documentary nature impertinently demands attention; but when regarded as documentary, its artistry intrudes" (92). Olin shows that Agee and Evans thus achieve a text that illuminates the "formative contradiction" of modern literature: the attempt to make of ostensibly hermetic art the engine of social change. Through the collaboration of camera and pen, Evans and Agee illuminate the reader's schizophrenic roles: as participant with the subjects, and therefore subjects themselves and, as spectator, able to appreciate a work of art that "presupposes distance and autonomy" (94). Authors, subjects, and readers are enmeshed in a web of intersubjectivity and then torn apart. But the aesthetic vision of the artists abruptly unravels that web, riveting our attention on the artistic object that has been created. The result, according to Olin, is a text that "repeatedly protests, down to its last sentence, that it is only about to begin" (112).

In the case of Hurston or Angelou, the result of this creation of schizophrenic roles for the reader is a tension between personally entering that realm and merely observing it, leading to a frustrating reading experience.

As noted above, the juxtaposition of different genres in literary texts is nothing new. DuBois, in *The Souls of Black Folk* (1903), in which each chapter is preceded by an epigraph of poetry juxtaposed to musical bars, created a unique example. His text is a model for modernism's alternating beckoning/rebuffing pose as well: beckoning us with the promise, rebuffing us with the practice of the so-called American Dream, and so envisioning for us that dream's disconnection with American lives. Wright's *12 Million Black Voices* (1941) is part of that legacy, too, comprised of prose juxtaposed to photographs. Unlike Agee and Evans, however, who worked in tandem, Wright describes photographs that were taken some ten years earlier, in the 1930s, by professional photographers (including Evans) during the Farm Security Administration. The text offers some historic comment upon the photographs, whereas the photographs serve as sole documentation of the text. Despite the fact that many do not provide a very compelling documentation, they do serve to render Wright's text another example of black authors' crossing of the boundaries of art forms.

Although no critics to date have noted the integration of the visual art into the literary in Hurston and Angelou, others have noted a crossing of *literary* genre boundaries, resulting in difficulty classifying authors' works. In her interpretation of the mule's "funeral" in *Their Eyes*, for example, Christine Levecq states, "Suddenly the novel skips out of the boundaries of its genre" (101). With respect to *Caged Bird* and other African American "autobiographies," Selwyn Cudjoe notes that they are formed from a convergence of traditions at variance among themselves and concludes that, as a result, "there is nothing in the autobiography that guarantees it will not be read as fiction or vice versa" (7). Nellie McKay illuminates "acts of cultural significance" in the alleged novel *Their Eyes*—"a sustaining connection to the roots of black culture" through its orality, its rich display of signifyin(g), and its centeredness in the community—that define "the nature of the Afro-American autobiographical impulse" (54). That impulse, she argues, is always present and subversive, blurring the boundaries between fictional and autobiographical work despite authorial intent to compose either one or the other. Levecq shows how that blurring alternately asserts, then undermines, the relative state of Janie's self-developing identity.

However, Levecq does not deal with what we propose to show, that Hurston's development of her persona's identity is revealed by an integration of the literary with visual art; but Levecq's title—"'You Heard Her, You Ain't Blind'"—strongly suggests the potential value of a study of that integration. We argue that both Hurston and Angelou, regardless of the genres in which the works we are studying supposedly reside, use the resulting multiplicity to achieve what Janet Varner Gunn calls an elastic process of reading "autobiography" [our emphasis]: one that is both participatory and "distantiating," an occasion of self-discovery as well as an experience of otherness (20).

Alfred Stone, however, in speaking of autobiographical literature ("factual fiction," he calls it), implicitly denies the validity of the inclusion of the visual although he agrees that crossing boundaries of genre clearly occurs in literature. He posits that reading autobiographical prose engages readers in two distinct responses—reality-testing and spectatorship, the signposts of nonfiction; and willing suspension of disbelief and participation, the signposts of fiction—which occur sometimes simultaneously and sometimes alternately, and thereby multiply the tensions already inherent in the reading process. But autobiographical writing (which we consider an accurate description of both *Their Eyes* and *Caged Bird*), according to Stone, is only verbal, originating as a "verbal artifact; its historical, psychological, and philosophical reconstructions are accomplished only by means of words," freeing autobiographers from "the physical constraints of the painter, and responsive to time and history in ways Rembrandt, Van Gogh, or Eakins cannot be" (324).

On one level, his view appears indisputable; in fact, however, we argue that its contrary is true: perhaps "factual fiction" writers use the physical constraints of the visual artist in their portraits so they can be liberated from the restrictions of *verbal* artifacts. Writers may fruitfully blur the so-called genre even more, by seeing how autobiographical fiction and fictional autobiography are not only innovatively verbal but characterized by visual art, as we show that Hurston does in *Their Eyes*.

The title page announcing the text of *Their Eyes* appears to negate the notions of Stone generally, and of McKay and Levecq specifically: "A Novel" it claims, as subtitle. What follows, however, holds that claim up for reconsideration, giving this text a complexity that not only defies classification as a single literary genre, as Stone et al. have predicted, but that also places the visual art in the foreground of the literary, sometimes drawing the reader in to see with the persona through a shared gaze, and then abruptly switching to a lofty authorial stance, but virtually throughout, more so than any other "novel" or "autobiography" (including Angelou's) that comes to mind, featuring the act of seeing.

The title exemplifies that feature and prepares us for the push and pull of the vision and the gaze as well: the third-person-plural subject safely distances us at once; "*their* eyes" do not seem threatening to engage and perhaps then engulf us. But the verb and direct object immediately bring us back: What is it to watch God? To watch an act of creation? To "see" that which is beyond the vision afforded by descriptive art? To participate, by virtue of that transcendent sight, in the creation of self? Whatever it means, the title renders uncertain that which we will "see," and what our stance will be, as we enter the text, but it also emphatically establishes the visual as both subject and object of the textual enterprise.

The opening passage further obfuscates what we may ultimately see, but the act of seeing—or not—is the distinguishing characteristic:

> Ships at a distance have every man's wish on board. For some they come in with the tide. For others they sail forever on the horizon, never out of sight, never landing until the Watcher turns his eyes away in resignation, his dreams mocked to death by Time. That is the life of men.
>
>   Now women forget all those things they don't want to remember, and remember everything they don't want to forget. The dream is the truth. They act and do things accordingly. (1)

As Henry Louis Gates has put it, "A man's [desire] . . . becomes reified onto a disappearing ship, and he is transformed from a human being into 'a Watcher'"; a woman's is controlled by her—by her ability to view it metaphorically and "control the process of memory" (171). As Gates has also pointed out, Hurston is signifyin(g) upon Frederick Douglass's similar passage in *Life and Times*, thus figuratively establishing an opposition in the nature of men's and women's desires: we see, in Hurston's signifyin(g), the prescience of the establishment of the fundamental opposition between the vision and the gaze. Expanding upon Douglass's description of the ships he watched as "so many shrouded ghosts, to terrify and torment me with my wretched condition" (qtd in Gates 170), Hurston magnifies their haunting of him and generalizes his experience to that of all men, as she provides us with a vision of the Watcher who becomes, at the same time, the gazer, immersed in and paralyzed by his gaze: the ghosts hold him in their grasp so that he cannot see to act; he is unable to turn his eyes away until he can do so only "in resignation." Ironically, the distance does not distance *men* from those ghosts; rather, it draws them in and paralyzes them in their gaze.

The metaphorical representation of desire by women, on the other hand—the naming of it as object rather than the objectification of self that occurs when a man is "transformed from a human being into 'a Watcher,'" as Douglass says—brings desire into intimate proximity, unlike the ships, but, at the same time, enables women to stand back and see it apart from themselves: as aesthetic vision.[2]

That opening passage also serves to announce emphatically what this book is about: watching, looking, seeing—and, to the extent that we (author/character/reader) enter into the process, creating.[3] Seeing as subject is borne out beginning on the very first page:[4] a woman comes back from the dead, one who, as the epigraph reveals, could not recognize herself in an object that was "real"—a photograph of herself. Her question "Where is me?" then, is what she will attempt to answer by locating herself through the course of the "novel." For her, the narrator unequivocally assures us, the "dream is the truth"—something she can "see" and thus becomes real in a way that a photograph, the vision that keeps us all at bay, is not.

From the first page of *Caged Bird*, too, Angelou offers a tantalizing invitation into her self—and then as promptly distances us from sharing that personal, all-of-a-sudden incommunicable, experience. This invitation to us to come in and gaze, then that sudden refusal to give us eye contact, is a process that recurs throughout the work. "What you looking at me for? I didn't come to stay . . ." (1). With these opening lines, the autobiography establishes a motif of gazing: willing members of the congregation of the Colored Methodist Episcopal Church, and readers who are willing, share a gaze with the young Angelou as she struggles to remember her memorized poem. Resembling the passages that appear in *Let Us Now Praise Famous Men* that Olin describes as incorporating three individuals—author, subject, reader—this direct invitation "takes the reader by the arm, exhorting 'you' to direct your gaze toward a photographed person" (105). But Olin warns that such an invitation is accepted at a price: "You are not going to be able to look 'this terrific thing in the eyes' unless you do so 'with all the summoning of heart you have'" (105). Gazing longer into the eyes of the child Angelou, as the author thrusts before us a repetition of the opening lines, we begin to grasp Olin's warning. Dolly McPherson has noted the importance of the opening lines in pointing to the importance of "something to look at" and has further suggested that since the persona is reciting an Easter poem, the "something to look at" is the persona as Christ (19). While the theme of cyclical renewal is present in the book, the prologue merely points to it. What the prologue actually augurs for and emphasizes is the suffering and descent preceding the rise and resurrection ultimately experienced by the maturing persona herself. And the narrative invites the reader to share this suffering and descent through sharing the gaze of the author and persona in the recreation of a poignant moment of childhood pain.

As the adult Angelou relates this experience, she acknowledges that her young self, a victim of "well-known forgetfulness" (1), had not forgotten the lines; instead, she had more important things to remember, which should be a cue that the opening of *Caged Bird* is more than the recreation pointed to above—that it will be a complexity created by a tension between narrator and subject, manifested by the tension between the vision of that adult and the gaze of the subject, the child.

Having been invited in to share the intensely personal gaze of young Maya, experiencing her pain with her as the shared gaze enables us to do, we participate in the text, in her embarrassment, in an entirely personal way.

Prompted to recall her lines, young Maya becomes so flustered that she runs out of the church, tripping over a foot stuck out from the children's pew, and then suffers the unforgettable—which she relates to us by letting us gaze into her eyes so that we are present:

> I stumbled and started to say something, or maybe to scream, but a green persimmon, or it could have been a lemon, caught me between the legs and squeezed. . . . Then, before I reached the door, the sting was burning down my legs and into my Sunday socks. I knew I'd have to let it go, or it would probably run right back up to my head and my poor head would burst like a dropped watermelon, and all my brains and spit and tongue and eyes would roll all over the place. (3)

But our gaze is abruptly interrupted: the narrative hand suddenly holds us at a distance, permitting us to view her plight objectively, not personally: "If growing up is painful for the Southern Black girl, being aware of her displacement is the rust on the razor that threatens the throat. It is an unnecessary insult" (1). First person becomes third; pronouns are almost entirely omitted. The metaphor of the rusty razor wrests our attention from the eyes and feelings of young Maya. Angelou seems to consciously grip the problem of modernism here: the potential to lose ourselves in the mesmerizing gaze of the subject and so become subjects ourselves, inaccessible to the artistic vision competing with that compelling gaze. She commandingly pulls us back to observe from a distance, shifting her tense and forcing us to shift our viewing perspective, away from a familiar and thus comforting place in Angelou's and our own pasts into a discomforting, disconcerting present that makes indirect object of what had been subject, grammatically separating us from the southern black girl and so insuring that we can "see" her. Our, Maya's and our, personal recollection of that morning at the Colored Methodist Episcopal Church yields to the reality of victimization and its social consequences—and an appreciation of the art of the metaphor and the power of language, without which we remain subject and only subject. The gaze that reverts to the vision, through the alterations of language alone, makes problematic, and so keeps supple, the position of the audience in *Caged Bird*.

There is a remarkable similarity between the opening lines of *Caged Bird* and the opening page of *Their Eyes:* Angelou writes, "I hadn't so much forgot as I couldn't bring myself to remember. Other things were more important" (1). Hurston's narrator observes, you will recall, "Now, women forget all those things they don't want to remember, and remember everything they don't want to forget" (9). The privilege of memory drives both books; and their common intertextuality is present via their common visual techniques.

As the passages above exemplify, technically the visual works in both texts to lure us in and then push us back into our chairs. Such shifts in the reader's visual stance occur most directly, however, in *Caged Bird:* Angelou's language alternately lures us in, almost seductively, to share a gaze—connect ourselves personally—with the subject. And then we are forced out of the connection by language that diverts our attention to a vision of how difficult that connection is to maintain, and how dangerous to the ultimate success of the text. Consider the familiar chapter of Angelou's school graduation. Beckoning us to personally enter the experience by looking not only into the eyes but into the soul of the subject, we feel with Angelou the anticipation of the ceremony, the gift-giving that precedes it, the excitement of beginning it:

> In the Store I was the person of the moment. The birthday girl. . . . My class was wearing butter-yellow pique dresses, and Momma launched out on mine. . . . I was going to be lovely. . . . I was headed for the freedom of open fields. . . . Years of withdrawal were brushed aside and left behind, as hanging ropes of parasitic moss. (144–145)

Unlike a similar section in Wright's autobiography in which the graduation exercise is recounted as an experience of isolation (see Kenneth Kinnamon's article for a complete discussion), Angelou's exercise invites us in through a technique of enabling us to share a communal gaze, even as we hear and experience the demoralizing effect of the invited white speaker's graduation address, and especially as we hear and experience the class valedictorian, "the conservative, the proper, the A student," lead the graduating class, in a totally unrehearsed gesture, in singing "the Negro national anthem" (156). The text invites us in, to gaze into the eyes of those graduates, as they gaze into ours, singing to us. We, with Angelou, hear "really for the first time" James Weldon Johnson's stirring words and, with her, as the song ends, "echoes of the song [shivering] in the air" (156).

Then abruptly, lest we become mesmerized in that gaze, unable to pull back and remember our ostensible job as reader to view the aesthetics of the text, Angelou cuts our close connection to the graduates, shifting tone and verb tense, and *audience,* to focus our vision on a larger view of artistic language itself and a contemplation of the larger community it speaks to, by singing her version of James Weldon Johnson's paean of praise. Giving Johnson center stage as she adds "known" to his "unknown bards" and expanding his focus on those "of long ago," Angelou as teacher here would lead us to seek Johnson's source:

There is a wide, wide wonder in it all,
That from degraded rest and servile toil
The fiery spirit of the seer should call
These simple children of the sun and soil. (Johnson 30)

She clearly does so in the voice of Angelou the poet-critic, the adult, the namer of experiences, into whose eyes, like the eyes of Johnson, we are *not* invited to gaze:

Oh, Black known and unknown poets,
how often have your auctioned pains sustained us?
Who will compute the lonely nights made less lonely by
your songs, or by the empty pots made less tragic by your tales?
(156)

Just as the last lines of Angelou's opening passage distance us who had been invited to gaze into the eyes of the young girl at the Colored Methodist Episcopal Church, lest we become mesmerized by the gaze and so become locked in wrestling with only the experience of that gaze, so do the last lines of this chapter pull readers back from the temptation of a subjective view, to contemplate the aesthetics of the work and its implications. We thus finally remain Other, separated by a linguistic averting of eyes, with only a *view* of the gaze that is shared by narrator and those black poets whose words she evokes.

This stance of Otherness is essential to the battle between detachment and involvement that is the challenge of modern art. Olin observes how Evans' photographs show extreme poverty, but "they do not tempt the reader to rearrange the mantle or to donate a silverware drawer and extra spoons to put in it" (99). It is surprising, she asserts, that *Let Us Now Praise Famous Men* communicates a dependence upon prayer as the only remedy for those who are photographed; and she posits that this Christian resignation reinforces the inactivity of the powerful. Throughout *Caged Bird,* especially in the chapter relating the revival meeting, Angelou suggests this same resignation and inactivity in which both observer and observed are immobilized by their own particular brand of passivity. As such, they are *both* visionaries: the powerful and the powerless locked in their visions of reality and unable to alter that reality.

Angelou frames the chapter of this visionary impasse with a photograph of people exhausted by the tedious, back-breaking activity to which they are forced, women with feet swollen to fit the discarded men's shoes they are wearing, and men with drooping shoulders and tired bodies. And yet these people are resigned to their fates, as Momma's words confirm: "Back where you started, bless the Lord" (110). As the chapter unfolds, the progression of the revival meeting, the colorful, enthusiastic congregation—those upon whom we gaze—dramatically demonstrates their belief in God and their gratitude to Him. "The minister's voice was a pendulum" swinging back and forth as he announces that the text for his sermon is "the least of these," and the people, mesmerized by this pendulum, know they are saved. As we gaze at the pendulum ourselves, we too become mesmerized in the moment.

But the chapter concludes with analysis, pushing us away from the community, distancing us and giving us pause:

> They basked in the righteousness of the poor and the exclusiveness of the downtrodden. Let the whitefolks have their money and power and segregation and sarcasm and big houses and schools and lawns like carpets, and books and mostly—mostly—let them have their whiteness. It was better to be meek and lowly, spat upon and abused for this little time than to spend eternity frying in the fires of hell. No one would have admitted that the Christian and charitable people were happy to think of their oppressors' turning forever on the Devil's spit over the flames of fire and brimstone. (110–111)

Young Maya, who had both participated in and observed the revival meeting, is recreated by Angelou, crafting her self-portrait in a manner that establishes a tension between the gaze and the vision, between a participation created by visual connectedness and the distance created by a focus only on the aesthetic. Whereas Angelou narrates the event at the beginning of the chapter so that readers are not only invited but beckoned to participate in her life story, she preaches at the end of the chapter, warning readers that the didactic voice of the autobiographer is delivering a sermon—not an invitation.

In *Their Eyes*, visual switches are equally prevalent, but many are less direct. For example, Hurston's language in the following passage invites the reader in, to share a gaze with Nanny—but only in an indirect manner: "She bolted upright and peered out the window and saw Johnny Taylor lacerating her Janie with a kiss" (11). Sharing her visual stance, the reader also indirectly shares a gaze with Nanny, but without the riveting of eye upon eye that could result in loss of the reader's identity. Authorial language immediately switches both narrator's and reader's stance, distancing us so that we have only a vision of Nanny, see her only as Other—"Nanny's head and face looked like the standing roots of some old tree that had been torn away by storm" (12)—for we now participate in the visual stance of Janie and would, were she to turn to us, have the opportunity to participate intimately in her gaze.

Uniquely, *Their Eyes*, unlike *Caged Bird*, takes such visual interplay as its very subject. Hurston has said that "black expression turns upon 'the interpretation of the English language in terms of pictures'" (qtd in Gates 199). The title of McKay's article ("Crayon Enlargements") implies, and Barbara Johnson states, that there is a remarkable preponderance of photography in the text. Johnson describes it as a series of snapshots of Janie, which differ so that her identity is never whole. Johnson credits Hurston for maintaining those divisions of identity—various poses, captured at various times—as the textual foreground: "There is no point of view from which the universal characteristics of the human, or of the woman, or of the black woman, or even of Zora Neale Hurston, can be selected and totalized" (210).[5] Expanding on McKay and Johnson, we argue that the principal action of this narrative is the visual. Turner was

> a vanishing-*looking* kind of a man as if there used to be parts about him that stuck out individually but now he hadn't a thing about him that wasn't dwindled and *blurred*. Just like he had been sandpapered down to a long oval mass. (137; emphasis added)

> Mrs. Tyler, hair all gray and black and bluish and reddish in streaks. All the capers that cheap dye could cut was *showing*. The corset gone and the shaking old woman hanging all over herself. Her chin hung from her ears and rippled down her neck like drapes . . . (emphasis added)

> Death, that strange being with the huge square toes . . . stands in his high house that *overlooks* the world. Stands *watchful* and motionless all day with his sword drawn back, waiting . . . (emphasis added)

"To share a gaze with Annie Mae Grudger" in Evans' photograph of her is to engage in an "epistemological" relationship with her (Olin 96). The photographs of Nanny, or Turner, or Death, or Mrs. Tyler, or the disintegrating Joe Starks—whom Janie's camera snaps as "bags hanging from an ironing board"—distance us from those characters, of course; but they provide us, indirectly again, the opportunity for an intimate gaze with the photographer: Janie. It will take Hurston the author to break that gaze with a view of her own aesthetic vision. Adding to the linguistic snapshots in virtually every instance is an abundance of language of seeing—or looking, anyway:

> She had come back from the sodden and the bloated; the sudden dead, their *eyes* flung wide open in judgment. (9; emphasis added)

Every morning the world flung itself over and *exposed* itself to the sun. (81; emphasis added)

They sat on the boarding house porch and *saw* the sun plunge into the same crack in the earth from which the night emerged. (31; emphasis added)

"Dis occasion is something for us all tuh remember tuh our dyin' day. De first street lamp in uh colored town. Lift yo' eyes and *gaze* on it." (emphasis added)

The gaze becomes shared in this work primarily as Hurston/Janie invites us in to share the process through which she answers that first question of the text, "Where is me?" She finds herself in the photographs she/Hurston "takes" and shows Phoeby/the community/the reader. Janie "knew that God tore down the old world every evening and built a new one by sun-up. It was wonderful to *see* it take form with the sun and emerge from the gray dust of its making" (44; emphasis added). That image of the world emerging as negatives do from slowly developing film announces what Hurston/Janie do to emerge through the development of this text: "When Joe died, his *eyes stared* unwillingly into a corner of the room. . . . Janie studied his *dead face* for a long time" (134–135; emphasis added). "Then she starched and ironed her face, forming it into just what people wanted to *see*" (135; emphasis added). "Joe's funeral was the finest thing Orange County had ever *seen* with *Negro eyes* . . ." (136; emphasis added). They engage us in the subjectivity of seeing, even a "dead face" which reveals the loss of the power of the vision of the gaze by Joe, by emphasizing its urgency to the passage.

As Levecq's title ("You Heard Her, You Ain't Blind") leads us to expect, talk is described as if it were an attribute of sight—more accurately, an attribute of Janie's (Hurston's) sight. But in all of these instances, the reader can only see the seeing, not directly gaze as participant in a shared understanding. When the unsought suitors came to call and speak to Janie of honor and respect, for example, "all that they said and did was *refracted* by her inattention and *shot* off towards the rim-bones of nothing" (88; emphasis added). And the reason Sop-de-Bottom thinks Tea Cake is lucky to have Janie has only to do with what he "sees" in her—or what others cannot see: "'Tea Cake, you sho is a lucky man,' Sop-de-Bottom told him. 'Uh person can *see* every place you hit her. Take some uh dese ol' rusty black women . . . next day nobody couln't *tell* you ever hit 'em. Dat's de reason Ah done quit beatin' mah woman. You can't make no *mark* on 'em at all'" (141; emphasis added). Interestingly, neither can anyone else share that gaze: refraction is the action.

In moments of biggest trouble, however, the action of seeing becomes circular, as in the moment the hurricane begins: "Even before the sun gave light, dead day was creeping from bush to bush watching man" (229)—who, since the narrator must have seen it to report it, was also watching "dead day." And the moment rabies gets Tea Cake in its grip, "Janie *saw* a changing *look* come in his face. Tea Cake was gone. Something else was *looking out* of his face" (269; emphasis added). He is gone, but there are still two subjects, engaged in a single shared act as watchers, *watching* each other *watch*. And a third—the reader—participates fully: "He gave her a *look* full of blank ferocity and gurgled in his throat. She *saw* him sitting up in bed and moving about so that he could *watch* her every move" (269–270; emphasis added). "She *saw* him stiffen himself all over as he leveled and took *aim*" (273; emphasis added). That is, he had her in his *sights*.

Still, the most intensely shared gaze occurs as Janie stands trial: "Then she *saw* all of the colored people standing up in the back of the courtroom. Packed tight like a case of celery, only much darker than that. They were all against her, she could *see*" (275; emphasis added). These instances of shared gazes do more than portray struggles between characters over opposing truths; they engage us intimately in those struggles, too, for they afford no outside view for the reader to assume. Reader as participant in the shared gaze, then as objective observer, facilitates the multiplicity of selves, the division of the outside and the inside Janie, which never become merged. As Johnson comments, "The task of the writer . . . would seem to be to narrate both the appeal and the injustice of universalization, in a voice that assumes and articulates its own, ever differing self-difference" (210). The tension between an alternating stance of perceiving the vision, then sharing the gaze, is the means.

Through its overwhelming concern with sight, Hurston in *Their Eyes* reverses the position of the anthropological spyglass, so that the folk she represents are both being represented and witnessing the representation of a personal self, as refracted through the recorder of her story, Phoeby. Hazel Carby cites the final passage as evidence that the tension between the two collapses, leaving a discourse existing "only for the pleasure of the self" (87) in which any sense of community is completely displaced: "The kiss of his memory made *pictures* of love and light against the wall. . . . She pulled in her horizon like a great fish-net. Pulled it from around the waist of the world and draped it over her shoulder. So much of life in its meshes! She called in her soul to come and *see*" (184; emphasis added). This collapse appears at first glance to be accompanied by a simultaneous collapse of any shared gaze to a single aesthetic vision: her horizon—that line, by definition, where the sun *looks* like it meets the earth—pulled away from the world's waist to adorn her shoulder only, so that her soul might see. Here, however, especially here, the tension between aesthetic vision and shared gaze is at work. Within her obviously divided self, the self-reflection is circular: as soul, she may both view the contents of her fish-net as a disinterested observant, which "called in" suggests she will do; but as definer of her own horizon, as synonymous with that self that will call her in, she is subject and must subjectively share the gaze, the responsibility for the truth of what is to be represented.

As the relationship between narrator and the community becomes diffused, that between author and narrator—and reader—becomes focused. "Ah betcha you don't never go tuh de lookin' glass and enjoy yo' eyes yo'self," Tea Cake says to Janie; "Naw," she replies, "Ah never gazes at 'em in de lookin' glass" (157). Perhaps she gazes at them in the photographs of the self that document her self-creation—and the reader's, to the extent that we share her gaze into her own eyes, through the visual art that permeates this text and the multiplicity of art forms that prevents its residing in any generic locale.

Frustrating as the tension between participant gaze and observant vision may be to the reader, particularly in *Caged Bird* where it is most pronounced, it is the engine that drives these texts, the energy that moves the reader from call to response. Agee wrote of the difficulties facing "one who sets himself to look at all earnestly, at all in purpose toward truth, into the living eyes of a human life" (99). Hurston and Angelou set themselves to look with that same earnestness (the anthropologist; the literary scholar), and their work is testimony to their dual point of view as well: the gaze of the participant as well as the vision of the spectator.

Given the centrality of this dual point of view to the technique of these two writers, we now turn to a preliminary exploration of intertextuality existing between them. In *Dust Tracks on a Road* (1942), Hurston foregrounds the visually artistic nature of what would become her work, a portent of the opening scene of *Their Eyes:* "I used to climb to the top of one of the huge chinaberry trees which guarded our front gate, and look out over the world. The most interesting thing that I saw was the horizon. . . . It grew upon me that I ought to walk out to the horizon and see what the end of the world was like" (44). In "Shades and Slashes of Light" (whose title itself points to the visual nature of her technique), Angelou describes her enterprise as that of capturing the sound of the black voice; but she includes even in this one passage distinctly *visual* images in the concluding two sentences:

> I write for the Black voice and any ear which can hear it. As a composer writes for musical instruments and choreographer creates for the body, I search for sound, tempos, and rhythms to ride through the vocal chord over the tongue, and out of the lips of Black people. I love the shades and slashes of light. Its rumblings and passages of magical lyricism. I accept the glory of stridencies and purrings, trumpetings and sombre sonorities. (3–4)

The shades into which we peer and observe may pull us further and further to peer into its depths, until we encounter its slashes of light, and must squint and turn away, lest the intensity of our gaze blind us from any other view. Those shades and slants of light may thus respond to the calls of the young Janie, the young Maya, in the epigraphs that began this essay: pulling us in with a tantalizing invitation to see and so locate their essence; then, through the intensity of the gaze, causing us to look away so we cannot own them, cannot make them stay.

In discussing the *Odu,* the Yoruba "biblical" text, and its duality as an oral tradition that is mediated to the recipient by a "reader" just as writing is, Gates notes, "We can privilege neither speaking nor writing in this system, since both . . . must be figured in terms of the other, existing only as a figure of the other in a bipolar moment of figuration within a system of differences" (40). Through such alternate moments of privilege, difference is both preserved and linked. In like manner, and as a legacy from the *Odu,* might the co-existence in these texts of the vision and the gaze, and their alternating moments of privilege, be the vehicle through which differences—the topic of the texts—are both preserved and resolved? Future studies may fruitfully examine them for points of intersection that we have yet to realize, that could expand our knowledge of those works' common roots, specifically their common source in the oral tradition.

In his study of the intertextuality he finds in Wright and Angelou, Kinnamon raises the possibility of intertextuality between Angelou and Hurston. Angelou herself, in an interview with Claudia Tate (2), acknowledged the influence that Hurston had had upon her. Further study should uncover whether the visual tensions in one text reflect upon those in the other: whether they visually connect to each other, as Mikhail Bakhtin claims novels connect by being in dialogue with each other through language that is always shared and never original; that how it is used in one instance always is tinged by past uses and tinges future uses since "it represents the co-existence of socio-ideological contradictions between the present and the past, between different socio-ideological groups in the present, between tendencies, school, and circles . . . [and they] intersect each other in a variety of ways" (291). The same interconnectedness may be achieved via the visual aspects of language and, we would argue, would be possible despite the fact that Hurston died before Angelou started writing: the experience which underlay their writing was the same.

Margaret Olin writes about a text that repeatedly protests, down to its last sentence, that it is only about to begin. The texts of Hurston and Angelou are not only about to begin, but their intersection is also an invitation to read other texts visually: looking at a distancing vision, and looking into a beckoning gaze.

Notes

1. By *gaze,* we do not mean the penetrating, degenerating probe of a seer on the seen, which feminist critics have rightly identified as the means of objectification of the person being viewed. Rather, we use the term as Margaret Olin does in her article on the "Privilege of Perception" which we discuss further on.

2. Dolan Hubbard identifies the passage as the "classical Biblical picture" in which we see "the looker standing before the horizon and wondering if she and the horizon shall ever meet" (169). According to Gates's claim of the signifying nature of black American literature, then Douglass signifies upon the Bible, appropriating it for the slave. If so, then Hurston reappropriates it for black American women.

3. Julia Watson and Sidonie Smith note as the essential enterprise of colonized autobiographers (women of color, for example) the adjusting, the reframing, the defiance of generic stabilization as "shifts in vision" that are the means of not only "seeing the world" but also of making it anew.

4. Gates puts it a little differently, seeing the subject of the text as the "emulation of the phonetic, grammatical, and lexical structures of actual speech" (196). But we think he essentially sees the subject as we do, for he describes that emulation as producing "the *illusion* of oral narrative" [our emphasis]—the viewing of it, then, via visual art forms.

5. William Ramsey's discussion of the text's "probings, discoveries, and tentative—even contradicting—critiques that resist shapely, formalist interpretive decodings" adds to Johnson's comments of its divisiveness (38). Alternating visual stances contribute to an understanding of that ambivalence that Ramsey describes.

Works Cited

Agee, James. *Let Us Now Praise Famous Men: Three Tenant Families.* Boston: Houghton Mifflin, 1969.

Angelou, Maya. *I Know Why the Caged Bird Sings.* New York: Bantam Books, 1969.

———. "Shades and Slashes of Light." *Black Women Writers (1950–1980): A Critical Evaluation.* Ed. Mari Evans. Garden City, New York: Anchor Press, 1984.

———. Interview. *Black Women Writers at Work.* Ed. Claudia Tate. New York: Continuum Publishing Company, 1983.

Carby, Hazel. "The Politics of Fiction, Anthropology, and the Folk: Zora Neale Hurston." *New Essays on* Their Eyes Were Watching God. Ed. Michael Awkward. Cambridge University Press, 1990.

Cudjoe, Selwyn R. "Maya Angelou and the Autobiographical Statement." *Black Women Writers (1910–1980): A Critical Evaluation.* Ed. Mari Evans. Garden City, New York: Anchor Press, 1984.

Dalgarno, Emily. "Ethnography in *Their Eyes Were Watching God.*" *American Literature* 74.3 (September 1992): 519–541.

DuBois, W. E. Burghardt. *The Souls of Black Folk: Essays and Sketches.* 1903. Rpt. Greenwich, Conn.: Fawcett Publications, Inc., 1961.

Gates, Henry Louis, Jr. *The Signifying Monkey: A Theory of Afro-American Literary Criticism.* New York: Oxford University Press, 1988.

Gunn, Janet Varner. *Autobiography: Toward a Poetics of Experience.* Philadelphia: University of Pennsylvania Press, 1982.

Holland, Norman. "Prose and Minds: A Psychoanalytic Approach to Non-Fiction." *The Art of Victorian Prose*. Eds. George Levine and William Madden. New York: Oxford University Press, 1968.

Hubbard, Dolan. "' . . . Ah said Ah'd save de text for you': Recontextualizing the Sermon to Tell (Her) story in Zora Neale Hurston's *Their Eyes Were Watching God*." *African American Review* 27 (Summer 1993): 166–178.

Hurston, Zora Neale. *Dust Tracks on a Road*. New York: Arno Press, 1969.

———. *Their Eyes Were Watching God*. Urbana, Illinois: University of Illinois Press, 1978.

Johnson, Barbara. "Metaphor, Metonymy and Voice in *Their Eyes Were Watching God*." *Black Literature and Literary Theory*. Ed. Henry Louis Gates. New York: Methuen, 1984.

Kinnamon, Kenneth. "Call and Response in Two Autobiographical Works by Richard Wright and Maya Angelou." *Studies in Black American Literature, Volume II: Belief vs. Theory in Black American Literary Criticism*. Eds. Joe Weixlmann and Chester J. Fontenot. Greenwood, Florida: The Penkevill Publishing Company, 1986.

Levecq, Christine. "'You Heard Her, You Ain't Blind': Subversive Shifts in Zora Neale Hurston's *Their Eyes Were Watching God*." *Tulsa Studies in Women's Literature* 1 (Spring 1994): 87–111.

McKay, Nellie. "'Crayon Enlargements of Life': Zora Neale Hurston's *Their Eyes Were Watching God* as Autobiography." *New Essays on* Their Eyes Were Watching God. Ed. Michael Awkward. Cambridge University Press, 1990.

McPherson, Dolly. *Order Out of Chaos: The Autobiographical Works of Maya Angelou*. New York: Peter Lang, 1990.

Olin, Margaret. "'It Is Not Going to Be Easy to Look Into Their Eyes': Privilege of Perception in *Let Us Now Praise Famous Men*." *Art History* 14.1 (March 1991): 92–115.

Ramsey, William M. "The Compelling Ambivalence of Zora Neale Hurston's *Their Eyes Were Watching God*." *Southern Literary Journal* 27.1 (Fall 1994): 36–50.

Stone, Alfred E. *Autobiographical Occasions and Original Acts: Versions of American Identity from Henry Adams to Nate Shaw*. Philadelphia: University of Pennsylvania Press, 1982.

Watson, Julia, and Sidonie Smith. "Introduction." *De/Colonizing the Subject: The Politics of Gender in Women's Autobiography*. Eds. Sidonie Smith and Julia Watson. Minneapolis: University of Minnesota Press, 1992.

Wright, Richard. *12 Million Black Voices: A Folk History of the Negro in the United States*. New York: Viking Press, 1941

SIPHOKAZI KOYANA

The Heart of the Matter:
Motherhood and Marriage in the
Autobiographies of Maya Angelou

It is indisputable that Maya Angelou's contribution to the autobiographical form in America remains unsurpassed. Angelou's unique probing of the interior self, her distinctive use of humour and self-mockery, her linguistic sensibility, as well as her ability to balance the quest for human individuality with the general condition of black Americans distinguish her as a master of the genre. While she breaks new ground by exposing issues such as rape and incest within the black community, she also uses her maturing understanding of family and community to project an individual's attempt to forge and maintain a healthy sense of self within a group that is undergoing a cultural transition. Focussing particularly on Angelou's use of the maternal trope as a controlling device in this regard,[1] this paper explores how racial, class, and gender oppression affect the experience of motherhood in the United States between the 1940s and 1960s.[2]

This essay argues that Angelou's experiences as a working-class mother "demythify" the socially accepted white notions of domesticated motherhood, the supremacy of the nuclear family structure, and the blissfulness inherent in the institution of marriage. All three factors challenge the "cult of true womanhood," a bourgeois Eurocentric perspective that has shaped how people think about family life in the United States.[3] By systematically reflecting on black women's roles as workers within their families and in societies at large,

The Black Scholar, Volume 32, Number 2 (Summer 2002): pp. 35–44. Copyright © 2002 The Black Scholar.

Angelou's womanist theories, as they are inscribed in autobiography, thus bring into relief the ideologies that serve to mythologize women's experiences as mothers and wives, as well as the hierarchical divisions that generate conflict and struggle within families. In essence, much more than bringing sexuality, childbearing, and child rearing practices into the domain of politics, Angelou's autobiographical works attempt to reveal the multiple and dynamic interconnections between households—home and family—and the larger political economy.

* * *

From the very beginning of her experiences as a teenage mother, Angelou wrestles with the need to work to provide for her baby. Given her racial and class background, it should come as no surprise that Angelou's experience of motherhood is so inseparably intertwined with work. As a black American woman, she comes from a long tradition of female independence and responsibility. Slavery never allowed for domesticity among slave women who had to work in the plantation house or the fields.

Raised first by her paternal grandmother, Momma, a daughter of ex-slaves, and a self-sufficient businesswoman and mother, Maya gives birth to her son, Guy, while living with her biological mother Vivian, a self-sufficient entrepreneur in her own right.[4] Momma is widowed and Vivian is divorced.[5] In neither home is there a male income provider in the traditional sense.[6] Even if there were, the women would still have to work to add to the often meager wages that internal colonialism ensured black men earned.[7]

Whereas motherhood was usually associated with domesticity and reproductive labor (work inside the home) for white women in America between the 1940s and 1960s, for black women and women of other racially oppressed groups, motherhood was, and always has been, inseparable from work, both productive (income-earning) and reproductive.[8] Describing this connection, Patricia Hill Collins uses the term "mother-work" to connote the need for racially oppressed women to "work for the day to come," whether for one's children, those of the community, or for those yet unborn.[9] Mother-work, capturing the inseparability of work from motherhood in oppressed communities, is a term that also reduces the dichotomies in feminist theorizing, which rigidly distinguish between private and public, family and work, the individual and the collective, identity as autonomous and identity growing from the collective self-determination of one's group.[10]

Collins also shows how the white feminists' dichotomous split of the public sphere (economic and political discourse) from domestic (private, non-economic, apolitical) regrettably distinguishes one domain as "male" and the other as "female" in a manner that disregards black women's realities.[11] Black mothers have always worked in both spheres. Working-class and racially oppressed women often work at home in many income earning activities (for example, letting out rooms, child minding, sewing, washing and ironing laundry) and are, therefore, never exclusively domesticated.[12] Thus, contrary to the white cult of "true womanhood" that was still upheld in the middle of the twentieth century—when productive work was seen as incompatible with motherhood—black motherhood always encompassed work.

* * *

Relying on her experience of black culture, wherein self-reliance and mother-hood are integrated, Maya rejects the option of seeking government assistance, a decision which leads to work situations that highlight how racist capitalism drives black women into a poverty that is not only financial but at times also moral.[13] In *Gather Together in My Name*, the sequel to *I Know Why the Caged Bird Sings*, Angelou writes about the problems she faced as a working teenage mother, an unprofessional black girl to whom only the most menial jobs are available. Because she has no skills and has refused Vivian's offer to take care of her son so she can continue with her education,[14] Maya ends up living along the periphery of society, "exploring the perimeter of the cage."[15] Here, in the post-World War II milieu, evil abounds. And, although the kings and queens of the underworld—gamblers and prostitutes, black-marketeers and boosters—may be the last to feel the pinch, poverty is everywhere. It is in such an environment that the need to support herself and her son leads Maya to some quick and easy choices.[16]

Being only a teenager, Maya is at an age where she is still very vulnerable, easily deceived, and has yet to define herself and her own morality.[17] At the book's lowest point she works as a prostitute with the hope of raising enough money to rescue her sugardaddy-pimp from debt. This, she innocently thinks, will enable him to divorce his wife and ultimately lead her to that most blissful state, marriage. Foolish as Maya's logic may be in these particular circumstances, the situation demonstrates how even black men have been willing to abuse the black woman's ability to work in that space in which the distinctions between the private and public spheres have been erased.

* * *

Maya's work experiences thus show how the lack of skills and the racist practice of excluding blacks from meaningful employment are the real culprits for despair and drug abuse, not working outside the home. A clear example of the exclusion of black mothers from constructive economic engagement arises when a white personnel supervisor fails Maya in a simple test that would qualify her to be a trainee operator. Consequently, she ends up as a "dumb" bus girl who must wait on the white girls who had been her classmates (*Gather Together*, 6–7).

This is one of the reasons for Angelou's unrelenting protest against racial injustice, which she records throughout her volumes. Her own life is evidence that the conditions that are allegedly due to being a working mother are rapidly improved when poor people are given jobs to earn a decent living.[18] For instance, when Maya is given an opportunity to appear in "Porgy and Bess," her life takes a turn for the better. Her financial situation improves and thereafter her whole life becomes more fulfilling. Not only is she now better able to provide for her son, she is then better able to contribute to society in general.

The long list of Maya's menial jobs, which includes those on the fringes of society, shows how the false assumption that working outside the home would liberate women from economic dependency on men was one of the major weaknesses of the later feminist movement of the 1960s and 70s.[19] This assumption was the main thesis of Betty Friedan's groundbreaking book, *The Feminine Mystique*.[20] Friedan's proposition obviously reflected the middle-class bias and composition of the feminist movement whose stance disregarded the fact that millions of black women, other women of color, and working-class white women had been working outside their homes for decades.[21] bell hooks also notes that the bourgeois assumption that working outside the home would bring women self-fulfillment did not take into account the nature of the work—that it is often demeaning, repetitive, so-called "menial" labor in which the majority of women from other racial and class backgrounds were already engaged.[22]

* * *

The assumption is that white middle class feminists limited their definition of work to high paying careers. As a result, the majority of women of color and working-class white women did not identify themselves with a movement that failed to address their desire to quit working, since the work they were doing (and still continue to do) was not liberating. The early feminist movement thus failed to arm the majority of women with strategies against economic exploitation and dehumanization.[23]

In this regard, Angelou's insertion of racially and economically oppressed women's motherwork to her revision of white middle-class maternal discourse is as necessary as her redefinition of family. If the former debunks the myth of domesticity, the latter "demythifies" the supremacy of the nuclear family structure. It would have been almost impossible for Maya to work full time if she did not have her mother and community "othermothers" to rely on for assistance with childcare.[24] It is precisely because extended family in black communities includes people outside of kinship lines who show loyalty and a sense of obligation, that Maya can leave her son with different care providers or friends while she searches for a viable career.[25]

Almost as important as self-reliance to the black mother is the under-standing that it occurs within a socio-cultural context in which self-reliance means sometimes relying on other people on the community.[26] This sense of community and the tendency to share mothering responsibilities are values which have also ensured the survival of other, immigrant, families.

* * *

Having shown us in her first autobiography how she came to have two mothers, Vivian and Momma, the pattern continues in her adult life when her own son is sometimes in his grandmother Vivian's care. As a black single mother, one who must provide both emotionally and financially for her child, Maya's experience of family, as recorded throughout the series of autobiographies, follows a set of rules that is distinct from that of middle-class white Americans. For Maya, family is neither nuclear, nor restricted to household. For middle-class white Americans, the ideal family is the archetypal middle-class nuclear structure with a father who earns enough to exempt his spouse and dependent children from work.[27] Being the sole income earner in his family, he exerts power over the women in the house-hold as much as over those in the workforce, since owing to his race, gen-der, and class, he earns more than they do.[28] This is the traditional pattern the ruling class has set up as the norm, the standard that others may wish to emulate.

On the other hand, traditional family structure in the black commu-nity in America has its origins in Africa. According to anthropologist Niara Sudarkasa, in African communities, marital and family stability are not the same thing. Lineages, rather than married couples, are the core around which the typical African extended family is built.[29] This form of family organiza-tion, Sudarkasa argues, is one of the traditional African retentions which have enabled the survival of the Afro-American people in the socially, economi-cally, and politically oppressive climate of the United States. Cautioning that the term "extended family" not be used as a euphemism for "disorganized" family," she points to the "extended family" structure's flexibility, adaptability, and inclusiveness as strengths that have ensured its continuity in America, despite the scarce resources, economic insecurity, and cultural assault blacks have faced.[30]

Sudarkasa points to the need to understand the traditional value placed on children and on their care within these structures.[31] Traditional "extended family" structures are usually established along patriarchal lines in which a male figurehead has more than one wife. This often ties women's authority within the family to their status as mothers. In such polygynous relationships, women often share the care of their children so that they can more efficiently perform other daily chores.

By demonstrating to us the traditional centrality of othermothers in black motherhood, Maya challenges the Western notion of children as property and demonstrates the importance of sharing one's children with other women in the community. She also shows how African and African-American communities have long realized that vesting one person with the full responsibility of mothering may not be wise, hence the role of othermothers.[32] Angelou's writing is thus a powerful attack on the nuclear family structure, especially in light of the studies that highlight the middle-class mother's isolation in the urban nuclear family.

* * *

Privileged white women and renowned psychoanalytic scholars, such as Nancy Chodorow, either worry about maternal isolation within the nuclear family or place emphasis on the all-powerful mother as the conduit for gender oppression.[33] Meanwhile, maternal separation from one's children (through work or death) is much more of an issue for racially oppressed women.[34] Collins asserts that it is precisely because white middle-class women do not suffer from physical starvation that such a lot of time has been devoted to their psychological and emotional health.[35] By contrast, women who are starving have to deal with issues of basic survival.[36] For the latter, it is not the isolation, but the physical or socio-cultural separation of mothers and children in social structures designed to disempower individuals and communities that is a much more pressing concern.[37] Thus, unlike the situation of the privileged nuclear family where struggling for power or for one's autonomy is defined as the main human enterprise,[38] for ethnic minority groups, the family is a unit of resistance to the oppressive system outside, rather than a sphere of conflict.[39]

* * *

Although Angelou's writing demands respect for the working mother, the extended family, and for othermothers, Maya's struggle demonstrates the tensions inherent in belonging to a group that values these notions of family, while living in a larger society that devalues them, as the drama underlying all five volumes. This tension is evident in Maya's feelings of rejection while she is a child in her grandmother's care as much as to her own frustrations when faced with the responsibility of raising Guy. While pursuing self-fulfilling career ambitions and living her own life often means relying on kin to help care for Guy, in the mid-twentieth century in America, the ethical ideological norm seems to be that good mothers are unselfish, meaning they put their children's needs before their own. In this context, therefore, Maya's confessed sense of guilt about leaving her son with relatives reflects the larger cultural expectations that a mother stays with her child at all times. Thus, while following in the footsteps of other "enraged" black mothers through her determination to protect and provide for her son against all odds testifies, the behavior this entails is not always seen as virtuous in the larger context.

Angelou projects the psychological split she experiences from this cultural dichotomy in two distinct ways. Firstly, she literally follows a pattern of departure from and return to family. Maya leaves and returns to her mother's and to Momma's homes a number of times throughout her life as recorded in her volumes.[40] Dolly McPherson sees Maya's cyclical movement as illustrating that journey which is a controlling metaphor in black American autobiography. For her it reflects Maya's quest for self-knowledge, allowing Maya to move from disorder (misunderstanding or chaos) towards order (reconciliation).[41] For McPherson, Maya's returning and leaving enable her to make peace with her past so that it is neither a sentimental haven nor a cage. Ultimately, the pattern records how her identity evolves as it synthesizes the extremes of her paternal grandmother and her biological mother.[42]

Secondly, Angelou presents her double-consciousness, her oscillation between her intrinsic Afro-American and her imposed Euro-American cultural identities, in literary terms, by contrasting reality with fantasy. This juxtaposition is most evident in her portrayal of the differences between her experience of marriage and its idealization in the larger American culture. Carol Neubauer also identifies the discrepancy between Maya's fantasy of marriage and the actual experience as one that shows how, despite the social propaganda, marriage fails to bring normality and stability to Maya's life.[43] Similarly, pointing to Maya's creation of imagined realities, which she identifies as central to the structural pattern and meaning of the work, McPherson argues that Maya, like other blacks, is trying to grasp the ever-elusive American Dream, the dream life she sees at the "movies."[44] That is why, for instance, she becomes L. D.'s "Bobby sock Baby," a prostitute hoping to attain romance and an easy life, as mentioned earlier.

* * *

When she was younger, Maya had often fantasized about growing up to be a housewife. For instance, she describes how at nineteen, when her life was "an assemblage of strivings and [her] energies were directed toward acquiring more than the basic needs," (*Singin' and Swingin'*, 16) she was nonetheless "as much a part of the security conscious fifties as the quiet young white girls who lived their pastel Peter Pan collared days in clean, middle-class neighborhoods" (*Singin' and Swingin'*, 16). But, unlike their white counterparts, girls in the black communities found themselves "too often unmarried, bearing lonely pregnancies and wishing for two and a half children each who would gurgle happily behind that picket fence while

we drove our men to work in our friendly-looking station wagons" (*Singin'
and Swingin'*, 16). Maya's romanticism, influenced by Hollywood and lyrics from popular music, is soon confronted with reality when, in 1949, she
marries her first husband Tosh Angelos, a Greek.

Having believed, in a "ferocious desperation," that "marriage would give
her a world free from danger, disease, and want" (*Singin' and Swingin*, 16),
Maya soon discovers that real life offers no such guarantees. As a housewife,
she is "legally a member of that enviable tribe of consumers whom security made fat as butter and who under no circumstances considered living by
bread alone, because their husbands brought home the bacon" (*Singin' and
Swingin'*, 33). However, as the head of the household, Tosh expects her to
give up her participation in the black church as well as her black friends. A
very private person and an atheist, he underestimates the role of the black
church in Maya's life. As a member of an oppressed group, it is her spiritual
life raft—something he apparently does not need—for, as a white man who
enjoys racial and gender privileges, Tosh does not appear to understand the
importance to Maya of religious faith.

* * *

Because Maya wants to live the dream, however, she compromises a lot of
herself and puts up with Tosh's demands. Yet, despite, or perhaps because
of surrendering all of her independence to Tosh, the marriage ends in 1952.
Even though Maya has been as perfect a wife as prescribed in women's magazines, Tosh can no longer bear the restrictions of this ideal nuclear structure he has created anymore than he can bear the strain of being part of an
inter-racial couple in the early 1950s.[45] Since there was little real stability for
Maya and her son once the novelty of it all wore off, it is no surprise that the
divorced Maya describes herself as a "saner, healthier person than the young,
greedy girl who had wanted a man to belong to"—a fantasy she admits was
"based on a Hollywood film, circa 1940" (*Singin' and Swingin'*, 51).

Maya's ideal of a glamorous Hollywood marriage is also a fantasy that
reflects her mother's influence on her.[46] When the seven-year old Maya first
meets her mother after a four-year separation, she is literally assailed by her
glamour and beauty. She "had never seen a woman as pretty as she who was
called 'Mother'" (*Caged Bird*, 60). Maya can only compare this enchanting blues
singer, who attracts men to her in a manner that makes her more than the aver-
age mother, to a movie star. Emphasizing this connection between Vivian and
the movies, Angelou recalls her early experiences at the cinema in which Kay
Francis, a white actress who closely resembles Vivian starred, thus:

> I laughed too, but not at the hateful jokes [the movie] made on
> my people. I laughed because, except that she was white, the big

movie star looked just like my mother. Except that she lived in a big mansion with a thousand servants, she lived just like my mother. And it was funny to think of the whitefolks' not knowing that the woman they were adoring could be my mother's twin, except that she was white and my mother was prettier. Much prettier.

The movie star made me happy. It was extraordinary good fortune to be able to save up one's money and go see one's mother whenever one wanted to. (*Caged Bird*, 118–119)

* * *

Having been so strongly impressed by her mother's physical attributes and talent as a child, it is easy to see why the older Maya is a "movie-star wanna-be." After being encouraged by Vivian to study dance and drama (Vivian teaches Maya her first dance steps and introduces her to the art of body movement in a bar), Maya's ideal of the mother/wife as performer/glamour girl is not totally incomprehensible, therefore. She emulates her mother, who, in many ways, presents her with an index of cultural assumptions about motherhood. In the final analysis, although Maya often finds Vivian's beauty and blues lifestyle oppressively competitive (Maya felt ugly, was often neglected, and felt inferior by comparison to Vivian), it is also her ticket to success, one that ultimately leads to her writing career. Having said this, it is important to add that Maya rejects some of Vivian's maternal practices. Unlike Vivian, who neglected her two children, Maya is very protective of her child.

* * *

Maya's second marriage is to a black South African political activist, Vusi Make. When she meets him, she is engaged to a divorced black American bail bondsman, Thomas Allen. Although she is a radical civil rights activist—a fundraiser and the northern co-ordinator for the Southern Christian Leadership Conference, Dr. Martin Luther King, Jr.'s organization—Maya is so desperate to marry Allen that she even entertains the idea of straightening her hair and wearing pretty hats with flowers and gloves so she can look like a nice, marriageable, potential homemaker, instead of the non-traditional career woman she really is. Intelligent as she is, she is willing to live the rest of her life in a marriage where conversation is limited to her shouting in the bedroom and his grunting at the dining-room table. In other words, although fully aware that Allen only wants sex and food from her, Maya is prepared to consider that as sufficient, as long as she has a husband. As a result, a few months into her relationship with him, she practically proposes marriage to him even though she knows that he is not the right man for her.[47]

Again, Maya is willing to compromise herself to attain the much-heralded state of marital bliss. Obviously, her desire for a stable male companion, though natural, is still shrouded by her long held fantasies. In real life, these fantasies, born of Maya's loneliness and socially constructed ideals, do not come to fruition. Instead, she marries Vusi Make and has another revealing encounter with the fantasies of marital bliss versus the real experience of marriage.

The following passage, which describes their courtship, captures Maya's idealization of their romance and demonstrates how Hollywood portrayals of Africa and the lifestyle of ease and glamour Vivian pursues influence Maya's decision to marry Make:

> At the dining table he spread before me the lights and shadows of Africa. Glories stood in thrilling array. Warrior queens, in necklaces of blue and white beads, led armies against marauding Europeans. Nubile girls danced in celebration of the victories of Shaka, the Zulu king. The actual earth of Africa was "black and strong like the girls back home" and glinted with gold and diamonds. African men covered their betrothed with precious stones and specially woven cloth. He asked me to forgive the paucity of the gift he had for me and to understand that when we returned to Mother Africa he would adorn me with riches the likes of which I had never imagined. When he led me into the darkened guest room and placed a string of beads around my neck, all my senses were tantalized. . . . The amber beads on my nut-brown skin caught fire. I looked into the mirror and saw exactly what I wanted to see, and more importantly, what I wanted him to see: a young African virgin, made beautiful for her chief. (*Singin' and Swingin'*, 150–151)

* * *

Make, like Tosh, also expects Maya not to work outside the home. Unlike Tosh, however, he seems to demand that a lot more of Maya's energy be spent on housework. If in her marriage to Tosh she was spiritually starved, in her marriage to Make, she is physically overworked. Make inspects and supervises her housecleaning to ensure that she has reached every nook under the bed and has removed dust from literally every surface. Expressing her frustration, Maya confesses, "I wanted to be a wife and to create a beautiful home to make my man happy, but there was more to life than being a diligent maid with a permanent pussy" (*Gather Together*, 168). Angelou describes her daunting routine thus:

> It seemed to me that I washed, scrubbed, mopped, dusted and waxed thoroughly every other day. . . . I wiped down the walls,

because dirty fingerprints could spoil his day, and ironed his starched shirts . . .

Each meal was a culinary creation. Chicken Kiev and feijoda, Eggs Benedict, and Turkey Tetrazzini.

A good woman put ironed sheets on the bed and matched the toilet paper to the color of the bathroom tile.

I was unemployed but I had never worked so hard in all my life. (*Heart of a Woman*, 166)

Whereas Maya meets her side of the bargain, Make, on the other hand, is not as good a provider as he would like to believe. A political activist whose unstable income depends upon donations from sympathetic sponsors, he cannot have the lifestyle he desires. His insatiable appetite for expensive furniture and classy decor consequently throws the family into debt and embarrassment. Although the excitement of the foreign and exotic initially masks the realities for Maya, before long she realizes that Make is neither faithful nor capable of supporting them. In Egypt she defies her husband's unrealistic attempts to put her on a pedestal, and starts to work outside the home.

Indeed, except for her short-lived marriage to Tosh, Maya has worked since she was sixteen years old. She has always known how much money she had, how to spend it, and when to pay her bills. Because Make keeps her in the dark about such crucial matters as the family's finances, she feels frustrated and powerless. Her rebellious decision to work not only demonstrates how successfully she reclaims her independence, but also her pragmatism as she faces her reality squarely, instead of perpetuating illusions of grandeur.

* * *

By trying to fit an African-American woman into his stereotypical idea of an African woman, Make shows no regard for Maya's cultural background. Niara Sudarkasa posits the notion that because Afro-American women have always worked and bought their own high priced items (cars, furniture and clothes), they have traditionally had a strong position within the home. In other words, because black men's earnings have not been able to provide more than half of the family's income, black women have always had more egalitarian relationships with their husbands than is often the case with white women.[48] In the same vein, after meeting African women in England, Maya realizes that, despite Make's portrayal, African women were not as docile, submissive, and powerless as his stereotypes held them to be.[49]

More than anything, Make's fantasy of African women as happy housewives, as much as his appetite for expensive furniture, shows the extent to which he has bought into Western ideals, ideals his career and socio-economic background do not enable him to fulfil. Ultimately, as well as underscoring the loss of her independence, Maya's second marriage proves her fantasy of marriage bringing her stability and security to be only that: fantasies. The dispelling of this marriage fantasy highlights the impossibility for black working-class mothers of being blissful housewives. In short, Maya's two failed marriages rid her of the notion that meeting the "right" man will liberate her from the need to work. Indeed, it is her healthy work ethic and her enterprising spirit that enable her to free herself from sexist husbands.[50]

* * *

Furthermore, because her need for a spouse is linked to her desire for a male role model for her son, by successfully raising Guy to be an independent, balanced, and well-rounded son, she proves that despite prevailing myths, the father's presence is not always necessary in the consolidation of identity. Never making it look easy, Angelou gradually illustrates that there is a greater sense of accomplishment when one pursues one's intellectual and career goals, goes beyond culturally prescribed boundaries of what mothers do, and does not allow oneself to be crippled by the absence of a husband.

Although more recent mainstream feminist autobiography has also challenged the traditional single-income, nuclear family as the only viable option, Angelou, writing between the late 1960s and the mid-1980s, set a new path by showing how black families often serve as barometers of social change and as forerunners of adaptive patterns that will be progressively experienced by the more privileged sectors of society as they lose their privileges. To the extent that white and black families in the United States now experience similar political and global economic pressures, they respond in similar ways, including the adaptation of family structures. Through questioning the prevailing myths about the black family, Angelou demonstrates that behaviors which may have initially seemed unacceptable, deviant, or pathological to middle-class whites (for example, teenage childbirth, single parent families, and working mothers), might actually be the "traditional" strategies that have enabled black families to survive the harsh economic realities.

* * *

In conclusion, by recognizing the centrality of remembering and rewriting the history of black mothers while underscoring the intricate connection between maternal concerns and the racial or economic politics of her country, Angelou radicalizes autobiography and acknowledges its contribution to the struggle for racial equality. Commenting on the importance of writing for Third World women, Chandra Talpade Mohanty emphasizes that "this process is significant, not merely as a corrective to the gaps, erasures, and misunderstandings of hegemonic masculinist history, but because the very practice of remembering and rewriting leads to the formation of politicized consciousness and self-identity."[51]

Ultimately, by analyzing her own experience of motherhood, Angelou is able to challenge the prevailing notions of maternity through questioning the feasibility of a domesticated motherhood for working-class black women, the supremacy of the nuclear family structure, and by dispelling the idealization of marriage. In the final analysis, although patriarchy exists in this moment of transition from traditional culture to feminism, Angelou demonstrates how she has always striven towards a self-empowering identity, one which can be seen as an inspiration for women (black or white) who confront "the heart of the matter."

NOTES

1. The significance of motherhood is a unifying element in Angelou's five volumes, since the interplay between mother and child creates thematic continuity. For instance, while the end of *I Know Why the Caged Bird Sings* marks the beginning of Maya's life as a mother, *Gather Together in My Name* relates her struggles as a teenage mother. In *Singin' and Swingin' and Getting Merry Like Christmas* she traces the tension between her pursuit of success as an entertainer and the guilt she feels as a mother who must leave her child to ensure a better future for both. Delineating her growth, in *The Heart of a Woman* she is a wiser, more mature woman and mother. Finally, in *All God's Children Need Travelling Shoes,* both Maya and son are adults and have established a healthy balance between dependence and independence as she leaves him at the university in Ghana while she returns to the United States.

2. This is the period of Angelou's motherhood in her first three volumes. It encompasses the post-World War II period in which many blacks migrated from the South to big cities in the North and the West of the country in search of better opportunities. This was followed by the Great Depression in the 1930s and the struggle for civil rights in the late 1950s and early 1960s.

3. Sometimes called "the cult of domesticity," this concept, which was developed in the mid-nineteenth century, refers to the notion that "the [so-called] true woman is self-contained within her nuclear family, with specific and separate roles for men and women, and with an economic dependence on men, in such a way that motherhood is one's true occupation" (Teresa E. Snorton, 1996:57, quoted in Trudelle Thomas, "'You'll Become a Lioness': African-American Women Talk About Mothering," *Journal of the Association for Research on Mothering* 2 (2), (2000:58–59).

4. To distinguish the protagonist from the writer, I use the first name to refer to the former. This is in line with Angelou's referral to "the Maya character," whom she envisioned as her invented self and as a "symbolic character for every black girl growing up in America." (See "'The Maya Character': Interview with Jackie Kay," *Conversations with Maya Angelou,* Jeffrey Elliot, ed. (Jackson: University Press of Mississippi, 1989), 194–200.

5. Vivian often has live-in lovers who help pay for her upkeep, but she never stops earning her own income. Even when she is married to a successful businessman, she continues to earn her own income by renting out rooms in her 14-room house.

6. Even within the black middle-class, women have had to work to keep the family's median income within the middle class bracket because even black middle-class men often do not earn enough for the wife to stay at home. (*Op. cit.*, 101).

7. Evelyn Nakano Glenn defines internal colonialism in the United States as that system which perpetuates discriminatory barriers and wage scales that keep minorities at the bottom of the economic scale, doing the dirtiest and the most menial jobs ("Racial Ethnic Women's Labor: The Intersection of Race, Gender, and Class Oppression," *Review of Radical Political Economics* 17 [3], 1985: 87).

8. Due to the history of slavery, "'labor' was therefore 'raced' as well as 'classed' in American culture. 'Ladies' did not labor, or if they did, were not to appear to have labored, according to the domestic ideology of the 'cult of true womanhood' which defined (white) women as domestic angels, and mothers of superior moral quality" (Harris, Jennifer, "Reading Mobility, Motherhood and Domesticity in Four African-American Women's Texts," *Journal of the Association for Research on Mothering* 2 (2), 2000: 201). Because black women slaves had had to work like their male counterparts, while their womanly virtues were exploited because they were not white ladies, black mothers expressed themselves in what scholars refer to as the trope of "the enraged mother." This means they had to be tough-minded in the protection of and provision for their children, due to their ready assumption that America is a foreboding and dangerous place for children and mothers.

9. Collins, Patricia Hill, "Shifting the Center: Race, Class, and Feminist Theorizing about Motherhood," *Representations of Motherhood*. Donna Bassin, et al., eds. (New Haven, CT: Yale University Press, 1994), 58.

10. *Ibid.*

11. *Ibid.*

12. Glenn, Evelyn Nakano, "Racial Ethnic Women's Labor: The Intersection of Race, Gender, and Class Oppression," *Review of Radical Political Economics* 17 (3), 1985: 102.

13. For a more recent study that shows that pragmatism, flexible sex roles, outside-the-home employment, and responsibility to and for one's extended family are certainties for most African-American women than for their white counterparts, see Trudelle Thomas, "'You'll Become a Lioness.'"

14. Driven by idealism, feigned independence, and pride, Maya did not trust Vivian, who had neglected her, to take sufficient care of her grandson. Later, however, she leaves her son with Vivian for a whole year when she goes on an international tour with "Porgy and Bess."

15. Hagen, Lyman, *Heart of a Woman, Mind of a Writer, and Soul of a Poet: A Critical Analysis of the Writings of Maya Angelou* (New York: University Press of America, Inc., 1977), 86.

16. *Op. cit.*, 77.

17. She is only 17 to 19 years old in this text.

18. Angelou once had a job scraping paint off cars by hand. Describing her poverty, she writes: "The tough texture of poverty in my life had been more real than sand wedged between my teeth" (*Singin' and Swingin'*, 18).

19. By the time she gets her first meaningful employment opportunity as a salesgirl in a record shop, Maya has also been a waitress, a short-order cook, R. L.

Poole's dance partner, a conveyor of stolen clothes, an assistant in a real estate office, and an assistant in a dress shop.

20. hooks, bell, *Feminist Theory: From Margin to Center* (South End Press: Boston, MA, 1984), 95.

21. *Ibid.*

22. *Ibid.* This kind of labor provided little financial freedom. At most, it enabled these women to supplement their husbands' meager incomes. In these conditions, husbands, also exploited in low-paying jobs, were not the enemy from whom the working women had to free themselves, but the partners with whom they had to collaborate to save for the deposit for the house, a car, or the children's college tuition.

23. *Op. cit.*, 97.

24. Patricia Hill Collins uses the term "othermothers" to designate women who assist bloodmothers by sharing mothering responsibilities. *Black Feminist Thought: Knowledge, Consciousness, and the Politics of Empowerment* (New York: Routledge, 1991), 119.

25. *Op. cit.*, 14.

26. McPherson, Dolly, *Order Out of Chaos: The Autobiographical Works of Maya Angelou* (London: Verago Press, Ltd., 1991), 36.

27. Collins, "Shifting the Center," 58.

28. *Ibid.*

29. Sudarkasa, Niara, *The Strength of Our Mothers: African and African American Women and Families* (Trenton, NJ: Africa World Press, 1996), xxi. Sudarkasa provides diagrams that show the strict rules and different arrangements that lineage ties follow in traditional West African societies.

30. *Op. cit.*, 1.

31. *Ibid.*, xxii.

32. Although some mainstream feminists are now attempting to redefine family and community, many still rely on the nuclear model of getting the father involved rather than depending upon extended family and othermothers.

33. Collins, "Shifting the Center," 65.

34. *Op. cit.*, 72.

35. *Op. cit.*, 61.

36. *Ibid.*

37. *Op. cit.*, 65.

38. *Op. cit.*, 58.

39. Glenn, 103.

40. More than once, she even relies on her mother for financial assistance. This is possible because in the extended family system, adulthood does not strictly mean establishing your own household. Single adults may live with parents or married siblings (Sudarkasa, 8). The positive values placed on generosity and reciprocity in this system (inter-family cooperation) often contrast with nuclear families, in which individualism, competition, selfishness, and separateness abound (*Op. cit.*, 9). Examples of separateness that are evident in real life (not the hypothetical ideal) nuclear family are the generation gap and the hating or rejection of one's parents (*Op. cit.*, 10).

41. McPherson, 18.

42. *Op. cit.*, 20.

43. Neubauer, Carol E., "Maya Angelou: Self and Song of Freedom in the Southern Tradition," *Southern Women Writers: The New Generation,* Tonette Bond Inge, ed. (Tuscaloosa: University of Alabama Press, 1990), 127.

44. McPherson, 69.

45. "A good wife had to be constant, faithful, clean (floors waxed and beaten rugs), economical, a good cook, and a compliant lover" (*Singin' and Swingin',* 45).

46. Vivian lives her life as though she is somebody wealthier than she actually is. She works in gambling salons, but lives as though she is a movie star.

47. Dolly McPherson's reference to Maya's folly of thinking that despite her success and independence she needs a man to make her life and her son's complete (McPherson, 98) disregards Maya's stated motive of warding off loneliness. Although the feminist ethic that McPherson is espousing here views male companionship as unnecessary, the Afro-centric ethic on which I am basing my thesis has a more realistic attitude towards the emotional and sexual needs of adults (See Sudarkasa, 9).

48. Sudarkasa, 298–299.

49. African women have always worked: farming in the fields, making crafts for sale, or as entrepreneurs in the market place. It was the patriarchal colonial policies of privileging men in education, training, and funding programs (based on the European models) that diminished their roles in the public sphere (Sudarkasa, xxiii). Consequently, African womanists look at the more marginalized and reduced relevance of the so-called modern African woman and articulate her disempowerment in the context of "dewomanization" (Nnaemeka, 10).

50. Feminist scholar bell hooks also laments that women often put too much value on interpersonal relationships instead of work. Consequently, even those women who have achieved economic self-sufficiency are often as unable to liberate themselves from oppressive relationships with sexist individuals as those women who do no wage labor and depend upon others for their economic survival (*Feminist Theory,* 105).

51. Mohanty, Chandra Talpade, *Third World Women and the Politics of Feminism* (Indiana University Press: Bloomington, 1991), 34.

Works Cited

Angelou, Maya, *All God's Children Need Travelling Shoes* (New York: Bantam Books, 1986).

————. *Gather Together in My Name* (New York: Bantam Books, 1975).

————. *I Know Why the Caged Bird Sings* (New York: Bantam Books, 1993).

————. *Singin' and Swingin' and Getting Merry Like Christmas* (New York: Bantam Books, 1997).

Chodorow, Nancy, *The Reproduction of Mothering: Psychoanalysis and the Sociology of Gender* (Berkeley: University of California Press, 1978).

Collins, Patricia Hill, *Black Feminist Thought: Knowledge, Consciousness, and the Politics of Empowerment* (New York: Routledge, 1991).

————. "Shifting the Center: Race, Class, and Feminist Theorizing about Motherhood," in *Representations of Motherhood,* Donna Bassin, et al., eds. (New Haven: Yale University Press, 1994).

Glenn, Evelyn Nakano, "Racial Ethnic Women's Labor: The Intersection of Race, Gender, and Class Oppression," *Review of Radical Political Economics* 17 (3), 1985.

Hagen, Lyman, *Heart of a Woman, Mind of a Writer, and Soul of a Poet: A Critical Analysis of the Writings of Maya Angelou* (New York: University Press of America, Inc., 1977).

Harris, Jennifer, "Reading Mobility, Motherhood and Domesticity in Four African American Women's Texts," *Journal of the Association for Research on Mothering* 2 (2), 2000: 200–210.

Hooks, Bell, *Feminist Theory: From Margin to Center* (Boston: South End Press, 1984).

McPherson, Dolly, *Order Out of Chaos: The Autobiographical Works of Maya Angelou* (London: Verago Press, Ltd., 1991).

Mohanty, Chandra Talpade, Ann Russo, and Lourdes Torres, eds., *Third World Women and the Politics of Feminism* (Bloomington: Indiana University Press, 1991).

Neubauer, Carol E., "Maya Angelou: Self and Song of Freedom in the Southern Tradition," *Southern Women Writers: The New Generation*, Tonette Bond Inge, ed. (Tuscaloosa: University of Alabama Press, 1990), 114–142.

Nnaemeka, Obioma, *Sisterhood: Feminists and Power from Africa to the Diaspora* (Trenton, NJ: Africa World Press, Inc., 1989).

Sudarkasa, Niara, *The Strength of Our Mothers: African and African American Women and Families* (Trenton, NJ: Africa World Press, 1996).

Thomas, Trudelle, "'You'll Become a Lioness': African-American Women Talk About Mothering," *Journal of the Association for Research on Mothering* 2 (2), 2000: 52–65.

MARY JANE LUPTON

"Spinning in a Whirlwind": Sexuality in Maya Angelou's Sixth Autobiography

In the summer of 1997 my husband Ken and I, thanks to the intervention of Professor Dolly McPherson, drove to Winston-Salem, North Carolina, for an over-night interview with Maya Angelou. We talked about many matters—her writing style and the continuity of her autobiographies, as well as her struggles with men and motherhood. Angelou seemed worried, distracted. She was making arrangements to go to New York City to visit Betty Shabazz, prominent Civil Rights worker and the widow of Malcolm X. Shabazz had been severely burned and died six days later, on Monday, June 23, 1997.

During the interview, the deaths of Malcolm X and of Martin Luther King, Jr., were much on Angelou's mind. I kept asking her about a sixth autobiography. The fifth, *All God's Children Need Traveling Shoes* (1986), had ended abruptly, with Angelou still in the Accra Airport getting ready to re-turn to the United States. "It is a series," I argued. "It's not finished. How would you complete it?"

She answered, "I want to be able to look at horror and not find a justifica-tion but a lesson. If I can find a lesson, I can live with it if I can put it in a place" (cited by Lupton, 10). Angelou then acknowledged that the two particular events had evoked such horror. One was the murder of her friend and associ-ate El-Hajj Malik El-Shabazz, formerly Malcolm X, in 1965. Malcolm X had

MAWA Review, Volume 18, Numbers 1–2 (June–December 2003): pp. 1–6. Copyright ©
2003 Mary Jane Lupton.

figured prominently in *All God's Children Need Traveling Shoes,* although there had been thorny moments in their relationship during his visit to Ghana in 1964. The other was the assassination of Martin Luther King.

In 1968, on her birthday, she was in California cooking party food when her close friend and biographer, Dolly McPherson, called. "Sister, have you listened to the radio? Have you listened? Don't do anything. Don't answer the phone until I get there" (cited by Lupton 10). McPherson told her that King had been killed.

These are two memorable stories, two appalling moments that affected Angelou after she had left Ghana for a racially torn America, moments that would stay with her forever. Nor, in the short duration of our interview, did she have time to talk about further horrors, such as the assassination of civil rights workers in the 1960's or the riots in Los Angeles, Detroit, Baltimore, and Watts. There are many deep scars on the face of America, scars that I suspected would be viewed under a microscope were Angelou to continue her autobiographical chronicle.

As to when her sixth autobiography would be written, she seemed un-certain. "I will do it, I say, but when? I still have to live a little longer and learn how to extract. I have to learn it. And the only way I can learn it is living" (cited by Lupton, 10).

I believe that Angelou has lived enough and learned enough to write *A Song Flung Up To Heaven* (2002), the final volume in the autobiographical series. I believe it when she told Valerie Webster: "After that it would just be writing about writing which is something I don't want to do" (180). But I get the awful feeling that she wrote this final volume under pressure—perhaps under pressure from Random House, more likely from an internalized pres-sure to reach closure. She told Lorraine Kee of the *St. Louis Post-Dispatch* that the unfinished series felt "as if a baby had been left in a room and not fed. I've fed it now" (1). It was perhaps born prematurely.

A Song Flung Up to Heaven does treat the deaths of Malcolm X and Martin Luther King, but it treats them without the passion or depth that she devotes to each man in *Heart of a Woman* (1981) and *All God's Children Need Traveling Shoes* (1986). The sixth volume is too perfunctory, too short. Angelou gives only five pages to King's assassination, most of it having to do with other people's responses rather than her own. Her mode as a reporter is not to confront but to withdraw. She describes the Watts riots as if she were a news commentator rather than a victim of racism: "Three police vans were filled and driven away as I stood on the corner of 125th and Vermont. I headed back to my car with an equal mixture of disappointment and relief" (77). The passive voice is telling ("vans were filled and driven away") as is her own inactivity ("I stood on the corner . . .").

It is not my intent to trash Angelou's new autobiography. That has already been done, quite viciously, by Hilton Als, a staff writer for *The New Yorker* who claims that she "aspired only to the traditional female roles (mother, wife) . . . " (75). Yet it is precisely this focus on women's lives that has earned Angelou her reputation as an autobiographer. Not everyone who writes is male.

The most disturbing negative reaction to Angelou's newest volume comes not from a defensive white male but from a Black woman poet, Wanda Coleman, who has been engaged in hot debate over *A Song Flung Up From Heaven* since shortly after its publication. On April 14, 2002, Coleman published a book review in the *Los Angeles Times* accusing the famous author of "dead metaphors," "empty phrases," "sweeping generalities," and "clumsy similes." Coleman continues: "Extravagant statements come without explication, and schmooze substitutes for action" (rpt. *Salon* 3, 10/21/2002).

Because of her harsh assessment of Angelou's book, a Black-operated bookstore, Esowon, dropped Coleman from its list of poets scheduled to read their works. E-mails poured into the bookstore, many in support of Coleman for her courage in questioning Angelou's pristine, non-racial orientation and her endless repetitions. "It has not escaped me," Coleman stated, "that to this date I have received more attention for my review of Maya Angelou's *A Song Flung Up to Heaven* than anything else I have ever written," a distinction for which she has received no satisfaction ("Black on Black" 12). Coleman retaliated in print for being ousted from the reading schedule and reaffirmed her position: "By applying my own standards to Angelou's *Song*, my answer was—and is—a resounding 'NO'" (*Salon* 5). Thulani Davis, writing for the *Village Voice* in the heat of the controversy, defended Coleman's "outlaw" evaluation and lamented that there really is no arena for Black poets conducting reasonable critiques of each others' works (September 4–10, 2002).

To my knowledge the debate continues, with considerable attention being paid to Angelou's weak writing in this text but without nearly enough emphasis on its sexuality. From *I Know Why the Caged Bird Sings* (1970), where she deliberately approached a young man to prove her femininity, to *All God's Children Need Traveling Shoes*, where she welcomes a handsome, rich African lover, Angelou is open about her heterosexual relationships and about her sexual needs as a woman. She was married three, some say four, times—first in 1951 or 1952, to a Greek sailor; then, unofficially in 1961, to a South African militant; and third, in 1973, to an English builder and writer (Lupton 7–14). Marriage, Angelou told Tricia Crane in 1987, is a serious personal commitment, trivialized by our shallow, soap opera culture. "So I no longer say I've been married X amount of times because I know it will not be understood" (177).

What amazes me is that few if any reviewers of *A Song Flung Up to Heaven* have recognized Angelou's open sexuality or have noticed it as a new freedom, a looseness, in this, particular phase of her autobiography. She is 39, going on 40. It is a good age for sexual fulfillment, particularly when she has just bid farewell to Guy, the son who has until this point been her major preoccupation, a source of pleasure but also of guilt and ambivalence, a theme that she most fully explores in her third volume, *Singin' and Swingin' and Gettin' Merry Like Christmas* (1976). Guy is staying on in Ghana to finish his degree, while Angelou is returning to America to a new life. And contrary to the reviews and the blurbs, that life has a focus that is more sexual than political, a life that explores the language of "frictional electricity," the language of folks who say, "I can hardly keep my hands off your body" (*Song* 160). "My body has always been slow-witted when it comes to that language," she writes (160). I wonder.

One delightful crisis that Angelou encounters in *A Song Flung Up to Heaven* is the occasional but persistent presence of her lover, someone she calls simply "The African." Als identifies The African as Gus Make, Maya's pretend husband and a South African freedom fighter. But that seems an unlikely guess, since she "divorces" Make in volume four after discovering his excesses—expensive furniture and other women. Coleman regrets that The African, "her most intriguing character," is "undeveloped" (*Salon* 3). My guess—I think an intelligent one—is that the unnamed African is Nana Nketsia, first African vice-chancellor of the University of Ghana and tribal chief of the Ahanta people. In the fifth volume, Angelou is summoned to his *Ahen-fie,* the magisterial "house of the Nana" (*Traveling Shoes* 108). She is critical of his self-righteousness and his boisterous voice, major characteristics of her African lover in volume six. Although Nketsia is at the airport when she leaves Ghana, she is discreet about any personal relationship that may have ensued, for reasons that remain her own or that I may have missed.

In volume six, an unidentified lover known as "The African" expects Maya to "fling up" the red carpet whenever he is in New York, providing food and entertainment for his coterie of dignitaries. He tells her on the phone that he will be teaching at one of America's "important universities" (161). He later tells her that he will be meeting Kwesi Brew (110), the poet who in *All God's Children Need Traveling Shoes* is the Chancellor's constant companion. Whoever the lover, all of this amorous play comes to a head when Angelou learns that "The African" is carrying on affairs with her and Dolly McPherson—at the same time, in the same America, but on two different coasts, lying to each about the other woman's supposed senility. In chapter 17 Angelou highlights the sexual nature of the text as well as the sisterly good-humor and bonding.

The chapter, which reads like a scene from a drama, takes place at the Manhattan apartment of novelist Rosa Guy. Angelou, again throwing a party, decides to invite McPherson, asking her to come early because she thinks McPherson is elderly. When the two women meet they realize that the African has been lying about their age and about the relationship. "The old goat," they laugh. The chapter ends with a sexual innuendo: "We were both intelligent women who had been had by the same man, in more ways than one (128–130).

In chapter 26, deciding to retaliate, McPherson stages an entrance during a party that Angelou is hosting for the African and his colleagues. She touches him on the shoulder while he is boasting about the fidelity of the African male. Stunned and angry, the lover from Ghana calls Angelou into the bedroom to say goodbye: "I saw hurt and embarrassment in his face. I had meant to prick him, not to pierce him . . . I knew he would never come back again" (171). Shifting the metaphor, Angelou concludes: "Well, sister, we couldn't swallow the big cat easily. He seems to have stuck in our throats" (171). Angelou's awkward use of metaphor in these and other passages substantiates Coleman's objections to her style. It seems likely that, having introduced a series of sexually charged images—prick, pierce, swallow—she retreats from their erotic meanings.

Angelou has become a bit trendy of late, having signed a contract with Hallmark to write greetings for a line of cards, vases and wind chimes (Weeks C1). At first I thought she might be imitating the supportive friendship, sludgy prose, and enormous popularity of Terry McMillan. During my retirement I waded breathlessly through *Waiting to Exhale,* published in 1992, ten years before *A Song Flung Up to Heaven.* I have concluded that there is really no influence and that Angelou is doing something quite different—more serious, less sexually graphic, less frictionally electric. I was amused, though, when Dolores suggests that "Black Women on the Move" get Maya Angelou or Oprah Winfrey to speak at a fund-raiser. "Do you know how much they'd probably charge?" one woman asked (*Waiting to Exhale* 246).

Making love for Maya Angelou is stronger than landing a steady Black man with a big penis. She also loves little men, even gay men, something that in *Waiting to Exhale* Terry McMillan is unable to imagine. Angelou's love for James Baldwin is a strong element in *A Song Flung Up to Heaven.* Like a caring mother, she worries about Eldridge Cleaver's derisive attitude towards Baldwin's homosexuality. Like a big big-sister, she defends her Bailey-like brother.

Angelou writes: "Jimmy Baldwin was a whirlwind who stirred everything and everybody. He lived at a dizzying pace and I loved spinning with him" (145). They go to bars together. Baldwin introduces her to his mother, Berdis, a "little lady with an extremely soft voice" (145)—the antithesis of

Angelou. If their sizes had been reversed, Angelou and Baldwin might have been the couple of the twentieth century. Maybe they still are.

At the end of the sixth and final autobiography Angelou suspects that Baldwin has spoken to Bob Loomis of Random House in her behalf about signing a contract for an autobiography. As several reviewers have pointed out, *A Song Flung Up to, Heaven* ends where *I Know Why the Caged Bird Sings* begins, with the same two sentences: "What are you looking at me for. I didn't come to stay." The sixth "song" spins backwards to become the first self, singing. Whatever her accesses and extravagances, Maya Angelou is here to stay.

NOTE

My 2003 speculations about the Chancellor of the University of Ghana have never been confirmed. (July 15, 2008)

WORKS CITED

Als, Hilton. "Songbird." *The New Yorker* (August 5, 2002): 72–76.

Angelou, Maya. *All God's Children Need Traveling Shoes.* New York: Random, 1986.

——. *Heart of A Woman.* New York: Random, 1981.

——. *I Know Why the Caged Bird Sings.* New York: Random, 1970.

——. *Singin' and Swingin' and Gettin' Merry Like Christmas.* New York: Random, 1976.

——. *A Song Flung Up to Heaven.* New York: Random, 2002.

Coleman, Wanda. "Black on Black: Fear & Reviewing in Los Angeles." *Ishmael Reed's KONCH Magazine.* 21 Oct. 2002: 1–12.

——. Review of *A Song Flung Up to Heaven. Los Angeles Times,* September 14, 2002. Rpt. wysiwyg://http://blgs.salon.com/0001118/2002/08.17.html.

Crane, Tricia. "Maya Angelou." *Conversations with Maya Angelou.* Ed. Jeffrey M. Elliot. Jackson: University Press of Mississippi, 1989. 173–178.

Davis, Thulani. "Slam Queen vs. Inaugural Poet." *Village Voice.* wysiwyg://16//http://www.villagevoice.com./issues/0236/davis.php. September 4–10, 2002: 1–6.

Kee, Lorraine. "Maya Angelou offers a perfect ending." *St. Louis Post Dispatch.* wysiwg://9/http://www.broomfieldnews.com/broomfield/news/18zbook2.shtml. 2 Oct. 2002.

Lupton, Mary Jane. *Maya Angelou: A Critical Companion.* Westport CT: Greenwood, 1998.

McMillan, Terry. *Waiting to Exhale.* New York: Simon & Schuster, 1992.

Webster, Valerie. "A Journey Through Life." *Conversations with Maya Angelou.* Ed. Jeffrey M. Elliot. Jackson: University Press of Mississippi, 1989. 179–182.

Weeks, Linton. "Hallmark of a Poet" *The Washington Post* (May 11, 2002): C1, C3.

ELEANOR W. TRAYLOR

Maya Angelou Writing Life, Inventing Literary Genre

The annual Heart's Day Conference of the Department of English at Howard University memorializes the venerable pioneer of the study of African American literature in the Academy, the late Howard University Professor Sterling Allen Brown. It also salutes African American writers who, like this year's honoree, sustain the legacy in thought, scholarship, and creative production for which Professor Brown stands. Evidence of this living legacy and heritage speak through two signature poems (among volumes) which link our honoree, Maya Angelou, a present day paradigmatic writer with the poet-founder of the most influential and provocative study of aesthetic and recorded life now prevailing. I find no more compelling way to present lines from these poems than by the example of Maya Angelou as reported in her fourth autobiographical narrative *The Heart of A Woman* (1981). This book is alive. It breathes as it pilots, pivots, taxis, and flies the lucky reader through a journey from San Francisco through New York to Egypt, landing in Accra, West Africa. Its motion wakes to literary resonance one of the many under-represented ascensions in the evolving aesthetics of African American and related creative productions which *Heart of A Woman* re-presents. And one of those was the Harlem Writer's Guild of which Maya Angelou with Paule Marshall, John O. Killens, John Henrik Clark, Sarah Wright, and Rosa Guy, among others, was a member. *Heart*

The Langston Hughes Review, Volume 19 (Spring 2005): pp. 8–21. Copyright © 2005 Eleanor W. Traylor.

of A Woman is, as well, a history of theatre during the late 1950's while it is foremost a biography of sensibility not alone in America: it highlights American and global response to the lurid murder of Patrice Lumumba in the Congo; the catastrophe at New York's Audubon Theatre, the murder of Malcolm; the horror at Memphis, the murder of Martin Luther King, Jr.; and the relentless sacrifice in South Africa before the walls came rumbling down at Robbins Island.

Like all of the Angelou narratives, *Heart of A Woman* is an account of how a personal life is guest and hostess on "the world stage" (*Complete Poems* 256). The narrative is also an enactment of individual genius as it engages the established genius preceding it. *Heart of A Woman* is, in fact, an aesthetic revelation: Miss Angelou is on the stage of the Apollo Theatre. She is billed as singer-performer. She knows the expectation of the Apollo audience. She understands and is a participant in "the cultural script" of the place and its "humanistic tradition" (Froula 18). Yet she proceeds with calculated deliberation to switch the code of the traditional aesthetics on the Apollo stage. We witness an instance when tradition is interrogated, re-visioned, and re-supplied. It is a second when surprise, the gem of creative expression, illumines what has gone before and asserts the innovation of refreshed continuity. The singer, Maya Angelou, asks the Apollo audience to *learn* a song. She has imported the song from West Africa. She also asks the audience to join her in refrain as she lines-out its verses. This call and response performance mode, common in West African singing, is also the ritualized ceremony of the Black Church. Now the singer stands on the Apollo stage amid cries of

> Why don't you do your act, girl
> If you can't sing come back on Wednesday.
> That's amateur night . . . Anyway
> if you like Africa so much, why don't
> you go back there.

The singer stands trembling but unmoving in the grip of "a grumble [. . .] in the balcony and [. . .] sounds of displeasure on the Main floor." Finally she hears an advocate shout, "Shut up there, you bastid"; others shout, "Let the woman sing," "yeah, you don't like it [. . .] get your ass down on the stage and do what you can do" (*Heart* 51–52). Well the Ayes have it, and tradition is renovated on the Apollo stage.

Now I risk grumbling and sounds of displeasure as I line-out a few lines from two signature poems which link the poetic enterprise of Maya Angelou with that of her predecessor Sterling Brown and ask you to supply the refrain:

You may write me down in history
With your bitter, twisted lies
You may trod me in the very dirt
But still, like dust . . . (Angelou, *Complete Poems* 163–164).

They dragged you from homeland,
They chained you in coffles,
They huddled you spoon-fashion in filthy hatches,
They sold you to give a few gentlemen ease . . .
You sang:
 Bye and bye
 I'm gonna lay down dis heaby load . . .
You sang:
 Walk togedder, chillen
 Dontcha git weary . . . (Brown, *Complete Poems* 56–57).

You may shoot me with your words,
You may cut me with your eyes.
You may kill me with your hatefulness,
But still, like air . . . (Angelou, *Complete Poems* 163–164).

One thing they cannot prohibit—
The strong men . . . coming on
The strong men gittin stronger.
Strong men
Stronger (Brown, *Collected Poems* 56–58).

The last two stanzas of the Angelou poem tell us how to read it. The poem calls attention to its aesthetic practice and the theory derived from the poetics of the tradition which it enters. The lines read:

Out of the huts of history's shame
I rise
Up from a past that's rooted in pain
I rise
I'm a black ocean, leaping and wide,
Welling and swelling I bear in the tide.

Leaving behind nights of terror and fear
 I rise
Into a daybreak that's wondrously clear
 I rise

Bringing the gifts that my ancestors
    Gave
I am the dream and the hope of the slaves.
    I rise
    I rise
    I rise (Angelou, *Complete Poems* 164).

This poem is alive. It "walks" and "springs" and "dances" and "leaps [...]" welling and swelling," recalling where it came from and identifying its present being. It styles itself as a bringer of gifts, "gifts my ancestors gave," it says. These gifts are its "diamonds" and "gold" of rhythm and sound and word. "*Rise,*" its constant refrain, its epitomized word, is an ancestral word. It is the rise of another ancestral signature poem, Margaret Walker's *For My People,* of which a line reads: "*Let a new earth rise.*" It is the rise sung in the sorrow song: "*The Lord loves a sinner / And she'll rise.*" Radiantly, the "I" of the poem exults as it faces "the rising sun of our new day begun" from James Weldon Johnson's song of joy *Lift Every Voice and Sing.* Finally, this "I" of "Still I Rise" is a performer whose performance is a lesson in reading and writing, practice, and theory. The poem's prosody of memory participates in the poetics of identity. It represents the lineage out of which its possibilities of being emerge. Its theory of perpetuity extends the premise of an antecedent theorizing artist. The artist who is the rag-time playing musician speaking from the night club scene in James Weldon Johnson's *The Autobiography of An Ex-Colored Man* (1912) tells us that "nothing great or enduring [...] has ever sprung from the brain of any master; the best he gives to the world he runs through the alembic of his genius" (*Autobiography* 100). Subsequently, this judgment defining the project of literary modernist poetics resounds in the famous essay of poet-critic T. S. Eliot's "Tradition and the Individual Talent" (1919), reminding us that "the conscious present is an awareness of the past in a way and to an extent which the past's awareness cannot show. [...] No poet, no artist of any art, has his complete meaning alone. His significance [...] is the appreciation of his relation to [his ancestors]" (*Selected Essays* 4–6). Indeed, the "I" of the poem assumes the identity of the contemporary poet as pronounced by the theorizing voice of Sonia Sanchez, saying "I am Time." (*Sister Sonji* 100–101).

The word *remember,* the predominant signifying word in the poetic production of Maya Angelou, also names the project of contemporary African American poetics not restricted to verse. Of the twenty thousand words that comprise the four volumes of the Angelou poetic canon so-far, ten thousand and fifty ring the word *remember* or its cognates. If these figures are incorrect, this hapless but wonderful audience must accept them, as no scholarship yet exists which challenges what may be an outrageously inaccurate assertion.

Indeed, if the word count is in error, I submit the error as a challenge to this conference. The hard fact is that after fifty-four years since the founder Sterling Brown established the study of African American literature in the Academy here at Howard, scholarship has yet to produce a single concordance of any African American poet, nor has it produced compendiums, indexes, encyclopedias, prosodies, glossaries of usage, or textual studies which offer the most fundamentally useful intelligence on literary practice in the foundational contemporary literature that we know as African American. The poetics of identity, which the Angelou canon advances, defines our immediate literary moment. But identity emerges from recognition or as Dr. Du Bois has put it from "a knowledge of the world that was and is and [our] relation to it ("The Talented Tenth" 170). In the Fanonian sense, the language of identity speaks as the ever-rising Angelou poem speaks to "assume a culture and bear the weight of a civilization" (*Black Skins* 17–18).

But in the sense of sheer pleasure by which a heritage ever rises, the poetics of identity is accomplished by what Sonia Sanchez calls "language sounds" (*Bum Rush* xv–xvii). "There is a music that takes place filled with metaphors and memories, madness and message" as today's younger poet-critic Tony Medina hears it. "It's the way we move" (*Bum Rush* xv). It's in the swing, said the grand Duke. It don't mean a thing if it ain't got that swing *do op, do op, do op*. The "it" for the Angelou speaker, in another signature poem, is a phenomenal occurrence in sound and movement:

> It's in the arch of my back
> The sun of my smile,
> The ride of my breast,
> The grace of my style. (*Collected Poems* 13)

This "Phenomenal Woman" poem swings. It paints a brand new image as it renovates the traditional ode. It is a praise song practicing the beat, the rhythm, the slide, the cadence, the be-bop, the assonance and dissonance, the jam session that embodies the poetics of identity. It triggers memory if you can hear in it the laughter and appeal of a ring-game poem or a hip-hop rap.

This conference addresses to scholarship the question raised by the venerable poet Paul Laurence Dunbar:

> Ain't you nevah hyeahd Malindy?
>   Blessed soul, tek up de cross!
> Look hyeah, ain't you jokin', honey?
>   Well, you don't know what you loss. (*Complete Poems* 131–132)

Of course, the "loss" or silence of scholarly response to the Angelou poetry of identity maybe accounted for in the assertion of Yale critic Harold Bloom in his introduction to the *Maya Angelou* volume of his *Bio Critiques* when he says, "Maya Angelou is *beyond* literary criticism. I [am] an admirer of a great personality" (1). Whether read as a compliment or a cop-out, the statement may be most generously understood as the awe inspired by Dunbar's exultant judgment of African American creative genius which his poem names "Malindy":

> Y'ought to hyeah dal gal a-wa'blin
> Robins, la'ks, an all dem things,
> Heish dey moufs an hides dey faces
>   When Malindy Sings . . .
> Heish yo' mouf, I hyeah dat Music
>   Ez it rises up an' mounts—
> Floatin' by de hills an' valleys,
>   Way above dis buryin sod.
> Ez hit makes its way in glory
>   To de very gates of God. (*Complete Poems* 131–132)

However awe-inspiring the achievement of a poet or her chosen antecedents or contemporaries, the job of scholarship, according to the visionary scholar-poet Sterling Brown, is not awe. The job is to create the *uncreated* in the study of literary texts. I have suggested that one of the untreated studies of African American poetry is the activity of an individual voice as it, like a ventriloquist, assumes other voices with whom it desires company. For example, in the Angelou poem titled "Weekend Glory" (as well as one titled "Here's to Adhering") we hear in the undersong the voice of Langston Hughes's Madam in his *Madam to You* poems. From Maya Angelou's "Weekend Glory,"

> Some dichty folks
> don't know the facts,
> posin' and preenin'
> and puttin' on acts,
> stretchin' their necks
> and strainin' their backs . . .
>
> My life ain't heaven
> but it sure ain't hell.
> I'm not on top
> but I call it swell
> if I'm able to work
> and get paid right

and have the luck to be Black
on a Saturday night. (*Complete Poems* 206–207)

From Langston Hughes "Madam's Past History," we hear

My name is Johnson
Madam Alberta K.
The Madam stands for business.
I'm smart that way. [...]
I do cooking,
Day's work too!
Alberta K. Johnson
Madam to you. (*Selected Poems* 210)

It is the *do-op,* the swing, the beat, not exact but close enough to hear the play and bring the smile. It is the discursive banter going on between the "weekend" speaker and Madam—the textual play—that is the wink of salute to the antecedent poet Langston Hughes.

The pronoun-antecedent relationship, especially intense in the African-American poetics of identity, has largely achieved an aesthetic of "reprise" or "the pleasure of your company." If the relationship of text to intertext understood by the readerly writer and the writerly reader constructs the cultural text or heritage, then as long as that understanding subsists, the heritage rises and rises, becomes stronger and stronger as it examines itself, revises, corrects, and renovates itself. But should a disconnection occur where the relationship is not understood or even not heard—where "the falcon cannot hear the falconer," then the legacy of heritage trembles on the precipice: the terrible verge of loss. This is the pedagogy of the Angelou poetic *oeuvre* from *Give Me a Cool Drink of Water 'Fore I Diiie* (1971); *Oh, Pray My Wings Are Gonna Fit Me Well* (1975); *And Still I Rise* (1978); *Shaker Why Don't You Sing?* (1993); *Now Sheba Sings the Song* (1987); *I Shall Not Be Moved* (1990); *Life Doesn't Frighten Me* (1993); and *On The Pulse of Morning* (the William Jefferson Clinton inaugural poem, 1993). These volumes continue the six predominant matters of African American poetry with their subsequent emphases, until now unnamed: the matter of Africa; the matter of mid-passage; the matter of slavery; the matter of America; the matter of "we folk" (home place, home speech, home agency, home critique, and home invention); and the matter of self-definition. The Maya Angelou poetic body also reengages the constant pedagogy of African American poetry and narrative, especially since mid-twentieth century as it points to now. This pedagogy is embraced in a continual exclamatory call to readers, as "claim the gifts the ancestor's gave." Or as another Angelou poem says it:

I beg you
Discover this Country. (*Complete Poems* 85–86)

I call for glossaries and compendiums; they aid discovery.

If the word *remember* signals the project of Maya Angelou's experiments in the poetics of identity, the six autobiographical narratives create a genre which actualizes what André Maurois has called "the magnificent poetry of life" ("Biography As a Work of Art" in Oates 1–17). I intervene to suggest that of this "magnificent poetry of life," Maya Angelou is Mistress. In his well-known study *Aspects of Biography* (1965), Maurois raises a touchstone question and supplies its answer:

> Can a biography [I insert autobiography] have a poetic value? I think it can. Poetry, in the wider sense, I conceive to be a transmutation of nature into some beautiful form, made intelligible by the introduction of rhythm. In poetry, in the stricter sense, this rhythm; in music, by the motif; in a book by the recurrence, at more or less distant intervals, of the essential motifs of the work. A human life is always made up of a number of such motifs; when you study one of them, it will soon begin to impress itself upon you with a remarkable force. In Shelley's life the water motif dominates the whole symphony. (Oates 16).

It is, of course, difficult to determine the dominant motif in a living author's life, for the last word is not written; another book may appear this afternoon. Yet through the five narratives extant (*I Know Why The Caged Bird Sings* (1970), *Gather Together in My Name* (1974), *Singin' and Swingin' and Gettin' Merry Like Christmas* (1976), *The Heart of A Woman* (1981), *All God's Children Need Traveling Shoes* (1986), and *A Song Flung Up To Heaven* (2002)), *motion*, by its recurrence, impresses itself upon a reader with remarkable force.

I suggest that rhythmic motion dominates the whole symphony heard in these narratives of being. At the outset, the titles of the narratives convey the language of motion. Of the narrative events that inform the books, readers have interpreted this motif as either geographical, physical, spiritual, psychological, intellectual or all of these informing intertextually. Some have emphasized the motif as *displacement, rootlessness, re-location, struggle* (as against the forces of life), *role-playing, embattlement, arrival, sojourn, departure, erosion* (as in a loss of faith in the American Dream), *transcendence*. Each of the five narratives justifies these readings. They also support the reading of early scholars such as that of the late and revered George Kent, whose 1975 essay "Maya Angelou's *I Know Why The Caged Bird Sings* and the *Black Autobiographical Tradition*" places the narrative within accounts of late 18th-century and 19th-century self-emancipated men and women, yet called slave narratives. In the 1980's Christine Froula reads the narrator of *I Know Why* back to Homer's silenced Helen, through Ovid's Philomela, Shakespeare's Lucrece and Freud's denial of the cultural daughter's story. Dr. Freud's decision "to privilege the cultural father's voice and story" and, therefore, preserve "the cultural script that protects the father's credit," (17) argues Froula, "ensures the dominance of patriarchal culture" (15) and, of course, saves Dr. Freud his career. The Froula reading also reminds us of Virginia Woolf's prediction in 1931 that it would be fifty years before "Woman's freedom to tell her own stories—and indeed [...] to know them fully herself would come" (13). In fact, the appearance of *I Know Why The Caged Bird Sings* in 1969 cuts short the predicted time by more than a decade. Accordingly, the scholar finds the narrative "to exemplify the breaking of women's forbidden stories into literary history, an event that reverberates far beyond their heroes' individual histories to reshape our sense of a cultural past and its possible future directions" (13). Professor Dolly A. McPherson's valuable 1990 book-length study *Order Out of Chaos: The Autobiographical Works of Maya Angelou* reads the narratives following *Caged Bird* as preceding readings principally had not. This study advances the now prevalent discourse of interiority brilliantly explored in Chinua Achebe's *Things Fall Apart* (1959). It characterizes the growth of the young narrator in *Caged Bird* as the epiphanic discovery of two worlds: the world of externality constructed as reality and the world of "St. Elsewhere"—the imagination—in which any thoughtful, much more, extraordinary consciousness must reside to find states of nurture.

Now at the outset of the millennium, it is the huge opportunity of scholarship to apply a revisionary lens for the exploration of the narratives which follow *Caged Bird* and to locate them as pioneers of contemporary life writing genres. *Gather Together in My Name, Singin' and Swingin' and Gettin' Merry Like Christmas, The Heart of A Woman, All God's Children Need Traveling Shoes*, and *A Song Flung Up To Heaven* are relentless interrogations of personal identity which reverberate to re-shape the public sense of self-awareness. These narratives of liberatory identity challenge the empire of constructed, entrenched, and imposed identity markers that James Baldwin, preceding Jean-Francois Lyotard, called "theologies which deny [one] life." *Woman, man, child, fool, wise, sinner, righteous, powerful, powerless* become questions in the Angelou life narratives where nothing is privileged and all is risked. Read as narratives of liberational identity, they interrogate the cultural text of the American dream which has heretofore characterized canonical American life-writing genres. Is the American Dream a vision of a journey from a "blood-stained gate to some clean, new, beautiful place" (Douglass 148)? If so, the Angelou narratives since *Caged Bird*, by their motion, ask where is that place? Is the American Dream the vision of Winthrop's "shining city on a hill"? If so, the Angelou life narratives since *Caged Bird,* by their rhythmic motion, ask "might that be Sugar Hill of Harlem or Hunter Hills of Atlanta or Beverly Hills of Los Angeles or Hillcrest of Washington, D.C."? Is the American Dream a journey from Horatio Alger's "rags to riches"? The Angelou narratives seem to ask "is the stock market forever stable?" Their judgment *remembers* the judgment of Zora Neale Hurston's Janie of Joe Starks, and the Angelou narrator muses: "Avarice cripples virtue and lies in ambush for honesty" (*Singin'*, 229). Is the American Dream the ideal of self-reliance? The motion of the daughter-voice seems to ask, "Is help never needed"? Is the American Dream the dream of Martin Luther King, the dream of Civil Rights and the dream of Black empowerment, the Dream of Stokely Carmichael (Kwame Ture)? The Angelou narratives supply an answering query:

> Now ain't we bad?
> An' ain't we Black?
> An' ain't we Black?
> An' ain't we bad?
> An' ain't we bad?
> An' ain't we bad?
> An ain't we Black?
> An' ain't we fine? (*Complete Poems* 165–166)

Yet the daughter-voiced narrator of *Caged Bird* continues in the later narratives to question what Hortense Spillers has cogently pointed to as a paternalistic cultural script in which the daughter must disappear "in deconstructing into wife and mother of his children" (127). The Angelou narratives return the daughter to visibility by realigning her with what Alice Walker has termed her "womanist" birth and lineage.

It is not simply that the narratives are peppered throughout with the chastening wit and the encouraging spark of Grandma Henderson, Grandma Baxter, and Mrs. V. B.—the lighting rod—saying: "Be the best of anything you get into. If you want to be a whore, it's your life Be a damn good one. Don't chippy at anything. Anything worth being is worth working for" (*Gather* 30). It is also that the daughter's voice gains recognition by its response to and reliance upon the brother: "My brother Bailey was my savior, a role he fulfilled most of my early years" (*Gather* 27). Most importantly, the daughter's respect for and recognition of the text of woman-wisdom is a central point of moral authority by which the daughter's story may be corrected, revised, and protected from delusional and destructive forces in these narratives of developing being. The Narrator of *Gather Together* tells us: "Our friendship was possible because Ivonne was wise without glitter, while I, too often glittered without wisdom" (*Gather* 60). And what of the Womanist dream? Is there not a canonical ancestral feminine dream that inheres in the American dream cycle? To borrow Deborah McDowell's on-point phrase, "It is not late-breaking news" (75) that black women scholars have cited this dream time and again. And could this dream be the reference of the Angelou speaker in lines from "On the Pulse of Morning" reading:

Lift up your eyes
Upon this day breaking for you
Give birth again
to the dream (*Complete Poems* 272)

This dream, needing a daughter's fulfillment, blueprinted the possibilities for all that can be called contemporary in life-writing and in the production of story. It is the foundation of the cultural daughter-cum-mother text, Harriet Jacobs' *Incidents in the Life of a Slave Girl* (1861). From *Incidents* we hear, "Reader, my story ends with freedom; not in the usual way, with marriage. I and my children are now free! We are as free from the power of slaveholders as are the white people of the North; and though that, according to my idea, is not saying a great deal, it is a vast improvement on my condition. [But] The dream of my life is not yet realized" (201). The freedom narrative, still called slave narratives by some, is a fully realized genre. An ever-enduring resonance is their paradigmatic liberating goal. Contemporary literature springs from this foundational paradigm. The Angelou "I" narratives enter this ancestral model in precisely the territory of the "not yet realized" dream. As Hortense Spillers has put it, that dream is the desire of woman "to become [her] own historical subject in pursuit of its proper object, its proper and specific experience in time" (105).

This conference builds upon the framing and shaping of Black women scholars, among them the late Claudia Tate, a former Chair of the Department of English at Howard. The theoretical lens, the critical approaches, the discourse-making landscape they have plowed constitute the premises for literary study today. By 1974, following Toni Cade Bambara's *The Black Woman: An Anthology* (1970), Beverly Guy Sheftall with her colleagues Roseann P. Bell and Bettye J. Parker published *Sturdy Black Bridges: Visions of Black Women in Literature* (1979). Its collection of creative and scholarly production by women over the diaspora and its liberating theses that "the primary definition of a group must come from the 'inside'" (Sheftall 292) articulated the direction of literary and social analysis before it and since. Just before *Bridges,* former Howard University President Joyce A. Ladner had released *Tomorrow's Tomorrow: The Black Woman,* a definitive sociological study that Mary Helen Washington cites as inspiration for her *Black-Eyed Susans: Classic Stories by and About Black Women* (1975). *Susans* followed *Bridges* by one year to be followed four years later by *Midnight Birds* (1980). In her essay "In Pursuit of our Own History" which introduces *The Stories of Contemporary Black Women Writers,* the subtitle of *Midnight Birds,* Mary Helen Washington affirms the Sheftall premise in *Sturdy Black Bridges* with the now patent understanding that "Black Women writers will first insist on their own name, their own space" (xvi). That they have is the brilliant scholarly revelation of Cheryl A. Wall's *Changing Our Own Words: Essays on Criticism, Theory, and Writing by Black Women* (1989). In this collection of womanly-leading scholarly voices, we learn that "It is not late-breaking news that literary criticism is another form of storytelling" (McDowell 75). Let us add that it is also not "late-breaking news" that storytellers are also theorists. Contemporary fiction by Black women writers has supplied and re-supplied theories of reading and writing. As wide a field of discourse-making insights that *Changing Our Own Words* realizes, Cheryl Wall generously reminds us: "yet there is other work for Critics to do" (9).

Entering upon the wings of this mind-expanding, spirit-lifting scholarship, I venture a thought which is also "not late-breaking news." In the creation of what was not before existing, Black women writers have realized new genres to enter into literature unrecorded ways of being. Maya Angelou's *Gather Together in My Name, Singin' and Swingin' and Gettin' Merry Like Christmas, The Heart of A Woman, All God's Children Need Traveling Shoes,* and *A Song Flung Up to Heaven* constitute a genre which dislocates received concepts of self and liberates an antecedent life-writing genre chained in time-bound categories of reductive designation. The narratives chart a continual motion of becoming, consciously interrogating every manifestation of an emerging and emergent self—"Marguerite," "Sister," "Rita," "Ritie," "Reet," Maya—asking who is she and who is she to me? These are not the bemused and bemusing "three faces of Eve"; they are clauses in the endless syntax of identity. They permit no end-punctuation because the self, insists the narratives, is a process. Navigated by the most circumstantial or capricious motivator of identity, desire is also the most educable. In the lineage of African American life-writing the desire of the mother-narrative was freedom from bondsmanship, to achieve a self-determination that leads to the un-bound regions of the imagination and to realize the un-yet-realized in the ongoing existential flux of life.

The mother-narrative frees the daughter-narrative to dare fate, disappoint destruction, determine the possibilities of destiny, and record the jazz—the magnificent poetry of life. The daughter-narrator of *Gather Together in My Name* tells us, "I had a heritage, rich and nearer than the tongue which gives it voice. My mind resounded with the words and my blood raced to the rhythms" (190). The motion of the Angelou-daughter narratives may dance with the movement that Albert Murray discovers as the blues narrative, and they may certainly move through phases of the migration narrative as discovered by Jasmin Farah Griffin. This kinship illustrates what Deborah McDowell calls "family matters" (*Changing* 75–97) in literary heritage. But kinship also discloses difference, and in this case, the wonderful difference that the daughter's voice makes. The Angelou daughter's life-story desires a proper name appropriate to what she has earned as a distinct way of being in the world. She has recorded the rhythmic passage that distinguishes her perilous quest for liberated identities showing that identity is not a solid static, but a fluid process. She has recorded this process in "ago time, now time" (Sanchez 100–101) for time to come. She is the *narrative of liberational identity* whose life encounters move paradigmatically through five characteristic experiences: assault, descent, navigation, development of a critical consciousness, and the recovery of a voice. *Assault*—the rape of the body and the psyche, tearing her body, paralyzing her voice, and disrupting her self-understanding: "I know that I was dying, and, in fact, I longed for death [. . .] I had to stop talking" (*Caged Bird* 80–85)—"I froze" (*Gather* 17); *Descent* into "the bottomless terror" (Spillers) of the "warping, dwarfing," (Johnson, 21) maiming and silly *yada yada* on race, class, color, hair, nose, feet, gender, sex—profiteering evangelisms which read all texts to justify hideous constructions of identity in service to the gargoyle face and bloated body of self-appointed righteousness and delusional, illegitimate power: "a woman called by a devaluing name will only be weakened by the misnomer" (*Wouldn't Take* 7); *Navigation* through destructive circumstances to discover the coping strategies conducted by the speaking, reading, writing, fighting, singing ancestry of heritage: "I needed to become an historian, sociologist, and anthropologist. I would begin a self-improvement course" (*Singin'* 36); Development of a *critical consciousness* which links the ethical with the beautiful in the constant interrogation of virtue and discovers the values of reading and writing to be those which unmask the project of pretentious tyranny thereby to revise and rename the possibilities of this world: "Since childhood I had often read until the grey light entered my room"; "I discovered the Russian Writers" (*Gather* 71, 65); and *Recovery* of a voice to sing the sublimity of being—the magnificent poetry of life: "Now Sheba sings her song."

As to the aesthetics of this narrative of liberational identity, the daughter's narrative gains the strategies of beauty from its ancestral forebears: the tortured, yet life-enduring holler from the field, the life-enhancing cadence of the spirituals, the shout of affirmation of the gospels, the dance of life cadence of the blues, the comprehensive vocabulary, the improvisational genius, the cool confidence of the jazz mode: "Music was my refuge. I could crawl into the spaces between the notes and curl my back to loneliness"; "The spirituals and gospel songs were sweeter than sugar. I wanted to keep my mouth full of them" (*Singin'* 1, 33). Finally, the daughter's narrative unchains the

time-bound and devaluing name of the mother narrative, changing it from
the slave narrative to the *narrative of liberational identity* and insists that the
terms of beauty are to be found in

> [. . .] the arch of my back
> The sun of my smile
> The ride of my breasts,
> The grace of my style [. . .] (*Complete Poems* 131)

whoever you are or think you are and whatever your liberated gender.

Works Cited

Angelou, Maya. *All God's Children Need Traveling Shoes.* New York: Random House, 1986.

———. *The Complete Collected Poems of Maya Angelou.* New York: Random House, 1994.

———. *Gather Together in My Name.* New York: Random House, 1974.

———. *The Heart of A Woman.* New York: Random House, 1981.

———. *I Know Why the Caged Bird Sings.* New York: Random House, 1970.

———. *Singin' and Swingin' and Gettin' Merry Like Christmas.* New York: Random House, 1976.

———. *Wouldn't Take Nothing for My Journey Now.* New York: Random House, 1993.

Bloom, Harold, ed. "Maya Angelou." *BioCritiques.* Philadelphia: Chelsea, 2002.

Brown, Sterling A. *The Collected Poems of Sterling A. Brown.* New York: Harper & Row, 1980.

Douglass, Frederick. *Narrative of the Life of Frederick Douglass.* New York: Dover, 1995.

Du Bois, W. E. B. "The Talented Tenth." *The Negro Problem: A Series of Articles by Representative Negroes of Today.* New York: J. Pott & Company, 1903.

Dunbar, Paul Laurence. *The Complete Poems of Paul Laurence Dunbar.* New York: Dodd, 1946.

Eliot, T. S. "Tradition and the Individual Talent." *Selected Essays.* New York: Harcourt Brace, 1932.

Fanon, Frantz. *Black Skins, White Masks.* 1952. New York: Grove, 1967.

Froula, Christine. "The Daughter's Seduction: Sexual Violence and Literary History." *Signs* 11.4 (Summer 1986): 621–644. Rpt. *Contemporary Literary Criticism.* Vol. 155: 12–23.

Guy-Sheftall, Beverly, et al., eds. *Sturdy Black Bridges: Visions of Black Women in Literature.* Garden City, NY: Anchor /Doubleday, 1979.

Hughes, Langston. *Selected Poems.* New York: Vintage, 1974.

Jacobs, Harriet A. *Incidents in the Lift of A Slave Girl.* 1860. Cambridge, Massachusetts: Harvard University Press, 1987.

Johnson, James Weldon. *The Autobiography of An Ex-Colored Man.* 1912. New York: Hill and Wang, 1960.

Maurois, André. "Biography as a Work of Art." In Oates.

McDowell, Deborah E. "Reading Family Matters." *Changing Our Own Words.* Ed. Cheryl A. Wall. New Brunswick: Rutgers University Press, 1989.

Oates, Stephen B. *Biography as High Adventure.* Amherst: University of Massachusetts Press, 1966.

Sanchez, Sonia. Foreword. *Bum rush the page: a Def Poetry Jam.* Ed. Tony Medina and Louis
    Reves Rivera. New York: Three Rivers Press, 2001.
———. "Sister Son/Ji." *New Plays from the Black Theatre.* New York: Bantam Books, 1969.
Spillers, Hortense. "The Politics of Intimacy." In Guy-Sheftall.
Wall, Cheryl A., ed. *Changing Our Own Words: Essays on Criticism, Theory, and Writing by
    Black Women.* New Brunswick, NJ: Rutgers University Press, 1989.

SUZETTE A. HENKE

Maya Angelou's Caged Bird
as Trauma Narrative

Since the publication of the first volume of her serial autobiography in 1970, Maya Angelou has frequently spoken out about the profound effects of childhood sexual trauma and her lifelong struggle to heal the shattered self through autobiographical acts of narrative reformulation. Angelou feels righteously indignant that American society refuses to imagine the powerful impact of traumatic assault on the psychological integrity of the Black female subject. News reports of rape and childhood sexual abuse are so prevalent in today's culture that their heinous perpetration seems to have fallen into the amorphous political space of "no woman's land," between the fissures of class and racial consciousness.[1]

In *I Know Why the Caged Bird Sings* (hereafter cited as *CB*), Angelou recreates her child-self in the persona of Marguerite Johnson (her birth name). She reclaims the horror of childhood sexual abuse from statistical anonymity through a poignant autobiographical account of the traumatic impact of physical violation on an eight-year-old victim, a young girl stunned and confused by a brutal sexual initiation and by the adult emotional betrayal that it signifies. Separated from her mother at the age of three, Marguerite Johnson felt haunted by the specter of parental absence. It is little wonder that Maya/ Ritie developed the naïve conviction that she existed as a racial changeling. Fed on celluloid fantasies of Shirley Temple beauty, the ingenuous child

The Langston Hughes Review, Volume 19 (Spring 2005): pp. 22–35. Copyright © 2005 Suzette A. Henke.

dissociated her subject position and personality from what she considered a dark, ungainly body with sludge-colored skin and nappy hair. Lost in Eurocentric fairy-tale fantasy, she harbored extravagant dreams of physical transformation and believed that, beneath an African American persona or mask, there resided a slim, cream-skinned, blue-eyed, blond-haired sylph—"one of the sweet little white girls who were everybody's dream of what was right with the world" (*CB* 1). Only no one knew the secret of her identity—not even God: "Wouldn't they be surprised when one day I woke out of my black ugly dream?" (*CB* 2).

Angelou's infantile version of Freud's family romance gave startling proof of the subaltern syndrome of "internalized inferiority" diagnosed by Franz Fanon in *Black Skin, White Masks* (1967). Interviewed by the journalist Bill Moyers, the adult Angelou explains: "I thought [. . .] maybe I'm really a white girl. And what's going to happen is I am going to wake up. I am going to have long blond hair and everybody is going to just go around loving me. [. . .] It's tragic" (*Conversations* 26). "How much of this is the pretense of self-rejection," asks Audre Lorde, "how much the programmed hate that we were fed to keep ourselves a part, apart?" (*Zami* 58). In response to the false self-system constructed for African Americans by southern white culture, Angelou declares: "I decided many years ago to invent myself. I had obviously been invented by someone else—by a whole society—and I didn't like their invention" (*Conversations* 88).

In Angelou's *Caged Bird,* negritude, and femininity make contradictory, irreconcilable demands on Ritie's sense of personal identity. The color of her skin, the kinkiness of her hair, and the fullness of her lips all contribute to socially engendered feelings of physical inadequacy bordering on self-hatred. During the 1930's, the American social ideal of white female beauty was touted in newspapers and in ladies' magazines and, most powerfully, in romantic cinematic representations. In the South at mid-century, there was little consciousness of the kind of African American pride that grew out of the Civil Rights movement of the 1960's. To be young, gifted, and Black in Stamps, Arkansas meant, quite simply, to be lonely and to be doubly marginal—twice removed from the dominant power group and handicapped by a burden of racial and gender stereotypes. "The Black female," Angelou insists, "is assaulted in her tender years by all those common forces of nature at the same time that she is caught in the tripartite crossfire of masculine prejudice, white illogical hate and Black lack of power" (*CB* 3).

The dominant tone of Ritie's narrative, modulated by wry humor and pervasive vitality, is one of shattering isolation: "If growing up is painful for the Southern Black girl, being aware of her displacement is the rust of the razor that threatens the throat" (*CB* 3). From early childhood, Marguerite feels uncomfortable with the societal role of specular object assigned her by Anglo-

America's racial constructions. She finds herself at the center of an alienating *regard*, a psychological location that makes her perpetually the object of another's critical gaze. As Mae Henderson observes, the "complex situatedness of the black woman as not only the 'Other' of the Same, but also the 'other' of the other(s) implies [. . .] a relationship of difference and identification with the 'other(s)'" (18). "What distinguishes black women's writing, then, is the privileging (rather than repressing) of 'the other in ourselves'" (19).

Maya/Ritie's perpetual struggle throughout *Caged Bird* is for acceptance, recognition, valorization, caring, and *love*. As a young Black girl, she desperately craves something more and different—a return to the welcoming arms of a fantasmatic (m)other figure, that sanctuary from which she feels painfully exiled. A mature Angelou nostalgically recalls, "my mother had left me when I was three and I saw her only once between the ages of three and thirteen" (*Conversations* 39). And so the resourceful Ritie must set out, from earliest childhood, to reinvent a matrifocal heritage by developing respect for the strength and beneficence of her paternal grandmother—a stalwart, patient, longsuffering matriarch imaginatively invested with Amazonian powers. In the tradition of Afra-American autobiography, Maya fashions an iconic figure identified by Joanne Braxton as the "outraged mother" who "sacrifices and improvises for the survival of flesh and spirit. [. . .] Implied in all her actions and fueling her heroic ones is outrage at the abuse of her people and her person" (1–2).

Angelou's early years were dominated by the pain of mother-absence, a source of bereavement that made her "so highly sensitive as to be paranoid" (*Conversations* 60). A loving Momma Henderson set about the task of socializing her granddaughter in the strict disciplinarian code of Black fundamentalist religion and time-tested principles of African American survival in the deep South. Cleanliness was godly, impudence impugned. Silence seemed a sensible tactic to confound the inscrutable white "ghosts," whose spectral lives of conspicuous consumption defined the parameters of African American indigence. "Momma intended to teach Bailey and me to use the paths of life that she and her generation [. . .] found to be safe ones" (*CB* 39), Ritie explains. And yet, paradoxically, this heroic grandmother continually triumphs over white racism through wise-woman strategies of faith, patience, self-respect, dogged persistence, enduring courage, and a tenacious adherence to principles of social justice. Through cunning silences and wicked locutions, she not only endures, but prevails in the face of outrageous bigotry. Her quiet, unassuming victory over the abominable dentist Dr. Lincoln, proves morally superior to, and more pragmatic than, the hyperbolic "Captain Marvel" scenarios her granddaughter conjures by dint of a vivid and fanciful imagination.

Bundled up and sent south by train at the age of three, Marguerite felt, along with her brother Bailey, a beleaguered sense of emotional abandonment.

How could her parents laugh and eat oranges in a paradise called "sunny California" while their children suffered the disciplinarian wrath of Uncle Willie, a crippled avuncular pedagogue teaching mathematics by the coal-stove method, and a loving but cantankerous grandmother whose religious sensibilities savagely bristled at the utterance of an innocent phrase like "by the way"? No, Ride concludes, her real mother had to be dead, laid in a beautiful white coffin and forever embalmed in the sweet sadness of mortality: "I could cry anytime I wanted by picturing my mother (I didn't quite know what she looked like) lying in her coffin. [. . .] The face was brown, like a big O, and since I couldn't fill in the features I printed M O T H E R across the O, and tears would fall down my cheeks like warm milk" (*CB* 43).

Since Maya/Ritie luxuriates in the possibility of entertaining nurturant maternal images at will, she feels stunned by the unexpected delivery of parental Christmas presents—a children's tea-set and a white, blue-eyed doll with "yellow hair painted on her head" (*CB* 43). Both gifts silently mock the poverty-stricken and astonished siblings who greet these offerings with wonder and incredulity. How could such affectionate parents have abandoned their progeny? Of what terrible sins were the children guilty, to be so cruelly punished? Marguerite and Bailey, in an act of consummate fury, angrily disembowel their white-skinned doll, whose blond hair mimics the Shirley Temple tresses that earlier entranced an infantile Ritie. The bewildered siblings cherish their tea-set, however, as a memento of the mother of their dreams, a figure to be worshipped and longed for but forever enshrined in the inaccessible world of the imaginary.

When Ritie and Bailey are finally delivered to "Mother Dear" in St. Louis by their inscrutable father (an apparently high-class gentleman, "the first cynic I had met," and reputedly the proprietor of "a castle out in California" [*CB* 45]), they both feel awestruck and seduced by the idealized figure of Vivian Baxter, who appears out of a mirage in the guise of an unapproachable Venus, light-skinned and lovely but too gorgeously erotic to function in the mundane role of maternal caregiver. Adoring and mute, Ritie proclaims: "To describe my mother would be to write about a hurricane in its perfect power. [. . .] My mother's beauty literally assailed me. [. . .] I knew immediately why she had sent me away. She was too beautiful to have children" (*CB* 49–50). Watching Bailey swept away by filial passion and intensely enamored of his long-lost mother/lover, Ritie becomes convinced that she herself must be an orphan, an abandoned waif adopted by the family to serve as an amusing companion for her gifted sibling. Vivian and Bailey, she tells us, "both had physical beauty and personality, so I figured it figured" (*CB* 50). Like a ghost or goddess, this newfound mother seems too beautiful to be nurturant, too remote and evanescent to offer her daughter the satisfactions of emotional attachment. And reunion with the long-lost female parent exacts a high price indeed, as Vivian's live-in boyfriend begins to express his jealous insecurities by sexually molesting his lover's daughter.[2]

Ritie's own uncanny experiences in St. Louis border on the unspeakable. Childhood sexual abuse takes the form of molestation, then rape, by her mother's frustrated and demented boyfriend, Mr. Freeman, whose confusing attentions initially mimic paternal expressions of physical affection. "From the way he was holding me," thinks the innocent girl, "I knew he'd never let me go or let anything bad ever happen to me" (*CB* 61). But when Mr. Freeman admonishes her not to "tell anybody what we did," lest he be forced to "kill Bailey" (*CB* 62), the benevolent father figure turns out to be a demonic predator enacting a torturous nightmare. "The child trapped in an abusive environment," explains Judith Herman, "must find a way to preserve a sense of trust in people who are untrustworthy, safety in a situation that is unsafe, control in a situation of helplessness. Unable to care for or protect herself, she must compensate for the failure of adult care and protection with the only means at her disposal, an immature system of psychological defenses" (102).[3]

Angelou's adult narrative voice recounts the experience of rape in a controlled style that is taut, laconic, and deliberately restrained by biblical allusion. She articulates the trauma in carefully modulated testimonial tones that compensate psychologically for the horror of the child's excruciating pain: "The act of rape on an eight-year-old body is a matter of the needle giving because the camel can't. The child gives, because the body can, and the mind of the violator cannot" (*CB* 6S). Through the helpless, vulnerable body of his lover's daughter, Mr. Freeman exacts both sexual satisfaction and pathological vengeance. Marguerite, the stunned rape victim, is so severely traumatized that she tries to keep the abuse a secret even from herself, since the only "means she has at her disposal are frank denial [...] and a legion of dissociative reactions" (Herman 102). As Janet Liebman Jacobs observes,

> In this retelling of the rape, Angelou reconstructs the child self who simultaneously experiences the suffering of the victim while responding to the remorse of the victimizer. Immediately after the assault, the perpetrator is [...] asking that she, the abused child, understand that he did not mean to hurt her. [...] In that moment of awareness, the physical and emotional boundary violations converge as the child feels both her pain and the pain of the abuser. Empathy is thus engendered under conditions of sexual violence. (62)

Accusing herself of tacit complicity, a traumatized Marguerite retreats into the silence of post-traumatic dysphoria. "What he did to me, and what I allowed, must have been very bad if already God let me hurt so much"

(*CB* 68), she reasons. "Participation in forbidden sexual activity,"Judith Herman tells us, "confirms the abused child's sense of badness. Any gratification that the child is able to glean from the exploitative situation becomes proof in her mind that she instigated and bears full responsibility for the abuse" (104). By uttering the unspeakable in court, and by denying that she initially took pleasure in Mr. Freeman's embraces, Marguerite believes that it was she who condemned her assailant to death. The young girl is bereft of language to articulate the double pain of rape and emotional betrayal. "I had in fact liked his holding me," she confesses (*CB* 65). And because she responded warmly to those brief moments of physical intimacy, Ritie fully expects to be punished as a biblical harlot. Reproducing infantile tones of shock and bereavement, the adult narrator recalls, "How I despised the man for making me lie. Old, mean nasty thing. Old, black, nasty thing" (*CB* 71). Ritie's only guide to the mysterious terrain of adult sexuality is the New Testament, a tract that would, she believes, condemn her to be stoned to death as an adulterous sinner.[4]

Sexual assault robs the prepubescent child of both dignity and language. She spoke, and a man was killed. Like Shakespeare's Iago, she determines never more to speak a word: "I had to stop talking. [...] I could talk to Bailey, but to no one else." "I knew that [...] if I talked to anyone else that person might die too. Just my breath, carrying my words out, might poison people and they'd curl up and die" (*CB* 73). Survivors of childhood sexual trauma, Herman explains, "face the task of grieving not only for what was lost but also for what was never theirs to lose. The childhood that was stolen from them is irreplaceable. They must mourn the loss of the foundation of basic trust" (193).

Brutally traumatized by rape and emotional betrayal, Maya responds by constructing a wall of protective silence around her imperilled ego. She exhibits the classic symptoms of post-traumatic stress disorder, delineated in the fourth edition of the American Psychological Association's *Diagnostic and Statistical Manual of Mental Disorders* as "recurrent and intrusive recollections of the [traumatic] event [...] or recurrent distressing dreams"; "[d]iminished responsiveness to the external world, referred to as 'psychic numbing' or 'emotional anesthesia'"; and a "markedly reduced ability to feel emotions especially those associated with intimacy, tenderness, and sexuality" (424–425). Other effects of severe psychological trauma include "self-destructive and impulsive behavior; dissociative symptoms; somatic complaints; feelings of ineffectiveness, shame, despair, or hopelessness; ... hostility; [and] social withdrawal" (425). As Judith Herman tells us, traumatic events "shatter the construction of the self that is formed and sustained in relation to others" and "cast the victim into a state of existential crisis" (51).

As an adult, Maya Angelou would later identify bitterness as a spiritual cancer that feeds upon its angry host: "It doesn't do a damned thing to the object of bitterness. Retention and exclusivity and isolation and distance do nothing to anyone but the person who set them up" (*Conversations* 174). The explicit purpose of Angelou's autobiographical project is defined in terms of self-conscious narrative recovery in the genre of *testimonio*.[5] As Daniel Schacter and Bessel Van der Kolk have shown, traumatic memories, obtrusive and haunting, are imprinted on the amygdala of the brain in the mode of infantile recollections that constitute an incoherent "prenarrative" that does not progress or develop in time but remains stereotyped, repetitious, and devoid of emotional content. These persistent iconic and visual images intrude on consciousness in the form of relentless traumatic flashbacks and terrible, repetitive nightmares. In the healing autobiographical project, the narrator plays both analyst and analysand in a discursive drama of scriptotherapy. According to Judith Herman, the organized narrative reformulation of traumatic experience can virtually restructure the mind's obsessive-compulsive processing of embedded personal scripts.

In the act of narrative articulation, the trauma story becomes a public, potentially communal testimony that sets the stage for psychic reintegration. It is the very process of rehearsing and emotionally reenacting a tale of survival and triumph that gives meaning to an otherwise meaningless experience of victimization and effects both psychological catharsis and reintegration into a sympathetic discourse community (Henke, *Shattered Subjects* xv–xix). In the words of Janice Haaken, the articulation of ineffable pain "anoints the survivor with an heroic status—as the bearer of unspeakable truths" (1083). In *Caged Bird*, Angelou successfully reconstructs the experience of incest trauma in the form of a coherent testimony, even as she heroically struggles to overcome obsessive-compulsive flashbacks by compassionately imagining the pathology of her perpetrator and "trying to understand how really sick and alone that man was." There has "not been a day since the rape 50 years ago," she confesses, "during which I have not thought of it" (*Conversations* 175).

When the young Marguerite Johnson, taciturn and traumatized, is sent back to Stamps, Arkansas and remitted to the sympathetic care of Momma Henderson, she inhabits a private cage of self-imposed silence until released by the skilled and patient tutelage of her mentor Bertha Flowers. Angelou recalls that "from the time I was 7 1/2 until I was almost 13, I didn't talk. I was persuaded to talk by a woman who knew I loved and memorized poetry" (*Conversations* 142). Because post-traumatic recovery must necessarily entail the "empowerment of the survivor and the creation of new connections," it is understandable that contact with a single "caring, comforting person may be a lifeline. [...] The reward of mourning is realized as the survivor sheds her stigmatized [...] identity" (Herman 133, 194).

When Marguerite slowly begins to regain hard-won mastery over speech and writing, her filial relationship with Bertha Flowers opens doors and worlds that stretch far beyond the limits of a small southern town in rural Arkansas. After Shakespeare and Dickens win Maya's intellectual commitment, she finds herself able to identify with a vast panorama of history that liberates her mind and fires her curious imagination. It is through literature, moreover, that she begins to discover a repressed African American heritage. When young Black children at a grammar school graduation are humiliated by a patronizing oration reminding them of white society's circumscribed expectations for their collective future, the poetry of James Weldon Johnson consolidates their energies into a sense of racial solidarity that inaugurates the first stirrings of political rebellion.

Ritie's adolescent rites of passage are acted out in relative seclusion. Searching for the freedom of personal expression, she must, as a Black woman, prove her competence in meeting a complex set of emotional challenges. Her narrative becomes a picaresque series of adventures, sometimes comic and sometimes dangerous and bizarre. In the slums of Los Angeles, she survives in a community of homeless, vagabond children who sleep in abandoned cars. On a pleasure trip across the border to Mexico, she rescues her inebriate father and learns spontaneously to drive an automobile. Through sheer persistence and stubbornness, she becomes the first Black ticket-collector on the San Francisco cable cars, and this socially inconsequential challenge to the unwritten color bar has, for her, the force of a momentous personal victory. If discrimination can be overcome by the patient self-assertion of a lone, determined teenager, what might racial solidarity and communal Black struggle for empowerment be able to achieve in combating entrenched American racism? Ritie feels that she has, by her own small step toward equality, taken a giant leap toward the cultural liberation of oppressed peoples everywhere.

I Know Why the Caged Bird Sings is not James Joyce's *Portrait of the Artist* nor does it claim to be. Many of Marguerite's battles, like those of Stephen Dedalus, have to do with adolescent sexual crises and the need for the young adult to construct a firm sense of gender identity from a curious army of bewildering possibilities. When Joyce's sixteen-year-old protagonist visits the red-light district of Dublin, he can luxuriate in furtive sexual acts, then atone for his transgression through the auspices of a kindly father-confessor. Angelou's alter-ego, in contrast, must face the painful ambiguities of female sexuality, physiologically interior and hidden from consciousness by a society that defines femininity through Freudian images of genital castration. Without the benefit of sex education, Ritie becomes panic-stricken at the sight of her own developing labia and comically confuses genital maturation with hermaphroditism. If, as Luce Irigaray suggests, society regards feminine sexuality as a "nothing-to-see," a hole or vessel to be filled by the phallus, then the maturing female has no positive model to explain her blossoming genitalia.

Baffled and panic-stricken, a teenaged Ritie feels compelled to engineer her own sexual researches, with the cooperation of an attractive young man willing to help choreograph her ritual defloration. In planning her sexual encounter with this neighborhood stud, Marguerite seems oblivious of the fact that such casual experimentation might well involve an obsessive-compulsive repetition of earlier trauma. Most survivors of childhood sexual abuse continue, through adulthood, to "feel unsafe in their bodies" (Herman 160). Ritie's astonishingly naive rhetoric, mimicking the ingenuousness of adolescence, might also mask the etiology of psychosomatic vulnerability, a syndrome that gives way to masochistic revictimization. In the wake of post-traumatic stress disorder, the rape victim continues to suffer from such low self- esteem that she unwittingly reduces her body to a specular object, an "other" from which she feels coolly detached, as she watches this sexual tableau from the safe location of post-traumatic disavowal. Angelou's teenaged self resembles those survivors of childhood abuse who, in the face of continued vulnerability, "choose actively to engage their fears" (Herman 197).[6]

Taking a gutsy initiative that startles even herself, Marguerite brashly invites an adolescent acquaintance to "have sexual intercourse" with her. Her detached tone of voice replicates the premeditated objectivity of a scientific experiment. Still suffering from symptoms of traumatic dysphoria, Ritie feels entirely removed from emotional affect and cannot cathect with the personal dimensions of sexual expression. When the boy she propositions eagerly complies, Marguerite at first feels delighted by her successful initiation into heterosexuality, then becomes anxiety-ridden over an unexpected pregnancy. In her own mind, she has taken control of an awkward and ungainly adolescent body through a bold act of wily seduction. But the audacious project to validate her feminine gender identity might also be interpreted in terms of obsessive-compulsive repetition, with Ritie desperately struggling to seize the initiative and to assume mastery over sexual confusion. Asserting her dubious sense of womanhood, she inadvertently reenacts the earlier trauma of childhood molestation. The results of Ritie's carefully choreographed "second defloration" are reassuring but life-transforming. "I had had help in the child's conception," the beleaguered teenager observes, "but no one could deny that I had had an immaculate pregnancy" (*CB* 245).

Luckily, Marguerite Johnson is *not* Hester Prynne, and no scarlet letter awaits her. African American communities have traditionally been more compassionate in matters of sexual fallibility than their white puritanical counterparts. Ritie's pregnancy is cause for temporary alarm, but no one in her immediate family interprets it as irreparable tragedy. After all, her lapse results in the birth of a beautiful, healthy baby. And Ritie finally attains through her infant son much of the emotional warmth and affection she has always craved. She has collaborated in the creation of a child whose presence reinforces something she instinctively feels: that Black is beautiful, or potentially so; and that she is worthy of a dignified place in a society of caring adults. As her mother affectionately assures her, "If you're for the right thing, then you do it without thinking" (*CB* 246).

The end of *I Know Why the Caged Bird Sings* is comic and triumphant. Unlike Joyce's Stephen Dedalus, who defines his manhood in proud opposition to family, church, and state, Marguerite Johnson realizes her womanhood by symbolic reintegration into the African American community that supports her. Her victory suggests an implicit triumph over the white bourgeoisie, whose values have been flagrantly subverted. Angelou writes in the tradition of African American authors who, according to Valerie Smith, "in their manipulation of received literary conventions [. . .] engage with and challenge the dominant ideology" (*Self-Discovery* 2). The final tableau of Ritie and her son offers a revolutionary paradigm of the Black anti-Madonna. As Joanne Braxton reminds us, the Black female autobiographer, unlike the solitary male hero, "uses language—sass, invective, impertinence, and ritual invocation—to defend herself physically and psychologically" (205–206).

At the conclusion of the first volume of her autobiography, Maya Angelou/ Marguerite Johnson has stopped serving white masters and, in the process, has become mistress of herself. In stunning metamorphosis, a proud Maya emerges from the cocoon enveloping a younger, trembling Ritie. Killing the celluloid specter of Shirley Temple, she gives birth not only to a healthy manchild but to a revitalized sense of herself as an African American woman spiritually empowered and psychologically liberated from the debilitating effects of childhood sexual abuse.[7] As Janet Jacobs declares, in "a very real sense, the birth of a child for the adolescent mother who has been victimized symbolizes the rebirth of the child self who can now be embraced and nurtured" (164).

Quoting from one of her poems, "Harlem Hopscotch," Angelou concludes her conversation with Bill Moyers by asserting a cryptic parable of narrative recovery: "the game is down. They think you lost and I think you've won" (*Conversations* 27). "If I have a monument in this world, it is my son," she proudly proclaims. "He is a joy, a sheer delight. A good human being who belongs to himself. [. . .] It's so thrilling to be here on this tiny blob of spit and sand, reading our own meaning into the stars" (*Conversations* 203). It is precisely the act of scriptotherapy, the candid and heroic autobiographical articulation of haunting trauma, that allows Angelou to read meaning into her own life-story and to reconstruct an enabling, communal testimonio from the shards of childhood tragedy.[8]

Notes

1. Janice Haaken notes: "While the voices of women of color in the survivors' movement are few, incest and sexual abuse are powerful themes in literary explorations of women's lives. [. . .] Black women writers [. . .] are more apt to place private enactments of violence within a broader dehumanizing context" (1072). Throughout this essay, I follow Maya Angelou's practice of using the uppercase *B* when referring to Black culture.

2. Because Mr. Freeman is clearly a father surrogate for young Ritie, his sexual abuse falls into the category of "incest trauma." Karin Meiselman notes that the perpetrator of incest, either a father or a father surrogate, often lacks "a secure sense of his masculine identity" and attempts "to compensate for his feelings of inadequacy" through the perpetration of sexual abuse on a powerless victim (91–92). He compensates for his own literal or metaphorical impotence by attacking a helpless child in a grotesque instance of aggression-displacement. "In certain kinds of abusive betrayals of children," Jennifier Freyd reminds us, "escape is not an option" (10). And Alice Miller observes in *Thou Shalt Not Be Aware* that infantile or childish "helplessness awakens a feeling of power in insecure adults" (6).

3. "On one level of imagination," hypothesizes Hortense Spillers, "incest simply cannot occur and never does. Under the auspices of denial, incest becomes the measure of an absolute negativity, the paradigm of the outright assertion *against*—the resounding no! But on the level of the symbolic, [. . .] incest translates into the unsayable which is all the more sayable by very virtue of one's muteness before it" (128).

4. Incest survivors, Alice Miller explains, "have a stake in keeping secret or covering up what has happened to them or in blaming themselves for it" (*Thou Shalt Not Be Aware* 7). Jennifer Freyd believes that secrecy itself constitutes a "secondary trauma" for the victim of sexual abuse (77–78). Sondra O'Neale writes that, at this point in *Caged Bird*, "the tenuous psyche of a gangly, sensitive, withdrawn child is traumatically jarred by rape, a treacherous act from which neither the reader nor the protagonist has recovered by the book's end. All else is cathartic: [. . .] even her absurdly unlucky pregnancy at the end does not assuage the reader's anticipatory wonder: isn't the act of rape by a trusted adult so assaultive upon an eight-year-old's life that it leaves a wound which can never be healed?" (32). Judith Herman reiterates the tragic dimensions of abuse, as a "profound sense of inner badness becomes the core around which the abused child's identity is formed, and it persists into adult life" (*Trauma* 105).

5. As John Beverley explains, the genre of *testimonio* "constitutes an affirmation of the individual self in a collective mode," whereby the narrator "speaks for, or in the name of, a community or group, approximating in this way the symbolic function of epic hero," and evoking "an absent polyphony of voices, other possible lives and experiences" (95–97). Throughout her autobiographical project, Angelou articulates the plight of an entire generation of African American women, as well as of those who have suffered the unspeakable wound of childhood sexual abuse.

6. Jennifer Freyd notes that incest survivors "commonly suffer damage to their ability to enjoy their sexuality. Their sexual behavior may be either excessively restricted or excessively promiscuous" (9172–9173). A number of survivors interviewed in Louise Armstrong's *Kiss Daddy Goodnight* testify to persistent anger

and insecurity, masochism, and self-destructive practices, including the impulsive choice of inappropriate sexual partners.

7. As O'Neale remarks, the "process of her autobiography is not a singular statement of individual egotism but an exultant explorative revelation that she is because her life is an inextricable part of the misunderstood reality of who Black people and Black women truly are" (26). Selwyn Cudjoe goes on to explain that the "Afro-American autobiographical statement emerges as a *public* rather than a *private* gesture," as "*me-ism* gives way to *our-ism* and superficial concerns about the *individual subject* usually give way to the *collective subjection* of the group" (10). In Angelou's case, who could have guessed that this talented single mother, defiant and unbowed, would one day read her poetry before millions of Americans at the 1993 presidential inauguration of Bill Clinton? For reasons of space and compression, I have limited my discussion to the inaugural volume of Angelou's multi-volume autobiography which continues to elaborate a similar chorus: "Black people Black women do not just endure, they triumph with a will of collective consciousness that Western experience cannot extinguish" (O'Neale 28).

8. Cheryl Wall notes: "Although *I Know Why the Caged Bird Sings*, the first volume of Maya Angelou's popular series of memoirs, partook more in th[e] mood of righteous anger and triumphant struggle, its dramatic center [. . .] was the rape of a girl. In a society ordered by hierarchies of power based on race, class, and gender, no one is powerless, hence more vulnerable, than a poor black girl. [. . .] Necessarily, the fierce young female characters who are survivors rather than victims are trenchant social critics" (3). Moving from issues of social ideology to linguistic dialogue, Mae Henderson suggests that contemporary Black women's writing amalgamates Mikhail Bakhtin's notion of heteroglossia with African-American religious practices of glossolalia to produce a unique combination of "testimony" and "testifying": "It is this notion of discursive difference and identity underlying the simultaneity of discourse which typically characterizes black women's writing. Through the multiple voices that enunciate her complex subjectivity, the black woman writer not only speaks familiarly in the discourse of other(s), but as Other she is in contestorial dialogue with the hegemonic dominant and subdominant or 'ambiguously (non)hegemonic' discourses" (20).

Works Cited

American Psychiatric Association. *Diagnostic and Statistical Manual of Mental Disorders*. 4th ed., rev. Washington DC: American Psychiatric Association, 1994.

Angelou, Maya. *Conversations with Maya Angelou*. Ed. Jeffrey M. Elliot. Jackson: University Press of Mississippi, 1989.

———. *I Know Why the Caged Bird Sings*. New York: Random House, 1970.

———. *Gather Together in My Name*. New York: Random House, 1974.

———. *Singin' and Swingin' and Gettin' Merry Like Christmas*. New York: Random House, 1976.

———. *The Heart of a Woman*. New York: Random House, 1980.

———. *All God's Children Need Traveling Shoes*. New York: Random House 1986.

Arensberg, Lilian K. "Death as Metaphor of Self." In Braxton, 111–127.

Armstrong, Louise. *Kiss Daddy Goodnight: A Speak-Out on Incest*. 1978; rpt. New York: Pocket Books, 1979.

Beverley, John. "The Margin at the Center: On *Testimonio* (Testimonial Narrative)." In Smith and Watson, *De/Colonizing the Subject*, 91–114.

Braxton, Joanne M. *Black Women Writing Autobiography: A Tradition Within a Tradition*. Philadelphia: Temple University Press, 1989.

———. *I Know Why Caged Bird Sings: A Casebook*. Oxford: Oxford University Press, 1999

Brodzki, Bella and Celeste Schenck, eds. *Life/Lines: Theorizing Women's Autobiography*. Ithaca: Cornell University Press, 1988.

Butterfield, Stephen. *Black Autobiography in America*. Amherst: University of Massachusetts Press, 1974.

Christian, Barbara. *Black Feminist Criticism: Perspectives on Black Women Writers*. New York: Pergamon, 1985.

Cudjoe, Selwyn R. "Maya Angelou and the Autobiographical Statement." In Evans, 6–24.

Evans, Mari, ed. *Black Women Writers (1950–1980)*. London: Pluto Press, 1985.

Fanon, Frantz. *Black Skins, White Masks*. 1952. New York: Grove, 1967.

Freyd, Jennifer. *Betrayal Trauma: The Logic of Forgetting Childhood Abuse*. Cambridge, MA: Harvard University Press, 1996.

Gilbert, Susan. "Paths to Escape." In Braxton, 99–110.

Haaken, Janice. "The Recovery of Memory, Fantasy, and Desire: Feminist Approaches to Sexual Abuse and Psychic Trauma." *Signs* 21.4 (1996): 1069–1094.

Henderson, Mae Gwendolyn. "Speaking in Tongues: Dialogics, Dialectics, and the Black Woman Writer's Literary Tradition." In Wall, 16–37.

Henke, Suzette A. *Shattered Subjects: Trauma and Testimony in Women's Life-Writing*. New York: St. Martin's/ Palgrave, 1998/2000.

Herman, Judith Lewis. *Trauma and Recovery*. New York: HarperCollins, 1992.

Irigaray, Luce. *Speculum of the Other Woman*. Trans. Gillian C. Gill. Ithaca: Cornell University Press, 1985.

———. *This Sex Which Is Not One*. Trans. Catherine Porter and Carolyn Burke. Ithaca: Cornell. University Press, 1985.

Jacobs, Janet Liebman. *Victimized Daughters: Incest and the Development of the Female Self*. New York: Routledge, 1994.

Lorde, Audre. *Zami: A New Spelling of My Name*. Freedom, CA: The Crossing Press, 1982.

Lupton, Mary Jane. "'Singing the Black Mother': Maya Angelou and Autobiographical Community." In Evans, 129–148.

McPherson, Dolly A. *Order Out of Chaos: The Autobiographical Works of Maya Angelou*. London: Virago, 1991.

Meiselman, Karin C. *Incest: A Psychological Study of Causes and Effects With Treatement Recommendations*. London: Jossey-Bass Ltd., 1978.

Miller, Alice. *Breaking Down the Wall of Silence: The Liberating Experience of Facing Painful Truth*. Trans. Simon Worrall. 1990; Rpt. New York: Dutton, 1991.

———. *The Drama of the Gifted Child*. Trans. Ruth Ward. 1979; rpt. New York: Harper Basic Books, 1990.

———. *Thou Shalt Not Be Aware: Society's Betrayal of the Child*. Trans. Hildegarde and Hunter Hannum. 1981; rpt. New York: New American Library, 1986.

Moore, Opal. "Learning to Live: When the Bird Breaks from the Cage." In Braxton, 49–58.

O'Neale, Sondra. "Reconstruction of the Composite Self: New images of Black Women in Maya Angelou's Continuing Autobiography." In Evans, 25–36.

Personal Narratives Group, ed. *Interpreting Women's Lives: Feminist Theory and Personal Narratives*. Bloomington: Indiana University Press, 1989.

Pryse, Marjorie and Hortense J. Spillers, eds. *Conjuring: Black Women and Literary Tradition.* Bloomington: Indiana University Press, 1985.

Schacter, Daniel L. *Searching for Memory: The Brain, the Mind, and the Past.* New York: Basic Books, 1996.

Smith, Sidonie. "The Song of a Caged Bird: Maya Angelou's Quest After Self-Acceptance" *Southern Humanities Review* 7 (1973). 368–375.

———. and Julia Watson, eds. *Decolonizing the Subject: The Politics of Gender in Women's Autobiography.* Minneapolis: University of Minnesota Press, 1992.

Smith, Valerie. "Black Feminist Theory and the Representation of the 'Other.'" In Wall, 38–57.

———. *Self-Discovery and Authority in African-American Narratives.* Cambridge: Harvard University Press, 1987.

Sommer, Doris. "Not Just a Personal Story: Women's *Testimonios* and the Plural Self." In Brodzki and Schenck, 107–130.

Spillers, Hortense. "The Permanent Obliquity of an In(pha)llibly Straight: In the Time of the Daughters and the Fathers." In Wall, 127–149.

Tate, Claudia, ed. *Black Women Writers at Work.* New York: Continuum, 1983.

Van der Kolk, Bessel A. "The Body Keeps Score: Approaches to the Psychobiology of Posttraumatic Stress Disorder." In Van der Kolk et al. *Traumatic Stress: The Effects of Overwhelming Experience on Mind, Body, and Society.* New York: Guilford, 1996. 214–241.

Vermillion, Mary. "Reembodying the Self." In Braxton, 59–76.

Wall, Cheryl A., ed. *Changing Our Words: Essays on Criticism, Theory, and Writing by Black Women.* New Brunswick, NJ: Rutgers University Press, 1989.

Willis, Susan. *Specifying: Black Women Writing the American Experience.* Madison: University of Wisconsin Press, 1987.

YASMIN Y. DeGOUT

The Poetry of Maya Angelou:
Liberation Ideology and Technique

If we were a people much given to revealing secrets, we might raise monuments
and sacrifice to the memories of our poets, but slavery cured us of that weakness.
It may be enough, however, to have it said that we survive in exact relationship
to the dedication of our poets (include preachers, musicians and blues singers).

Despite the ongoing publication of her poetry beginning in 1971, and including at least six volumes, two independently printed texts and *The Collected Poems of Maya Angelou* (1994), critical attention to the creative canon of Maya Angelou has focused overwhelmingly on her autobiographical production. The range of issues addressed in these texts and others in the Angelou autobiographical canon, as well as their reception in the critical arena, substantiates not only the depth and breath of Angelou's perception and writing talent, but also the liberating ideology contained therein.[1]

By contrast, while the poetry of Maya Angelou has been included in films, turned into children's books, recited at school ceremonies, offered as greeting cards, and mounted on posters, it has received less critical attention. Fairly few critical pieces spoke to its content and technique prior to 1993, among these Pricilla R. Ramsey's "Transcendence: The Poetry of Maya Angelou" (1985) and Robert B. Stepto's "The Phenomenal Woman and the Severed Daughter" (1980). At the beginning of the Clinton presidency in January of 1993, however, Angelou's inaugural poem, "On the Pulse of

The Langston Hughes Review, Volume 19 (Spring 2005): pp. 36–47. Copyright © 2005 *The Langston Hughes Review*.

Morning," brought her poetic voice and practice into the national arena and into the national consciousness. This inclusion not only elicited its own critical response, as seen in Minoo Moallem's "Multicultural Nationalism and the Poetics of Inauguration" (1999) and A. R. Coulthard's "Poetry as Politics: Maya Angelou's Inaugural Poem" (1998), but also encouraged a critical response to the larger canon of Angelou's poetry, as seen in dissertations such as Leila A. Walker's "'Touch Me, Life, Not Softly': The Poetry of Maya Angelou" (1994) and Kathy Mae Essick's "The Poetry of Maya Angelou: A Study of the Blues Matrix as Force and Code" (1994). Despite this additional attention, the poetic practice of Maya Angelou remains understudied, despite discourse on her autobiographical canon, on the importance and liberating potential of poetry itself.

In *I Know Why the Caged Bird Sings* (1970), Angelou not only reveals the importance of literature to the development of her sensibility during her formative years, but also presciently instructs her future readers on the liberating discourse that would evolve in her own poetic canon. In her discussion of "meeting" and "falling in love with" Shakespeare, she reveals that literature can be the context for racial pride: "I saved my passion for Paul Laurence Dunbar, Langston Hughes, James Weldon Johnson and W. E. B. Du Bois's 'Litany of Atlanta'" (16). It can be the point of disruption of allegiances based on the social construction of race: "[Shakespeare] was my first white love. Although I enjoyed and respected Kipling, Poe, Butler, Thackeray and Henley" (16). It has the potential to create boundless affinity and identification. It allows her "into the private lives of strangers, to share their joys and fears," and "tears of love filled [her] eyes at [her] selflessness" (80).

Many scholars have scrutinized Angelou's autobiographical narratives in this manner. The project of this paper is to turn such scrutiny to Angelou's poetic works, as solicited by her own rendering of the power and uses of poetic language and literary production. Borrowing the terms already applied to her canon in the critical arena, this paper seeks to uncover the strains of liberation, survival, self-acceptance, and transcendence in the verses of Maya Angelou. It seeks to discover the ways in which her own poetry elicits racial pride, disrupts false allegiances, provides healing community, creates boundless affinity, yields individual consciousness, allows triumph, ensures survival, and serves as political intervention—that is, the manner in which it contains and enacts liberation ideology. The poetry of Maya Angelou defies categorization within a single listing of reductive themes or poetic techniques. In fact, in seeking to uncover the liberation ideology in the Angelou canon, this paper will offer evidence that the liberating content and the poetic technique in which it is couched become an inseparable discursive practice in the poems of this author.

Many of the poems in the Angelou canon, specifically those in her first two collections, *Just Give Me a Cool Drink of Water 'fore I Diiie* (1971) and *Oh Pray My Wings Are Gonna Fit Me Well* (1975), are personal, introspective pieces that may at first appear to lack the overt empowerment themes of Angelou's later, better known works, most particularly those included in *And Still I Rise* (1978) and *I Shall Not Be Moved* (1990). As seen in her autobiographical writing, however, a particular gift of the Angelou muse is the translation of personal experience into political discourse. "The Zorro Man" here serves as an example of this practice and of the textured liberation found throughout Angelou's poetry. The poem begins: "Here / in the wombed room / silk purple drapes / flash a light as subtle / as your hands before / love-making" (1.1–6)[2]. The first stanza uses the catachresis "wombed room" to establish the primary pun (and conceit) of the poem: its imaging of both sexual intimacy, which is taking place in the "room of the womb" and of the contemplative woman, who is remembering her "lover" in a quiet and woman-identified space. The imagery of sexual intimacy is further contained in the "purple drapes" of the "womb" and in the description of the light as "subtle / as your hand," and it is and further continued in the next stanza: "Here / in the covered lens / I catch a / clitoral image of / your general inhabitation / long and like a / late dawn in winter" (2.1–7). The covering of the "lens," of the womb, expands the imagery of women's sexuality, as do the description of light "as subtle / as your hands before / love-making" and of her lover's presence as "inhabitation / long and like a / late dawn."

Such use of concrete imagery and abstract symbolism through which to render both the sexual and emotional experience is characteristic of the Angelou muse. At the same time, this poem about the recollection of love, can be read through a second layer of meaning, one in which the room is personified as a woman-centered space of memory. Because the persona is "trap[ped] . . . unwillingly / in a gone time," the speaker conveys both that she is imprisoned by her own memory and that she is filled with a sense of loss, mourning the time in which she was "[the object of] love." In this case, "The Zorro Man" of the poem's title is "thief in the night," stealing into the speaker's room and into her memories. While "The Zorro Man" may seem to lack the obvious liberation ideology of, say, "Phenomenal Woman," the subtle poetic techniques and the themes situate this poem within the liberating discourse of the Angelou canon and allow it to precede and compliment the author's more overly empowering pieces. By centering her speaker in a woman-centered space, Angelou challenges the male-centered and militaristic messages of the Black Arts Movement, a rhetoric that pervaded the poetry (even that of women poets) in the years leading up the publication of *Just Give Me A Cool Drink* in 1971. Angelou thereby precedes the African American women poets and dramatists of the 1970's in turning her attention to women's experience, and she challenges the gender codes of previous eras by celebrating women's sexuality and drawing this component of women's experience into her poetry's broader discourse on self-acceptance.

The piece liberates women from gendered constraints by centering upon women's sexual aegis in the depiction of women's desire, in the use of the women's bodies (and sexuality) as the "lens" through which to view sensual and erotic experience, in the depiction of the persona's imaginative (re)creation of sexual intimacy, and in the rendering of women's erotic pleasure. Such attention to the rethinking of sex-gender codes is also addressed in pieces such as "To a Man," "Chicken-Licken," "Remembrance," "To a Suitor" and "Shaker, Why Don't You Sing?" In depicting intimacy and women's sexuality through images such as "silk purple drapes," and a "clean mirror," Angelou excavates it from derogatory assessments, specifically through use of hieratic style and imagery that de-familiarizes it, allowing new interpretation. In fact, though the persona is depicted as "unwillingly" trapped in the "mirror"—in a memory—the language of the poem situates women's sexuality as the site of power, power to "flash" and to photograph even when the lens is capped. Conversely, though her lover is "booted and brave" in her recollection, he is also "trembling for [her]," an image that beyond its sexual connotations, moves toward deconstruction of the patriarchal assumption of male control over the sexual act. Moreover, in its use of visual imagery—the light flashing in the purple drapes, "the covered lens," and the "clean mirror"—the poem rewrites traditional aesthetics (a topic also addressed in pieces such as "Black Ode" "Sepia Fashion Show" and "Communication I"). Rather than the female body through the male gaze or even the male body through the female gaze, what is eroticized is sexual intimacy itself: foreplay (the movement of "hands before / love-making"), penetration ("general inhabitation / long and like a / late dawn"), and sexual arousal ("trembling").

"The Zorro Man," while at first glance might seem to reinforce selected societal constructs pertaining to gender—imaging women as sexual body parts, depicting men in the chivalric mode of Zorro ("booted and brave")—in effect, the poem both produces a rendering that transcends racialized perception of the human condition and creates an individual consciousness, a woman's interiority. In doing so, the poem allows a readership (specifically one of women) to identify with the celebration of women's sexual experience beyond identification with racial sub-groups and forces the reader into the private space of the persona, one in which perceptions of intimate experience reaches beyond social prescriptions. In the yielding of independent assessment of such intimacy, the poem enacts political intervention into limiting sex-gender codes. In short, such a piece, while not an obvious example of the liberation discourse in the Angelou canon, does, in fact, enact empowerment by liberating the reader from stigmas placed on women's sexuality from gender assumptions of male (sexual) power, and from racialized notions of women's experience.

A similar example of Angelou's strategy is provided by "The Couple," first published in *Oh Pray My Wings Are Gonna Fit Me Well* (1975). Present here is the merging of liberation ideology and poetic technique to question gender constructs and class aspiration as false components of identity formation, beginning with notions of womanhood: "Discard the fear and what / was she? Of rag and bones / a mimicry of woman's / fairy-ness / Archaic at its birth" (1.1–5). Line length is used to create ambiguity and aporia in each stanza of the poem. Here, the first stanza suggests that without fear, the woman being identified is nothing more than her 'mimicry' of notions (the "fairy-ness") of women found in children's stories or fairytales, notions that were outdated as they came into being. The ambiguity created by the line break allows it to function as both a statement and part of a question, both a command (that the culture be rid of such reductive notions of women) and a call to question our own perceptions of gender and power. As Robert Young's assessment of the works of Homi Bhabha suggests, "Mimicry at once enables power and produces the loss of agency" (147). Angelou calls this power into question and reveals the loss of not only agency but also identity in the mimicry of gender norms; the persona is reduced to "rags and bones."

The second stanza—"Discharge the hate and when / was he? Disheveled moans / a mimesis of man's / estate / deceited for its worth" (2.1–5)—offers a similar assessment of "masculinity" and introduces the first clear reference to class-based notions of identity integral to gender and social positioning. While the first line creates a double meaning parallel to that of the first stanza, it is the use of the word "estate" and its multiple meanings—"condition," "social status," "social or political class," "fortune," and "landed property" *(Merriam-Webster)*—that links the enactment of "manhood" to notions of economic status and that therefore defines it as false imitation (or "bad faith"). The falseness of the notion is conveyed by the word "mimesis," which also suggests that the notion is a social construction, mirroring the allusion to fairy tales in the first stanza. Further, "mimesis" implies that such constructs are what Jean Baudrillard defines as simulacra, "the map that precedes the territory" (166). The critique is contained in the description itself and through the figurative language of the phrase "deceited for its worth," which implies that the male subject has been made into a dissemblance or falsehood both by the "hate" of the perceiver and by the "hate" he himself contains, and also by a false value placed on his estate, that is, "*its* worth" rather than "his worth; (emphasis added). In fact, in challenging such constructs, Angelou challenges the referential status between the models of the constructs and the adaptation of them. As Baudrillard argues: "feigning or dissimulating leaves the reality principle in tact: the difference is always clear, it is only masked; whereas simulation threatens the difference between 'true' and 'false' [sic] between 'real' and 'imaginary'" (168).

The final stanza—"Dissolve the greed and why / were they? Enfeebled thrones / a memory of mortal / kindliness / exiled from this earth" (3.1–5)—mirroring the first two in its use of ambivalence, suggests the political urgency to end such class-based notions of identity in order for a return to humanism. The kind of Marxist discourse in this piece is found elsewhere in the Angelou poetic canon, for example, in pieces such as "Worker's Song." Here, however, it is linked to a discussion of gendered identity that calls for the liberation of human beings from both classist ideology and gendered constructs. In addition, "The Couple," by calling for such rethinking in a de-racialized manner, seeks liberation not only in relation to gender and class but also in relation to race, thereby disrupting false allegiances based on class, gender and race, and arguing for a boundless affinity across human experience (an issue overtly addressed in pieces such as "Human Family" but most often conveyed through the more subtle de-racializing and 'positioning' processes undertaken here). The poem also disrupts false allegiances by focusing on the shared human emotions that are structurally shown to motivate such positioning: "fear," "hate," and "greed." The shift called for in the piece thereby mirrors Fantz Fanon's need to "set man free" (9) by removing the "uniform" of race (114), though here expanding the call to include class and gender. By identifying such a stance as producing "enfeebled thrones" (12), Angelou suggests that alternative values and notions are required in order to ensure greater human survival.

Several of the techniques used in "The Couple" and in "The Zorro Man" are characteristic of that strand of poems where Angelou makes use of the hieratic style of writing, conveying their meaning through more "literary" imagery and denser vocabulary. These techniques including catachresis (seen in "Tears," "Request," "Woman Me," and "Plagued Journey"), ambiguity (also seen, for example, in "After," "Woman Me," and "For Us, Who Dare Not Dare"), and personification (evident in "Faces") to name only a handful. To suggest that such techniques become inseparable from the liberation ideology contained in the poems is, in fact, to suggest that such techniques function in the Angelou canon as they function in all poetic discourse.

The mixed metaphors (the catachreses) found in "wombs rooms" and "[d]isheveled moans" de-familiarize the subject for the reader, allowing the poem to re-present experience (gendered, class-based, personal, racial) in a manner that creates the distance required for the reassessment being made. The personification likewise causes de-familiarization but also allows Angelou to depict both the physical effects of human ideology and the manner in which ideology (or challenge to it) can reconstruct human perception of the material world. Similarly, the ambiguity contained in Angelou's works, the epitome of her poetic genius, forces the reader's engagement in the decipher-ing process and thereby insists that the reader take an active role in the learn-ing process afforded by the poems. In short, Angelou's very use of language in-and-of itself liberates her reader from traditional perceptions of human experience and hegemonic values pertaining to her variety of issues.

In each work, Angelou's poetry calls for a rethinking of the notions that limit human beings or thwart humanism. As conveyed in "A Plagued Jour-ney," first published in *Shaker, Why Don't You Sing* (1983), the Angelou muse seeks to inspire each reader to engage actively in not only the poem but also the socio-political struggles that allow liberation of the human spirit. The speaker in "A Plagued Journey," who knows that "[s]afe in the dark prison, / light slides over / the fingered work of a toothless / woman in Pakistan" (3–6), is "invaded" in her seclusion and despair by "sunrise, with Hope / its arrogant rider" (20–21). The effect is a reengagement with the human con-dition and humanism: "My mind / formerly quiescent / in its snug encase-ment, is strained / to look upon their rapturous visages, / to let them enter even into me. / I am forced / outside myself to / mount the light and tide joined with Hope" (22–28). The suggestion here is that hope allows action and forces engagement with the world. The converse is implied through in-terpolation—that without such activism, if we do not refuse "that quiet path" ("Artful Pose"), there is no hope.

While analysis of specific poems uncovers the manner in which libera-tion ideology in the poetry of Maya Angelou is constituted through poetic technique, broader strategies, those not specific to poetry or to written dis-course, are best evidenced through their repetition throughout the body of the author's work. Among the recurrent strategies through which Angelou conveys liberation ideology, are the representation of interiority and personal experience in a manner that provides a community of healing; the use of the demotic style (that is the use of more accessible vocabulary and/or of the vernacular) to celebrate various communities and to reach a broader audience; and both direct and intertextual references to cultural heroes in order to elicit racial pride.

Many of Angelou's poems are introspective pieces that render the per-sonal experiences of their speakers. While such pieces often do not convey overt liberation ideology and, in fact, frequently reveal the despair, loss, and hardship of their speakers, taken as group, it is clear that Angelou represents interiority and personal experience in a manner that provides a community of healing, the type of community Shakespeare provided for her as described in *Caged Bird*. Such pieces depict the woman used for sexual intimacy who is left behind when each man returns to his wife ("They Went Home"); the sorrowful memory of lost love ("When You Came to Me"); attention to do-mestic abuse ("A Kind of Love, Some Say"), the experience of rape ("Men"),

the horror of child abuse ("To Beat the Child Was Bad Enough"); the experience of letting a child grow up and leave home ("Known to Eve and Me");
and other important themes such as the destruction of rage within the African American community as seen in "Riot: 60's," "Harlem Hopscotch," "The
Pusher," "A Georgia Song," and others.

While these poems may appear to invert the tone and effect of empowerment, they do quite the opposite. By creating a community of listeners of
witnesses, those who share in the pain or trauma of the speaker, such pieces
undertake the healing process by creating a community of healers—those
whose acknowledgement of the pain of the speaker allows healing to occur.
The pieces also offer such healing to readers who share similar stories. One
may call this part of the blues mode in the Angelou canon. Such pieces not
only create affinity among actual readers of the work, they also imply a community of listeners (whether actual readers or not)—what Benedict Anderson
would call an "imagined community"—simply through the assumption that
the pieces will find sympathetic listeners. As Anderson points out, the benefit
of the "imagined community" is that it assumes a "deep, horizontal comrade-
ship" strong enough that its members would willingly die for the group (7).
Anderson's piece is also relevant here in that his discussion of the "imagined
community" focuses on the rise of nationalism and on the manner in which
identity must be narrated when it cannot be remembered (204). Here then,
examples pertaining to shared racial experience and a shared community of
healers within the African American community maybe read within the context of black nationalism and in the context of the need to narrate an identity
(like that of the nation) that spans centuries, an identity that forms a sustaining sense of self for the black subject.

While the pieces relating the shared experience of racial oppression and
black rage may be more obvious in their assumption of a shared community that is healed and encouraged through the sharing of their trauma and
struggle, such creation also may be seen in a more novel way in a poem such
as "Poor Girl" first published in *Oh Pray My Wings*. The speaker of the poem
has been left by her lover, who has found another woman, and while the
speaker wishes to warn the new woman that this man will also "leaver her too"
(3.1.), she knows she will not be believed: "If I try to tell her / what I know /
She'll misunderstand / and make me go / Poor Girl / just like me" (2.5–10).
All that the speaker of the poem can offer is her sympathy: "She'll cry and
wonder / what went wrong / Then she'll begin / to sing this song / Poor Girl
/ Just like me" (3.5–10). While the new lover is unaware of the old one, the
poem imaginatively creates a shared community between them in which their
mutual experience has the potential to stop the oppression taking place and
provide a healing outlet for the pain.

In representing interiority and personal experience in a manner that provides a community of healing and in using this technique as a vehicle of the liberation ideology and empowerment offered by her poetry, Angelou foreshadows later black women writers of the 1970s, who, like Angelou, are clearly drawing upon the strategies of the Black Arts Movement in which poetry was performed for the shared enlightenment and motivation of black audiences. Ntozake Shange's *for colored girls who have considered suicide / when the rainbow is enuf* (1975), for example, casts the sharing of race-gender experience as a "laying on of hands" and yields "the holiness of myself released" (62). The choreopoem creates a community of black women on the stage, a community of which the audience becomes a part. In the works of Angelou an allegiance across communities of women facing gender oppression, across communities of African Americans facing racial oppression, and across communities of human beings who have been affected by a host of hardships, engenders a boundless affinity.

Angelou's employment of the demotic style allows for the celebration of various communities and the engagement of a broader audience. Pieces such as "Riot: 60's," "Africa" and the "The Pusher," as well as a host of others are poems that convey their message through everyday language, black vernacular, black musical sounds and forms, and even the variety of rhetorical techniques prevalent in Black Arts poetry and drama, including shocking language, profanity (rare but seen, for example, in "Riot: 60's"), and traditionally unacceptable subject matter.[3]

"The Pusher," first published in *Oh Pray My Wings* is an obvious example: "He bad / O he bad / Make a honky / poot. Make a honky's / blue eyes squint / anus tight" (1–6). While "The Pusher" ultimately calls for an end of drug dealing and destructive drug use ("Pry free the hand / Observe our Black present,") (7.1–2), the piece also reveals the manner in which use of the vernacular allows Angelou to celebrate black culture: "His Afro crown raises / eyes" (2.3–4), and "He sleek / Dashiki / Was-printed on his skin / remembrances of Congo dawns / laced across his chest [. . .] 'Black IS!' / 'NATION TIME!'" (3.1–5, 6.1–2). Ironically, while use of the demotic style in general and the vernacular in particular are not the overriding strategies in Angelou's poetic canon, they are the overwhelming techniques of her more popular and most obviously liberating poems, proof that this technique achieves its given purpose by allowing her to reach a broader audience with her empowerment message. At the same time, while such pieces clearly undertake the projects of the Black Arts Movement,[4] her broader discourse, by transcending race in its inclusion of the call for wider affinity, also, ironically, challenges such projects.

Finally, Angelou also makes use of both direct and intertextual references to cultural heroes in order to elicit racial pride, another primary focus of the liberation ideology found in her poetry. "The Pusher," and its resonance with pieces by Haki Madhubuti and other Black Arts poets, may stand as an example, as would Angelou's homage to Paul Laurence Dunbar in "Caged Bird," to Langston Hughes in "Son to Mother," to Sterling Allen Brown in "Willie" and to Countee Cullen, to whom "Lord, in My Heart" is dedicated. Other references to cultural heroes include "Vesey, Turner, Gabriel, / dead Malcom, Marcus, Martin King" ("My Guilt" 7–8); Harriet Tubman and Frederick Douglass, to whom "Elegy" is dedicated and of whom it speaks; and the eponymous "Ailey, Baldwin, Floyd, Killens, and Mayfield." Of the later group, writes Angelou, "Our souls / dependent upon their nurture / now shrink, wizened" (4.4–7). A vein of Angelou poems are odes to the people in the author's own life, not known to us but who reflect strength or racial pride. Most interesting are the pieces that reference unnamed or representative cultural heroes in order to elicit racial pride and thereby liberate her readership from racist discourse within dominant ideology. Such pieces occur throughout her oeuvre and include such gems as "Times-Square-Shoeshine-Composition," "When I Think About Myself," "To a Freedom Fighter," "Woman Me," "Song for the Old Ones," "Through the Inner City to the Suburbs," "Willie," as well as "Weekend Glory" and "Worker's Song"

As seen in these examples; the poetic canon of Maya Angelou makes use of traditional literary and poetic techniques—the use of catachresis, ambiguity, personification, and hieratic style being only examples—as well as techniques that reach beyond these: creation of a community of healing, demotic style and vernacular language, and the inclusion of cultural heroes. These techniques each enhance the capacity of her poetry to heal, liberate, and empower her readers. The themes of 'liberation,' 'survival,' 'self-acceptance,' and 'transcendence' are prevalent in the verses of this author as well as her prose, and her poetry elicits racial pride, disrupts false allegiances, provides healing community, creates boundless affinity, yields individual consciousness, allows triumph, ensures survival, and serves as political intervention. At times Angelou's poems are explicit in their conveying the poet's liberation ideology, in pieces such as "Phenomenal Woman," "Still I Rise," "Ain't That Bad?," "Life Doesn't Frighten Me," and "Our Grandmothers" which names women who are cultural heroes. At other times, the manifestations are less obvious. While Angelou's poems can never be reduced to a short list of themes, liberation ideology in a variety of manifestations is constant in her sites of empowerment and survival.

NOTES

1. Robert J. Saunders's "Breaking Out of the Cage: Autobiographical Writing by Maya Angelou" (2000), Dana C. Carpenter's "Strategies of Survival: Narrative Patterns as Self-Portraiture" (2000), and essays in Harold Bloom's anthology on

Caged Bird, such as Sidonie A. Smith's "The Song of a Caged Bird: Maya Angelou's Quest after Self-Acceptance" (1998), to name only a few such pieces published over the last few years, confirm the complexity and importance of Angelou's work, explain its continued use in high school and college classrooms, and point toward the broader liberation theory and practice embedded in the canon of this author-performer-activist-writer-educator.

2. Citations refer to stanza and line(s).

3. See Haki Madhubuti (Don L. Lee) "Toward a Definition."

4. See Neale.

Works Cited

Anderson, Benedict. *Imagined Communities: Reflections on the Origins and Spread of Nationalism.* 1983. New York: Verso, 1991.

Angelou, Maya. *The Complete Collected Poems of Maya Angelou.* New York: Random House, 1994.

———. *I Know Why the Caged Bird Sings.* 1970. *The Collected Autobiographies of Maya Angelou.* New York: The Modern Library, 2004. 1–222.

Baudrillard, Jean. "Simulacra and Simulations." 1981. Trans. Paul Foss, Paul Patton and Philip Beitchman. New York, Semiotext(e), 1983. Rpt. *Jean Baudrillard: Selected Writings.* Stanford: Stanford University Press, 1988. 166–184.

Carpenter, Dana Chamblee. "Strategies of Survival: Narrative Patterns as Self-Portraiture in the Works of Eudora Welty and Maya Angelou." Diss. University of Mississippi, 2000. DAI 61.9 (2001): 3562A.

Coulthard, A. R. "Poetry as Politics: Maya Angelou's Inaugural Poem, 'On the Pulse of Morning.'" *Notes on Contemporary Literature* 28.1 (Jan. 1998): 2–5.

Essick, Kathy Mae. "The Poetry of Maya Angelou: A Study of the Blues Matrix as Force and Code." Diss. Indiana University, 1994. DAI 55.8 (1995): 2389A.

Fanon, Frantz. *Black Skin, White Masks.* 1952. Trans. Charles Lam Markmann. New York: Grove Wiedenfeld, 1967.

Johnson, Barabara. "Metaphor, Metonymy, and Voice in Zora Neale Hurston's *Their Eyes Were Watching God.*" *Black Literature and Literary Theory.* Ed. Henry Louis Gates, Jr. Rpt. *Textual Analysis: Some Readers Reading.* Ed. Mary Ann Caws. New York: MLA, 1986. 232–244.

Madhubuti, Haki. (Don L. Lee) "Toward a Definition: Black Poetry of the Sixties (After LeRoi Jones)" *The Black Aesthetic.* Ed. Addison Gayle. New York, 1971. Rpt. *Within the Circle: An Anthology of African American Literary Criticism for the Harlem Renaissance to the Present.* Ed. Angelyn Mitchell. Durham: Duke University Press, 1994. 213–223.

The Merriam-Webster Dictionary. New Ed. Springfield, MA: Merriam-Webster, 2004.

Moallem, Minoo "Multicultural Nationalism and the Poetics of Inauguration." *Between Women and Nation: Nationalisms, Transnational Feminisms, and the State.* Ed. Caren Kaplan. Durham: Duke University Press, 1999. 243–263.

Neale, Larry. "The Black Arts Movement." *The Drama Review* 12.4 (1968). Rpt. *Within the Circle: An Anthology of African American Literary Criticism for the Harlem Renaissance to the Present.* Ed. Angelyn Mitchell. Durham: Duke University Press, 1994. 184–198.

Ramsey Pricilla R. "Transcendence: The Poetry of Maya Angelou." *A Current Bibliography on African Affairs* 17.2 (1985): 139–159.

Saunders, Robert James. "Breaking Out of the Cage: Autobiographical Writing by Maya Angelou." *Twayne Companion to Contemporary Literature in English.* Ed. R. H. W. Dillard and Amanda Cockerell. New York: Twayne, 2002. 11–20.

Shange, Ntozake. *for colored girls who have considered suicide / when the rainbow is enough.* New York: Macmillan, 1975.

Smith, Sidonie Ann. "The Song of a Caged Bird: Maya Angelou's Quest after Self-Acceptance." *Maya Angelou's I Know Why the Cadged Bird Sings.* Ed. Harold Bloom. Philadelphia: Chelsea House, 1998. 3–13.

Stepto, Robert B. "The Phenomenal Woman and the Severed Daughter." *Parnassus: Poetry in Review* 8.1 (1980): 312–320.

Walker, Leila Andrea."Touch Me, Life, Not Softly: the Poetry of Maya Angelou." Diss. Florida State University, 1994. DAI 56.1 (1995): 196A.

Young, Robert. *White Mythologies: Writing History and the West.* New York: Routledge, 1990.

CHERRON A. BARNWELL

Singin' de Blues, Writing Black Female Survival in I Know Why the Caged Bird Sings

The blues is an impulse to keep the painful details and episodes of a brutal experience alive in one's aching consciousness, to finger its jagged grain, and to transcend it, not by the consolation of philosophy but by squeezing from it a near-tragic, near-comic lyricism. As a form, the blues is an autobiographical chronicle of personal catastrophe expressed lyrically.

—*Ralph Ellison*

When the Modern Library paid tribute to her life writing with its publication of her six-volume autobiographical series in a handsome one-volume edition titled *The Collected Autobiographies of Maya Angelou* (2004), Dr. Angelou's place in America's literary and cultural traditions was reaffirmed. Angelou's autobiographies are monumental memoirs of inspiration, celebrating life and encouraging survival. Dr. Angelou launched her canon of life writing with the 1970 publication *I Know Why the Caged Bird Sings.* A coming-of-age story, fashioned after the slave narrative, recalls the experience of a Southern black girl, in the throes of an imprisoning and chaotic socialization, growing up in segregated Stamps, Arkansas during the 1930s, and ends with her becoming a teenaged single mother frightened but determined to face the world and fulfill her duty of motherhood. It is the foundational text in her six-volume autobiographical series, which introduces to the black

The Langston Hughes Review, Volume 19 (Spring 2005): pp. 48–60. Copyright © 2005 *The Langston Hughes Review.*

133

autobiographical genre a powerfully candid, bordering-the-absurd, style of writing about true-life black woman's tragedy, trauma, and survival. The style Angelou brings to black autobiography is aptly described by George Kent, in his essay titled, "Maya Angelou's *I Know Why the Caged Bird Sings* and Black Autobiographical Tradition": *Caged Bird*'s place within the black autobiographical tradition is cemented for "its use [of] forms that exploit the full measure of imagination necessary to acknowledge both beauty and absurdity" (20).

Many of us, having read Angelou's *Caged Bird,* find it no surprise that her work would be accorded the prominence of *American* (meaning, white mainstream) literary status. Critics have steadfastly granted it attention. They praise her autobiographies for the universal sense of self that emanates from them, claiming as does Harold Bloom that "[. . .] [T]he secret of Angelou's enormous appeal to American readers, whether white or black [. . . is] her remarkable literary voice [, which] speaks to something in the universal American 'little me within the big me'" (1). And, while readings of the Americanness of Angelou's *Caged Bird* are valid, and the institutional accolades accorded her autobiographies appreciated, for this writer, the greatness of *Caged Bird* is rooted in is its blackness. It is Angelou's drawing of that which is beautifully universal in black culture that propels her into canonization.

Caged Bird has been examined over and anon for what it owes to other elements in the African American cultural tradition, such as Negro spirituals, the blues, black vernacular, and of course black poetry. Sidonie Smith, in a 1973 essay titled, "The Song of a Caged Bird: Maya Angelou's Quest after Self-Acceptance," acknowledges that *Caged Bird* is indebted to "the earliest form of black autobiography, the slave narrative, which traced the flight of the slave northward from slavery into full humanity" (qtd. in Bloom 5); Joanne Braxton in *Black Women Writing Autobiography: A Tradition Within A Tradition* (1999) finds traditional black American women's autobiographical themes in *Caged Bird,* themes such as "the importance of family and the nurturing and rearing of one's children, as well as the quest for self-sufficiency, self-reliance, personal dignity, and self-definition" (127); regarding black vernacular and traditional linguistic influences, in "Con Artists and Storytellers: Maya Angelou's Problematic Sense of Audience," Francoise Lionnet's finds that in "gesturing toward the black community," *Caged Bird* uses a duplicitous language of survival traditionally understood by oppressed peoples (143). My celebration of *Caged Bird*'s distinct black forms, then, is a revival of sorts, a project that aligns me with these precursory readings of *Caged Bird.*

Of the African American cultural elements present in the text, the blues is most influential in *Caged Bird.* The blues shapes its form and content, and in using the blues aesthetic, Angelou meets the challenge of writing autobiography as literature. Descending from the Negro spiritual, the blues is a music native to America, having its genesis in the African American culture; it is expressive of blackness encountering that which is commonly called American. Amiri Baraka's classic text, *Blues People: Negro Music In White America* (1963) articulates this understanding of the blues. "[B]lues could not exist if the African captives had not become American captives" (17), asserts Baraka. Moreover, the blues is valued for both its music and meaning. Its polyphonic rhythms, loud and brass timbers accent the history of black America's uprooting encounters and cultural ransacking. The whoops and hollers scream out the pain of being the nation's exploited laborers who have been denied the right to possess even the vestiges of a ransacked ancestral cultures. To ascertain a textual sign system of Angelou's blues aesthetic in the literariness of her autobiography, a semiotic examination of *Caged Bird*'s prefatory opening and specifically chapter 23, is helpful.

Houston A. Baker Jr.'s *Blues, Ideology, and Afro-American Literature: A Vernacular Theory* (1984), supports theoretical readings of black writing that use "readily discernible Afro-American expressive cultural referents" (89). For Baker, the African American literary critic, who is "versed in the vernacular and unconstrained by traditional historical determinants, may well be able to discover blues inscriptions and liberating rhythms" (115). Blues forms in *Caged Bird*, then, are its liberating rhythms, re-inscribing (or replacing) Angelou's socialized sense of placelessness with American literary prominence. A semiotic analysis makes evident the traits of *Caged Bird* that anticipate blues forms as the aesthetic in Angelou's other autobiographies.

It is necessary to note here that the blues functions as an autobiographical act. At the heart of the blues are individualizing features comparable to those in autobiography. Baraka offers an explanation: "Though certain techniques and verses came to be standardized among blues singers, the singing itself remained as arbitrary and personal as the shout. [. . .] The music remained that personal because it began with the performers themselves, and not with formalized notions of how it was to be performed" (Baraka 67). Through the formal techniques of the blues, Angelou enters into an inner-retrospective meditation on her life experiences and depicts the self that obtains from such meditation. This self-understanding is in an image of a blues Priestess endowed with self-healing, life-affirming powers.

As Sidonie Smith states about any good autobiography, the opening defines its narrative strategies. *Caged Bird* consists of a prefatory opening, and 36 episodic chapters that chronicle the life of a southern black girl growing up in the 1930s, aware of her feelings of displacement and a debilitating socialization. Right away in its prefatory opening the work sings the blues. It is young Maya's blues. She is at an Easter Sunday recital, standing before the children's section of the Colored Methodist Episcopal Church in Stamps, Arkansas, trying to remember the lines of a children's poem. On this dreaded Easter Sunday, young

Maya wears a "cut-down from a white woman's once-was-purple throwaway" dress, a dress she imagined as beautiful, and hoped would transport her out of her blues reality and turn her into "one of the sweet little white girls who were everybody's dream of what was right with the world" (2). But, young Maya's lavender-taffeta, ruffled-hem dress failed her. Even the Easter's early morning sun betrayed her, showing her dress to be plain ugly and her to be a "too-big Negro girl, with nappy black hair, broad feet and a space between her teeth that would hold a number-two pencil" (3). So, young Maya, "painfully aware of her displacement" (4) had a blues to sing: "What you looking at me for? / I didn't come to stay [...] / What you looking at me for? / I didn't come to stay [...] / Ijustcometotellyouit'sEasterDay" (1). Angelou thrusts us right into this blues by the way the lines from the poem are actually quoted. Those of us who recognize the poem as a blues form might even hum the quoted lines as a blues tune while reading it. The first two lines are the same, quoted in intervals between autodiegetic narrative; the third line, consisting of nine words, is quoted but with all nine words slurred together. All three quoted lines together form closely a "classic" blues of 12-bars, 3-lines, AAB structure with the third line, B structure, ensuring that we read it as a blues in its capturing syntactically the style Baraka calls "'blueing' the notes." He explains this as "sliding and slurring effects in Afro-American music, the basic 'aberrant' quality of a blues scale" (25). The quoted lines from song or poetry patterned into blues forms are textual signs in Angelou's blues aesthetic.

Because the three lines are set in quotation marks as direct speech, they evoke with immediacy Angelou's present-writing situation and thereby signal the new intended meaning(s) and function she gives them. In quotation marks, the poem signals not merely a present speech act but rather a present act of expression—a present blues, if you will. The word "you" in the line "What you looking at me for," along with the immediacy of the quotation marks, connects *Caged Bird* to its readers, marking what Baker calls "an invitation to energizing intersubjectivity" (5). Thus, the quoted lines are inviting in the same ways the blues invites its audience to share in the experiencing of it. The children at the Colored Methodist Episcopal Church had no choice but to look at young Maya, identify her, and complete her sense of self when she declared "What *you* looking at me for" (emphasis added). Recited in *Caged Bird,* however, the same line calls to present-writing Angelou's black readership (who themselves have sat in the children's section of their black churches) to "look" at young Maya's childhood experience in the black church and recall their own, thereby asking them to identify with her. They are encouraged to sing their blues. Thus, the blues function as an autobiographical act and allows *Caged Bird* to exhibit what Joanne Braxton observes about black women's autobiography: "Black women's autobiography is [...] the occasion for viewing the individual in relation to those others w/whom she shares emotional, philosophical, and spiritual affinities, as well as political realities" (9). As such, *Caged Bird*'s opening produces an intersubjectivity that is black, female, and in relation to the black community.[1]

Furthermore, the inviting qualities the blues forms give to Angelou's autobiographical act require readers, to complete present-writing Angelou's sense of self just as the children of the Colored Methodist Episcopal Church did; and after readers identify with Maya's childhood experience, they become attuned to their own childhood experience and the sense of self that obtains. Baker explains,

> The blues singer's signatory coda is always *atopic*, placeless: "If anybody ask you who sang this song / Tell 'em X done been here and gone." The signature is a space already "X"(ed), a trace of the already "gone"—the fissure rejoined. Nevertheless, the "you" (audience) addressed is always free to invoke the X(ed) spot in the body's absence. (5)

So, while the "you" in the line "What you looking at me for" immediately addresses black readers who are thus encouraged to identify with young Maya's childhood experience(s), the "I" in the line "I didn't come to stay" encourages readers to invoke self-understanding and understanding of what Angelou is (or should be) in the transient "I" space. Readers are made ever cognizant of the present-writing Angelou attempting to recapture her childhood experience(s) as already changed—for young Maya has grown up—as readers superimpose our understanding of the experience onto present-writing Angelou's self-understanding. Black experience is universalized, but not as a constant. It is understood as a changing same, which the prefatory opening predicts will be dramatized inside the covers of *Caged Bird*.

As a way to begin the autobiography, then, the quoted line from a children's poem, "I didn't come to stay," signals that movement and placelessness will be a motif throughout *Caged Bird*. It is a transience that marks the transformative and thus transforming nature of the blues, or what Baker describes as "a phylogenetic recapitulation of experience" (5). Therefore, Angelou's self-representation will be transforming as well as transformative; as phylogenetic as a blues song.[2]

The remainder of the autobiography's opening sings Angelou's blues of black survival as rendered in the embarrassing moment when she runs out of the church urinating. After she recited her poem, she suddenly had to go to the bathroom, barely able to hold back her urine. She found herself caught in a quandary for if she did not urinate "it would probably run right back up to [her] head and [her] poor head would burst like a dropped watermelon, and all the brains and spit and tongue and eyes would roll all over the place" (3–4). Urinating freely as she ran home, young Maya experienced the joy of release and relief "not only from being liberated from the silly church but from the knowledge that [she] wouldn't die from a busted head" (4). Of this humorously ironic past experience, Angelou sings a hysterically releasing blues. There is sadness and humor. There is defiance, symbolized in "urinating," towards her feelings of humiliation and displacement. Baker's further description of the blues applies here: Angelou's blues of embarrassment is ironic self-accusation, which "seamlessly fades into humorous acknowledgement of duplicity's always duplicitous triumph" (4). *Caged Bird*'s opening, therefore, forecasts the ways in which past experience will be made into episodic anecdotes that teach survival of a blues reality: life-lessons are found in ordinary, everyday experiences of black life; and, like every blues song, the condition can be transcended. It can be survived.

Following the prefatory opening, the narrative proceeds to the episode of three-years-young Maya along with her one-year older brother, Bailey, traveling alone on a train-ride from Long Beach, California to Stamps, Arkansas to stay with their Grandmother Henderson. Angelou's earliest memory of feeling abandoned and displaced is captured. She states that she doesn't remember the trip, but she remembers that "Negro passengers, who always traveled with loaded lunch boxes, felt sorry for 'the poor little *motherless* darlings' and plied [her and her brother] with cold friend chicken and potato salad" (5 emphasis added). These feelings were not solely her own. Angelou ensures us in this first episode that she shared these feelings with many black children growing up during the depression and the great black migration: "Years later I discovered that the United States had been crossed thousands of times by frightened Black children traveling alone to their newly affluent parents in Northern cities, or back to grandmothers in Southern towns when the urban North reneged on its economic promises" (5–6). In retelling young Maya's migration South, Angelou gains understanding of the experience as a traumatizing social condition of all black Americans in the 1930s. The child's migration is retold as a symbolic act recalling social displacement in the African American historical experience. The experience is a blues. It is an experience that imparts self-understanding to the present-writing Angelou because she treats the experience as transformative. While the motif of movement is influenced by the slave narrative, the blues form treats movement as transforming. Angelou's phylogenetic recapitulation of young Maya's migration South and signals the change to be dramatized in her coming-of-age autobiography.

Each chapter of the autobiography contains an episode of displacement and trauma, which ends in a further understanding of self, usually how the self overcomes the trauma. Stories of the retired white sheriff's warning Grandmother Henderson of the Klan's random, lynch-law escapades, which led to the night crippled Uncle Willie hid in a bin beneath layers of potatoes and onions; of grandmother Henderson's maintaining her dignity before the "powhitetrash" children's insults and mocking gestures, shape the body of *Caged Bird* into episodic anecdotes of survival and transcendence of a blues reality. Of course, the most drastic episode is Angelou's sexual molestation and rape by her mother's boyfriend Mr. Freeman. The segments detailing her vow to live in silence and thus remain mute for several years after learning of Mr. Freeman's death; her "life-line" friendship with Ms. Flowers who gave her the gift of self-love and voice; the violent fight with her father's pretentious "white-airs" girlfriend; and driving her father's car and getting herself back to town because a drunk father couldn't, all touch upon issues of displacement, self-doubt, self-hatred, and resilience, thus survival, in the face of adversity. Of the 36 chapters, Chapter 23, Graduation of 1940, demonstrates most apparently the semiotics of Angelou's blues aesthetic at work.

Chapter 23 recounts twelve year-old Maya's graduation from Lafayette County Training School. Angelou remembers this was an exciting day for the whole Stamps' black community, especially the youth:

> The children in Stamps trembled visibly with anticipation. Some adults were excited too, but to be certain the whole young population had come down with graduation epidemic. Large classes were graduating from both the grammar school and the high school. Even those who were years removed from their own day of glorious release were anxious to help with preparations as a kind of dry run. [...] Even teachers were respectful of the now quiet and aging seniors, and tended to speak to them, if not as equals, as beings only slightly lower than themselves.

Just days before graduation, young Maya took possession of a new happiness; she took to "smiling more often [so that her] jaws hurt from the unaccustomed activity," Angelou recollects (172). On the day of graduation, she believed that her youthful prayers had been answered. She recounts:

> I gave myself up to the gentle warmth and thanked God that no matter what evil I had done in my life He had allowed me to live to see this day. Somewhere in my fatalism I had expected to die, accidentally, and never have the chance to walk up the stairs in the auditorium and gracefully receive my hard-earned diploma. Out of God's merciful bosom I had won reprieve. (175)

The haunting fatalism foreshadows *Caged Bird*'s thematic expectations resulting from the semiotic of episodic anecdote, as the story takes a turn for the worse and a blues develops. The sunshine day of Graduation 1940 turns into clouds of ugliness when guest speaker, the white Donleavy, delivered the customary, racist speech he reserved for southern black schools' graduating ceremonies. It was laden with half-hearted inspirations representative of a larger, mainstream society's low expectations of black people. Donleavy's spirit-killing speech was successful: "Constrained by hard-learned manners [she] couldn't look behind [her], but to [her] left and right the proud graduating class of 1940 had dropped their heads" (179), recalls Angelou. The speech conjured up again her feelings of displacement and the collective consciousness of Stamps' black community: "It was awful to be Negro and have no control over my life. It was brutal to be young and already trained to sit quietly and listen to charges brought against my color with no chance of defense. We should all be dead" (180).

After Donleavy's spirit-killing speech, valedictorian, Henry Reed, delivers his address to Graduation Class 1940 as planned. Angelou recalls that Reed's address possessed the promise of great fortune for the black graduates in spite of Donleavy's statement to the contrary. Little Henry Reed had the mind and wherewithal to restore black pride to and self-determination in his fellow graduates. The epitome of self-determination, he states in his address, "I am the master of my fate, I am the captain of my soul" (181), and he turned to his audience and began to sing the Negro National Anthem, "Lift Ev'ry Voice and Sing." The graduating class joined him; the audience joined them. Everyone joined in song and sermon, overcoming their feelings of displacement. Through the healing forces of the Negro National Anthem, faith, pride, and self-determination were restored. Young Maya was proud again not only to be a member of the Graduation Class 1940, but also of the "wonderful, beautiful Negro race" (184).

Quotations from the Negro National Anthem are patterned into a blues form as the lines, interspersed with autodiegetic narrative, take the shape of a blues, this one closer to what Baraka describes as primitive blues, a musical form which precedes classic blues, succeeds the work song, and issues directly from the spiritual. Like the classic blues, primitive blues reflects the social and cultural problems plaguing African American life; however, a new self-determination is part of this experience, and the primitive blues sings of it as a changing sense of being, asserts Baraka:

> There was a definite change of direction in the primitive blues. The metaphysical Jordan of life after death was beginning to be replaced by the more pragmatic Jordan of the American master: the Jordan of what the ex-slave could see vaguely as self-determination. [...] [T]he American Negro wanted some degree of self-determination where he was living. [...] The Negro began to feel a desire to be more in this country, America, than chattel. (64–65).

The lines quoted from the anthem sing of African American historical determination:

"Lift ev'ry voice and sing
Till earth and heaven ring
Ring with the harmonies of Liberty [. . .]
Stony the road we trod
Bitter the chast'ning rod
Felt in the days when hope unborn had died;
Yet with a steady beat,
Have not our weary feet
Come to the place for which our fathers sighed?" (182–183).

These lines are reflective of the primitive blues form as they celebrate social transcendence rather than spiritual or religious transcendence.

Because the anthem is a transformative song, quoting the passages that best capture this, Angelou reconstitutes the experience of displacement and all its complexity into a blues matrix composed of converging negative and positive feelings. Within the covers of *Caged Bird*, the anthem is understood as a song of survival, by the use of blues strategies, making concrete the transient experience of displacement conjoined by the healing properties of song.

Indeed, *Caged Bird*'s blackness rings with the harmonies of liberties, beckoning its black readers socialized by the Negro National anthem to join present-writing Angelou in song. At the end of chapter 23, the apostrophe to black poets and blues singers best illustrates the chronotopic collapse of narrative and thus the difficulty of distinguishing young Maya from writerly Angelou:

Oh, Black known and unknown will poets, how often have your auctioned pains sustained us? Who will compute the lonely nights made less lonely by your songs [. . .] less tragic by your tales? If we were a people much given to revealing secrets, we might raise monuments and sacrifice to the memories of our poets, but slavery cured us of that weakness. It may be enough, however, to have it said that we survive in exact relationship to the dedication of our poets (include preachers, musicians and blues singers). (184)

At this juncture, *Caged Bird*, once again, is self-reflexive, calling attention to its blues form. Inasmuch as Angelou's apostrophized survival is "in exact relationship to the dedication of our poets, preachers, and blues singers" so too is the work's. *Caged Bird*'s textures and themes intersect and interanimate to unfold a self-conscious autobiographical act, producing an intersubjective Angelou who is well aware of the cultural referents that shape her.

Knowing the Maya Angelou that is a poet whose auctioned pains have sustained many, *Caged Bird*'s, readers see how the apostrophe summons an understanding of Angelou. It functions as an inviting energizing intersubjectivity: Angelou's autobiographical act. Through the apostrophe, she is cast in the image of a Black poet/blues priestess, who, as Baker describes: "[L]ustily transform[s] experiences of durative landscape [. . .] into the energies of rhythmic song. Like [a] translator of written texts, [the blues priestess, Angelou . . .] offer[s] interpretations of the experiencing of experience" (7). The result is an intersubjective Angelou, who is created (or rather completed by her readers) as she creates. Furthermore, the life-sustaining powers of the quoted spiritual infuse *Caged Bird,* shaping graduation 1940, into an episodic anecdote of survival and transcendence of a blues reality. Maya and her classmates survived their momentary blues reality of socialized displacement chanted to them in Donleavy's speech. In the moment of retelling the phylogenetic experience of socialized displacement, Angelou transforms into a blues Priestess whose auctioned pains sustain us, her readers.

Because Chapter 23's first line of the apostrophe, alone, signifies on James Weldon Johnson's poem titled *"Black and Unknown Bards,"* in the way *Caged Bird*'s title signifies upon Paul Laurence Dunbar's *"Sympathy,"* Caged Bird does more than sing young Maya's blues. Signifyin' upon Dunbar's and Johnson's poetry and music, respectively, Angelou makes her autobiography resonate with these renowned African American creators' praiseworthy stylistics. While joining this canon on the one hand, on the other, her six-volume autobiographical series, indeed makes Dr. Angelou a canon unto herself. *Caged Bird* lays the foundation for this canon, using a life writing blues aesthetic, which can be traced in the other volumes. Because readers know Dr. Angelou has written five more autobiographies after this initial one, because they know the self undergoes five more transformations, they know her blues aesthetic proves successful.

In *Gather Together In My Name* (1993), for example, the semiotics of Angelou's blues aesthetic allows her to dramatize again her life as a story about surviving displacement with pride and dignity, and to do so in the image of black poet/blues priestess. *Gather* recounts teenaged, single-mother Maya's struggle to find her niche in life while raising her son alone. Particularly in chapter 16 of *Gather,* episodic anecdote of survival and transcendence of a blues reality shapes the chapter and foregrounds Angelou's self-understanding. Chapter 16 recounts an instance at the Dew Drop Café, when a male-friend/suitor, L. C. rescues single-mother Maya from a drunken humiliation planned surreptitiously by people she thought were her friends. Angelou remembers the episode with the force, energy, and complexity of the blues so that her readers can partake in the experiencing of her blues reality:

Well, I ain't got no
special reason here.
No, I ain't go [sic] no
special reason here.
I'm going leave
'cause I don't feel welcome here (67).

Quotations of song or poetry patterned into blues form are used again here as they were in *Caged Bird,* making *Gather* sing her blues in its present writing situation. The lyrics foreshadow the outcome of the Dew Drop Café episode. Once Maya finds out from L. C. that she was the butt of her "friends'" joke, the "unwelcomeness" or feelings of displacement *Gather* sings about is actualized. The blues captures Angelou's understanding of the experience as another one that shapes her into a blues Priestess who sings about surviving life's cruel and humiliating moments with pride and dignity.

Angelou's third autobiography, *Singin' and Swingin' and Gettin' Merry Like Christmas* (1976) modifies her textual sign system of a blues aesthetic by reinforcing self-signifying as a practice. *Singin'* continues with the life-story of finding her artistic niche in pursuing a show business career as dancer, singer, performer. When in chapter 8, the Garden Allah episode, she recounts how three white women, who pressured the owner of Garden Allah to put Maya on notice approach her with their phony well-wishes, *Singin'* signifies on, the episode in *Caged Bird* when Momma Henderson remained dignified and withstood the "powhitetrash" girls' disrespectful jeers. Here, self-signifying constructs Angelou's autobiographical series into a canon that must be read in its entirety.

It is in autobiography number four, *The Heart of a Woman* (1981), that the semiotics of Angelou's blues aesthetic addresses the issue of gender and thus takes on a feminized structure. In *Heart* Maya is now thirty years old and her son, Guy, is fourteen years old; she has acquired some show-business fame, and is involved in the Civil Rights struggle as one of Dr. Martin Luther King's coordinators. It is no wonder for the reader who appreciates Angelou's blues aesthetic that Angelou opens *The Heart of a Woman* showcasing Billie Holiday. Though Billie might be thought of more as a jazz than blues singer, through evoking her presence, Angelou clearly assumes the self-image of a female blues singer whose stature equals Lady Day's.

To the semiotics of Angelou's blues aesthetic is added self-signifying, which allows the transformative nature of the blues to modify Angelou's blues priestess self-image in *All God's Children Need Traveling Shoes* (1986). Angelou attributes the survival of the black community to the African American intellectual community, as well as the black poet, preacher, musician, blues singer. *All God's Children* recounts Angelou's recovering her independence and spiritual solitude after giving too much of herself in a failed marriage to an African revolutionary. Specifically in the episode describing the protest march she and her fellow "Revolutionist Returnees" arranged in Ghana to coincide with Dr. King's famous August 1963 March on Washington at 7:00 a.m., Angelou remembers W. E. B. DuBois' death. People broke out into song. Angelou quotes from the song, explaining her understanding of the moment. Her explanation is self-referential:

> We were singing for Dr. DuBois' spirit, for the invaluable contributions he made, for his shining intellect and his courage. To many of us he was the first American Negro intellectual. We knew about Jack Johnson and Jesse Owens and Joe Louis. We were proud of Louis Armstrong and Marian Anderson and Roland Hayes. We memorized the verses of James Weldon Johnson, Langston Hughes, Paul Laurence Dunbar and Countee Cullen, but they were athletes, musicians, and poets, and White folks thought all those talents came naturally to Negroes. So, while we survived because of those contributors and their contributions, the powerful White world didn't stand in awe of them. Sadly, we also tended to take those brilliances, for granted. But W. E. B. DuBois and of course Paul Robeson were different, held on a higher or at least on a different plateau than the others.

There is no mistaking the apparent echo this passage has to the apostrophe in *Caged Bird*. Signifyin' on her first volume, Angelou modifies her understanding of self. No longer is it only the black poets, preachers, musicians, and blues singers whom she commemorates for their life-sustaining forces. Now, she commemorates the African American intellectual, represented by W. E. B. DuBois and Paul Robeson, for their contributions to the survival of the black community. The self-referential nature of this passage endows Angelou with the voice of the African American intellectual. As blues priestess, now, she sings with the shining intellect and courage possessed by DuBois and Robeson.

In her final autobiography, *A Song Flung Up to Heaven*, Angelou makes it clear through the self-reflexive elements and a consciousness of the writing process, that her six autobiographies are to be treated as a series. In the closing description of James Baldwin's encouraging her to write, *A Song* explains Angelou's purpose for writing poetry. As such, *A Song* reinforces the self-image Angelou creates in her other five autobiographies, the image of blues priestess contributing to the survival of the black community. The African American community has sustained itself, as Angelou quotes Baldwin, because

> We put surviving into our poems and into our songs. We put it into our folk tales. We danced surviving in Congo Square in New Orleans and put it in our pots when we cooked pinto beans. We wore surviving on our backs when we clothed ourselves in the colors of the rainbow. We were pulled down so low we could hardly lift our eyes, so we knew, if we wanted to survive, we had better lift our own spirits. (197)

Autobiography, for Angelou, serves the same purpose: to teach survival and invoke the sense of transcendence of blues reality. It lifts her spirit and her autobiography lifts ours.

In using the blues in a textual sign system, Angelou patterns her six-volume autobiographical series into a canon of life-sustaining songs which situate her firmly in the black literary and cultural canon of black survival. Her autobiographies present her in the image of blues priestess who auctions her pains for the survival of her community. Her songs echo those of the black poet, preacher, musician, blues singer, African American intellectual. Alone Angelou's body of life writing has its own unique significance as inspirational literature that is monumental. And, so, to the list of contributors of black survival commemorated in *Caged Bird* and again in *All God's Children Need Traveling Shoes* should be added the black autobiographer. For using the autobiographical occasion to share cultural, historical, socio-political, and spiritual affinities, which upon inner-retrospection imparts self-understanding, Angelou ensures the longevity of a significant genre as well as the survival of a monumental black humanity.

NOTES

1. In its prefatory opening there is a pact formed between with those of us who read *Caged Bird* for its blues blackness. Angelou and her readers agree to share in her autobiographical enterprise because any dramatization of a blues reality must be inviting and energizing.

2. Movement as motif in *Caged Bird* has usually been attributed to the slave narrative's influence. And, yes, the slave narrative does offer *Caged Bird* a theme of movement, of "enslavement from which the black self must escape" (Bloom 5); but, here in the quoted lines patterned in blues form, the movement motif, as influenced by the blues forms, signals an autobiographical act whereby Angelou is granted an intersubjectivity, which is at once transient and shared.

Works Cited

Angelou, Maya. *I Know Why The Caged Bird Sings*. 1970. New York: Bantam, 1997.

——. *Gather Together In My Name*. New York: Bantam, 1993.

——. *Singin' and Swingin' and Gettin' Merry Like Christmas*. New York: Bantam, 1976.

——. *The Heart of a Woman*. New York: Random House, 1981.

——. *All God's Children Need Traveling Shoes*. New York: Vintage, 1991.

——. *A Song Flung Up to Heaven*. New York: Bantam, 2003.

Baker, Jr., Houston A. *Blues, Ideology, and Afro-American Literature. A Vernacular Theory*. Chicago: University of Chicago Press, 1984.

Baraka, Amiri. (LeRoi Jones). *Blues People: Negro Music in White America*. New York: Perennial, 1963.

Bloom, Harold, ed. *Maya Angelou*. Philadelphia: Chelsea House, 1999.

Braxton, Joanne M., ed. *Maya Angelou's I Know Why The Caged Bird Sings: A Casebook*. New York: Oxford University Press, 1999.

Brooks, Tilford. "The Blues." *America's Black Musical Heritage*. Englewood Cliffs, NJ: Prentice-Hall, 1984. 51–60.

Ellison, Ralph. "Richard Wright's Blues." *Shadow And Act*. New York: Vintage, 1972. 77–94.

Megna-Wallace, Joanne. *Understanding I Know Why The Caged Bird Sings: A Student Casebook to Issues, Sources, and Historical Documents*. Westport, CT: Greenwood, 1998.

REMUS BEJAN

Nigrescence: Mapping the Journey in Maya Angelou's I Know Why the Caged Bird Sings

The history of the American Negro is the history of this strife—this longing to attain self-conscious manhood, to merge his double self into a better and truer self. In this merging, he wishes neither of the older selves to be lost. (Du Bois, *The Soul of Black Folk*)

Of the many categories that mark autobiographical identity, race has remained an ever-present lens through which the world is viewed, and has continued to be a primary force that determines the shifting nature of subject positioning. Though it has changed character several times, raceness has never been an arbitrary term. Expressions like "Black" or "African American" mirror particular human experience and mediate it in relatively consistent ways, which necessarily produce common understandings. Moreover, once constructed, such discursive systems tend to take on lives of their own, which may help to explain the persistence of "blackness" as a mechanism in American life. Nigrescence, as a speculative notion involves a "theory" without which we could not make sense of, or explain, a central feature of American society.

The specific positionality and perspective of African-Americans provide their self-fashioning with a characteristic and consistent mode of perceiving and behaving, largely generated by their construction of whites as alien and hostile others. Identity has always presented itself as an open problem

---

Romanian Journal of English Studies, Number 4 (2007): pp. 200–207. Copyright © 2007 Romanian Journal of English Studies.

to them, not only because "questions of identity are always questions about [negotiating] representation" or "exercises in selective memory", but because Black Americans live "in a place where the centre is always somewhere else", in other words, they are a divided selves (Hall 1995: 5). For African Americans, racial identity is bound up in both the historically specific politics of representation and experience and the effects of repression that occur upon entry into the symbolic structures of language and culture, the social and political relations of everyday life, and active involvement with the racial projects of American society. The system of racial stratification characteristic of the American society has deep roots in eighteenth century European classification schemes, in the eugenics movement and the racialized history of imperialism. Slavery exaggerated existing ideas of racial difference and the inferiority of color people, serving as a rationalization of the exploitation of Africans in America. That same racist ideology continued, in metamorphosed form, after the emancipation of slaves, guaranteeing their subordinate status for generations. This particular experience has produced in time a number of competing representations of the Nigrescence.

The most resilient is the image of *the Negro as damaged*, described by Kardiner and Ovesey (1962) as "a psychologically tormented individual, whose entire identity was dictated by white racism" (qtd. in Mama 1995: 49). Also captured by Black protest writers like Ralph Ellison, James Baldwin, and Richard Wright, the Negro as 'scarred', was meant to demonstrate the injustice and viciousness of racism. The political mediation is clearly exposed by Malcolm X in *Malcolm X Speaks* (1966):

> [The Whites] very skillfully make you and me hate our African identity, our African characteristics. You know yourself that we have been a people who hated our African characteristics. We hated our heads, we hated the shape of our nose, we wanted one of those long dog-like noses, you know; we hated the color of our skin, hated the blood of Africa that was in our veins. And in hating our features and our skin and our blood, why, we ended up hating ourselves. And we hated ourselves. (169)

Negromachy, the term that Thomas C. W. coined (in 1970) for *the Negro as self-hating*, which he describes as "being symphonized by confusion over self-worth, over-dependency on white society for self-definition, compliance, subservience and over-sensitivity to racial issues" (qtd. in Mama 1995: 58), draws on the earlier work of W. E. B. Du Bois on black alienation.

In the 1960s, against the backdrop of the intensifying struggle and suppression, when the pacifism of the Civil Rights Movement was superseded by the militancy of the Black Power Movement, a new image, i.e., of *the Negro as empowered,* emerged. Now, inquiry centered on the assertion of a black identity, as distinctively different and separate. Whiteness was rejected as corrupt and undesirable, and a philosophy that concentrated on the acquisition of power by black people was asserted. Black writers posited an alternative construction of Black "reality", under the slogan "Black is beautiful" underpinning the ideological assumptions of Western constructions of African-American subjectivity.

In literature, through the appropriation of experiences of Black life, African-American writers challenged, deconstructed and dismantled dominant Western modes of representing Black reality, while also advancing new definitions of Blackness. A problematic aspect of that the new Black discourse was its representation of (Black) women. Not only the rewriting of the racial narrative, but a significant reconceptualization of feminist discourse was needed to accommodate the new politics of race (Butler 1989: 40).

In this emancipatory struggle, autobiographical writing played an important role. Kenneth Mostern even insists that "African-American literary history begins with the self-consciously politicized autobiography" (7), because, John Paul Eakin convincingly argues, self-construction and empowerment relate to processes of narration:

> When it comes to autobiography, *narrative* and *identity* are so intimately linked each constantly and properly gravitates into the central field of the other. Thus, narrative is not merely a literary form but a mode of phenomenological and cognitive self-experience, while self—the self of autobiographical discourse—does not necessarily precede its constitution in narrative. (1999: 100)

Conflicting discourses therefore inscribe self-referential Black narratives, which are marked by violent ruptures and tensions, as black authors try to articulate their inner drive towards selfhood. However, while black male authors' life writing tends to be "totalizing", black women's representation of it, constituted itself in opposition even with this model (cf. Peter Brooke, qtd. in Butler 1989: 3). Against the divided female subjectivity, trying to resist the hegemonic impulses of race and gender, in their attempts to construct and narrate an identity, Black women writers pursue various approaches that attempt to resolve these conflicts.

Maya Angelou's *I Know Why the Caged Bird Sings* directly addresses the relations among personal experience and racial construction. Significant in her narrative is the manner in which specific textual strategies construct a Black female subject torn by allegiances to race and gender politics and engaged in acts of self-assertion and affirmation.

Her autobiography opens with a passage in which a young, discomfited child dressed in a long cut-down faded purple, taffeta gown, stands anxiously before an Easter congregation in Stamps, Arkansas, asking, "What you looking at me for?" She can't bring herself to remember the next lines. The minister's wife whispers to her the forgotten lines eventually. She mumbles them into the congregation and then stumbles out of the watching church, "a green persimmon caught between [her] legs." Unable to control the pressure of her physical response, she urinates, then laughs "from the knowledge that [she] wouldn't die from a busted head." But laughter, Sidonie Smith perceptively comments, does not silence the real pain that is this experience: her "diminished self-image", distorted and mystified by the standards of a community (Black) adjusted to white standards of physical beauty (3). In her imagination, grows an ideal (white/ned) self instead:

> I was going to look like one of the sweet little white girls who were everybody's dream of what was right with the world . . . Wouldn't they be surprised when one day I woke out of my black ugly dream, and my real hair, which was long and blond, would take the place of the kinky mass that Momma wouldn't let me straighten? My light-blue eyes were going to hypnotize them, after all the things they said about "my daddy must of been a Chinaman" (I thought they meant made out of china, like a cup) because my eyes were so small and squinty. Then they would understand why I had never picked up a Southern accent, or spoke the common slang, and why I had to be forced to eat pigs' tails and snouts. Because I was really white and because a cruel fairy stepmother, who was understandably jealous of my beauty, had turned me into a too-big Negro girl, with nappy black hair, broad feet and a space between her teeth that would hold a number-two pencil. (2)

In this primal scene, the black child testifies to her imprisonment in her bodily and racial confinement. She *is* a "black ugly" reality, not a "whitened dream":

> Easter's early morning sun had shown the dress to be a plain ugly cut-down from a white woman's once-was-purple throwaway. It was old-lady-long too, but it didn't hide my skinny legs, which had been greased with Blue Seal Vaseline and powdered with the Arkansas red clay. The age-faded color made my skin look dirty like mud, and everyone in church was looking at my skinny legs. (2)

What makes this early experience particularly significant is that it suggests how the claim for self-worth will be clarified later in the autobiography, as well as the terms in which one's relationship with the community is going to be conceived. Angelou's choice of a narrative strategy,—a linear narrative that reminds the typical design of a *Bildungsroman*—, is the result of the writer's attempt to reconcile her fragmented, split self, with racial and gender politics.

Our assessment of young Maya depends on how we interpret her growth throughout the autobiography, and how we define the relationship between her ability to understand and her emotional capacity to respond to her own location and to her own, or the Black community's traumatic experiences. Only in the context of this expanded capacity can we understand the trajectory of the central argument that informs and organizes the narrative. As readers, we have to pay constant attention to the voice in the story, which frequently shifts, from the girl of limited experience and perspective but growing to consciousness of herself and the limits of her world, to that of the experienced, confident, and (occasionally) didactic writer who speaks with the authority of truths. The different voices of the narrator,—loving or loathing, forgiving or biting, vulnerable or confident—, suggest the complexity of coming to know oneself or the community, through sustained emotional labor.

There is an episode in the book when a few white girls come from the school to Momma's store, in Stamps. Maya begs her grandmother to go inside, and she will deal with the girls. Momma, however, insists on standing outside the door as they come; the girls mock her and are rude, and then one does a handstand, showing off the fact that she is not wearing any underwear. Maya is enraged at the girls' behavior, but Momma stands there and does not say anything; and when the girls leave, she even calls them "Miz," and says goodbye to them. Maya is confused and does not think her grandmother should have demeaned herself this way:

> . . . I burst. A firecracker July-the-Fourth burst. How could Momma call them Miz? The mean nasty things. Why couldn't she have come inside the sweet, cool store when we saw them breasting the hill? What did she prove? And then if they were dirty, mean and impudent, why did Momma have to call them Miz? (27)

Momma's situation reminds us that someone's humanity is itself measured in terms of personal ethics, and a capacity for self-determination, which the institution of slavery had denied the slave. Though totally mystified, young Maya seems to glimpse, somehow dimly and vaguely, this 'reality':

> She stood another whole song through and then opened the screen door to look down on me crying in rage. She looked until

I looked up. Her face was a brown moon that shone on me. She was beautiful. Something had happened out there, which I couldn't completely understand, but *I could see that she was happy* (27).

Maya's experience does not bring forth self-evident meanings, for they are in part mediated by social narratives. She cannot really claim herself morally until she has reconstructed her collective identity. This involves her making discoveries about what the Black community stands for, what its continuity consists in, that cultural meanings are in fact materially embodied and fought for. Maya's initial rage at her people's complacency with their powerlessness and their shoring up with subdued hominess in fundamental faith, subsides in time, and makes room for a more congenial understanding. What she discovers intuitively or, better, feels, is that these too are a sign of her people's resilience and resistance. Stuart Hall aptly reminds us that

"the symbolic language for describing what suffering was like, it was a metaphor for where they were, as the metaphors of Moses and the metaphors of the train to the North, and the metaphors of freedom, and the metaphors of passing across to the promised land, have always been metaphors, a language with a double register, a literal and a symbolic register" (Hall 1995: 13).

This reconciliation with her own people and with herself ultimately, is as much an intellectual growth as it is an emotional acknowledgment of her indebtedness to Momma, to her family, and to the Black community. Maya is forced to continuously redefine the contours of "her world". Such experiences temporarily dislodge her from her old world-view, making her vulnerable to new interpretations of her own identity and condition. The girl comes to self-knowledge by discovering or understanding features of the social and cultural arrangements of her world that define her sense of self, the choices she is taught to have, the range of personal capacities she is expected to exploit and exercise.

The self-inquiry and self-knowing in autobiography is always relational, as Paul John Eakin (1999: 43–98) argues. Maya's story is bound up with that of many others, suggesting that the boundaries of an "I" are often shifting and flexible. Momma is one of those "significant others" (Smith 2001: 66) whose stories are deeply implicated in the narrator's, and through whom the narrator understands her own self-formation. Then, there is the delicate Mrs. Flowers, through whose intervention young Maya gradually develops a sense of self-worth and respectability after a long period of silence generated by tragic personal events. One gesture, however, is very much an expression of her growing acceptance of her own self-worth. For a short time Maya works in the house of Mrs. Viola Cullinan, who assaults her ego by calling her Mary rather than Maya. Against such a devastating sign of disrespect for her humanity, Maya rebels by deliberately breaking Mrs. Cullinan's most cherished dish. At this particular moment, the girl assumes the consciousness of rebellion as a stance necessary for preserving her individuality and affirming her self-esteem. Freed from the whites' values and stereotypes, Maya is then ready to confront their system. The Mexican adventure and the junkyard of abandoned cars where she finds herself in a community of homeless, runaway children, signal the resolution of conflicts between the old and the new world-views characterized by self-confidence, psychological openness, pluralistic and non-racist perspectives:

> After hunting down unbroken bottles and selling them with a white girl from Missouri, a Mexican girl from Los Angeles and a Black girl from Oklahoma, I was never again to sense myself so solidly outside the pale of the human race (247).

Needless to say, the remembering that is essential to Angelou's autobiography is never easy, nor is the moral growth that is tied with it irreversible. While making salient certain characteristics of existing racial models of identity, other qualities or experiences seem to have been excluded. Distinctly African ways hardly affect her portrayal of character, either individually and collectively. In *I Know Why the Caged Bird Sings* Angelou describes Momma's reluctance to be questioned or to tell all she knows as her "African bush secretiveness and suspiciousness" which has been only "compounded by slavery and confirmed by centuries of promises made and promises broken" (164). She relates the habits of address, calling neighbors "Uncle," "Sister," "Cousin" to a heritage of tribal belonging. In the economy of the book these however do not count too much.

The same collective experience seems responsible for the Black people's 'blindness' to another drama of marginality, very similar to their own—the forced relocation of Japanese from San Francisco in wartime, which Angelou explains as follows:

> The Black newcomer had been recruited on the desiccated farm lands of Georgia and Mississippi by war-plant labor scouts. The chance to live in two- or three-story apartment buildings (which became instant slums), and to earn two- and even three-figured weekly checks, was blinding. For the first time he could think of himself as a Boss, a Spender. He was able to pay other people to work for him, i.e. the dry cleaners, taxi drivers, waitresses, etc. The shipyards and ammunition plants brought to booming life by the

war let him know that he was needed and even appreciated. A completely alien, yet very pleasant position for him to experience. Who could expect this man to share his new and dizzying importance with concern for a race that he had never known to exist?

Another reason for his indifference to the Japanese removal was more subtle but was more profoundly felt. The Japanese were not white folks. Their eyes, language and customs belied the white skin and proved to their dark successors that since they didn't have to be feared, neither did they have to be considered. All this was decided unconsciously. (178–179)

In *I Know Why the Caged Bird Sings*, young Maya relates to a number of female characters that are particularly powerful: Momma, Vivian Baxter, or Grandmother Baxter. Yet, in portraying these models of female Black identity, the autobiographer remarks that she knew few expressions of tenderness. Momma was embarrassed to discuss any emotions not associated with her religious faith; the mother imparted power but not tenderness: "To describe my mother would be to write about a hurricane in its perfect power" (49). Critics (Gilbert 1998: 89) have also noted that absence of significant male figures in Angelou's autobiography.

From the conflicts of black and white worlds, Maya finally finds the strengths that lead her beyond them. Her 'story' thus comes to a sense of an ending: the Black American girl, now a sixteen-year old mother, frees herself from the natural and social bars imprisoning her in the cage of her own diminished self-image by assuming control of her life and fully accepting her Black legacy. In addition, *I Know Why the Caged Bird Sings* seems to demonstrate that the very act of writing can hold in place a self (Black) that is otherwise existentially marked by an inner split.

WORKS CITED

Angelou, Maya. 1971. *I Know Why the Caged Bird Sings*. New York, Toronto, London, Sydney, Auckland: Bantam Books.

Butler-Evans, E. 1989. *Race, Gender, and Desire: Narrative Strategies in the Fiction of Toni Cade Bambara, Toni Morrison, and Alice Walker*. Philadelphia: Temple University Press.

Du Bois, W. E. B. [1903] 1996. "The Soul of Black Folk". *The Oxford W. E. B. Du Bois Reader*. Eric J. Sundquist, editor. New York: Oxford University Press. 97–240.

Eakin, P. J. *How Our Lives Become Stories: Making Selves*. Ithaca and London: Cornell University Press, 1999.

Gilbert, Susan. 1998. "Maya Angelou's *I Know Why the Caged Bird Sings*: Paths to Escape". *Modern Critical Interpretations: Maya Angelou's I Know Why the Caged Bird Sings*. Edited and with an introduction by Harold Bloom. Philadelphia: Chelsea House Publishers, 1998. 81–92.

Hall, S. 1995. "Negotiating Caribbean Identities" in the *New Left Review*. Volume: a. Issue: 209. 3–14.

Malcolm X. 1966. *Malcolm X Speaks*. New York: Grove Press.

Mama, Amina. 1995. *Beyond the Masks: Race, Gender and Subjectivity*. London and New York: Routledge.

Mostem K. 2004. *Autobiography and Black Identity Politics Racialization in Twentieth-Century America*. Cambridge, UK: Cambridge University Press.

Smith, Sidonie. 1998. "The Song of the Caged Bird: Maya Angelou's Quest after Self-Acceptance". Maya Angelou. *I Know Why the Caged Birds Sings. Modern Critical Interpretations*. Harold Bloom, ed. Philadelphia: Chelsea House. 3–14.

Chronology

1928	Maya Angelou is born Marguerite Johnson on April 1 in St. Louis, Missouri, the daughter of Bailey and Vivian Baxter Johnson.
1931	Her parents divorce; Angelou and her four-year-old brother are sent to live with their maternal grandmother, Annie Henderson, in Stamps, Arkansas.
1936	During a visit to her mother in St. Louis, Angelou is raped by her mother's boyfriend. The man is beaten to death by her uncles and Angelou does not speak for almost five years. She returns to Stamps and discovers literature under the tutelage of an educated neighbor, Mrs. Flowers.
1940	Graduates from the eighth grade at the top of her class. Her mother, now a professional gambler, takes the children to live in San Francisco.
1940–1944	Attends George Washington High School in San Francisco and takes dance and drama lessons at the California Labor School.
1945	While still in high school, becomes the first black woman streetcar conductor in San Francisco; graduates from Mission High School at age 16; one month later, gives birth to a son.
1946	Works as a cook for $75 per week at the Creole Cafe; with $200 she moves to San Diego.

1947	After becoming involved in prostitution as a madam, Angelou returns to Stamps. She upbraids a rude white store clerk; her grandmother, fearing reprisals from the Ku Klux Klan, sends her back to San Francisco.
1948	Joins a nightclub dance act; then works as a restaurant cook; spends several days as a prostitute, until her brother threatens violence if she continues.
1950	Marries Tosh Angelos; they divorce three years later.
1953	Angelou resumes her career as a dancer at the Purple Onion.
1954–1955	Joins a twenty-two-nation tour of *Porgy and Bess,* sponsored by the U.S. Department of State.
1955	Returns to care for her young son, Guy; becomes instructor of Modern Dance at the Rome Opera House and at Hambina Theatre, Tel Aviv.
1957	Appears in a play, *Calypso Heatwave.* Makes a commitment to become a writer and black civil rights activist; moves to Brooklyn and participates in the Harlem Writers' Guild, a group that included John Henrik Clarke, Paule Marshall, James Baldwin, and social activist author John Killens.
1959–1960	Succeeds Bayard Rustin as northern coordinator of Martin Luther King Jr.'s, Southern Christian Leadership Conference.
1960	Appears in the Off-Broadway production of *The Blacks;* produces and performs Off-Broadway in *Cabaret for Freedom,* written with Godfrey Cambridge.
1961–1962	Associate editor of the *Arab Observer,* an English-language newspaper in Cairo, Egypt.
1963–1966	Assistant administrator of the School of Music and Drama at the University of Ghana's Institute of African Studies at Legon-Accra, Ghana. Feature editor of the *African Review;* contributor to the Ghanian Broadcasting Company.
1964	Appears in *Mother Courage* at the University of Ghana.
1966	Appears in *Medea* and *The Least of These* in Hollywood; lecturer at the University of California, Los Angeles.

1970	Writer in residence at the University of Kansas; receives Yale University fellowship; *I Know Why the Caged Bird Sings* is published and nominated for a National Book Award.
1971	A volume of poetry, *Just Give Me a Cool Drink of Water 'Fore I Diiie* is published and nominated for a Pulitzer Prize.
1972	Television narrator, interviewer, and host for African-American specials and theater series.
1973	Receives a Tony Award nomination for her Broadway debut in *Look Away*. Marries Paul Du Feu in December; they divorce in 1981.
1974	*Gather Together in My Name* is published; directs the film *All Day Long;* appears in the adapted Sophocles play *Ajax* at the Mark Taper Forum; named distinguished visiting professor at Wake Forest University, Wichita State University, and California State University.
1975	A volume of poetry, *Oh Pray My Wings Are Gonna Fit Me Well*, is published; appointed by President Gerald R. Ford to the American Revolution Bicentennial Council; member of the National Commission on the Observance of International Women's Year; becomes member of the board of trustees of the American Film Institute; appointed Rockefeller Foundation Scholar in Italy; receives honorary degrees from Smith College and Mills College.
1976	*Singin' and Swingin' and Gettin' Merry Like Christmas* is published; directs her play, *And I Still Rise;* named Woman of the Year in Communications; receives honorary degree from Lawrence University.
1977	Appears in the television film *Roots*, and receives a Tony Award nomination for best supporting actress.
1978	*And Still I Rise* is published.
1981	*The Heart of a Woman* is published. Angelou receives a lifetime appointment as Reynolds Professor of American Studies, Wake Forest University.
1983	*Shaker, Why Don't You Sing?*, a volume of poetry, is published. Angelou is named one of the Top 100 Most Influential Women by the *Ladies' Home Journal;* receives the Matrix Award.

1986   *All God's Children Need Travelin' Shoes; Mrs. Flowers: A Moment of Friendship; Poems: Maya Angelou* are published.

1987   *Now Sheba Sings the Song* is published; receives the North Carolina Award in Literature.

1988   Directs Errol John's *Moon on a Rainbow Shawl* in London.

1990   A volume of poetry, *I Shall Not Be Moved* is published.

1993   The inaugural poem *On the Pulse of Morning; Soul Looks Back in Wonder,* poems and *Wouldn't Take Nothing for My Journey Now* are published. Angelou contributes poetry to the film *Poetic Justice.*

1994   *My Painted House, My Friendly Chicken, and Me* and *Phenomenal Women: Four Poems Celebrating Women* are published.

1995   *A Brave and Startling Truth* is published.

1996   *Kofi and His Magic,* a children's story, is published.

1999   Angelou is presented Lifetime Achievement Award for Literature and is named one of the 100 best writers of the twentieth century by *Writer's Digest.*

2000   A new edition of *Phenomenal Woman: Four Poems Celebrating Women,* edited by Linda Sunshine and with paintings by Paul Gaugin is published, and Angelou is presented the National Medal of Arts.

2002   *A Song Flung up to Heaven,* the final volume of Angelou's biography, is published and she wins a Grammy Award for her recording of it.

2004   *I Know Why the Caged Bird Sings: The Collected Autobiographies of Maya Angelou* is published.

2005   *Amazing Peace* is published.

2006   Angelou's *Amazing Peace* wins Quill Award for poetry.

Contributors

HAROLD BLOOM is Sterling Professor of the Humanities at Yale University. He is the author of 30 books, including *Shelley's Mythmaking* (1959), *The Visionary Company* (1961), *Blake's Apocalypse* (1963), *Yeats* (1970), *A Map of Misreading* (1975), *Kabbalah and Criticism* (1975), *Agon: Toward a Theory of Revisionism* (1982), *The American Religion* (1992), *The Western Canon* (1994), and *Omens of Millennium: The Gnosis of Angels, Dreams, and Resurrection* (1996). *The Anxiety of Influence* (1973) sets forth Professor Bloom's provocative theory of the literary relationships between the great writers and their predecessors. His most recent books include *Shakespeare: The Invention of the Human* (1998), a 1998 National Book Award finalist; *How to Read and Why* (2000); *Genius: A Mosaic of One Hundred Exemplary Creative Minds* (2002); *Hamlet: Poem Unlimited* (2003); *Where Shall Wisdom Be Found?* (2004); and *Jesus and Yahweh: The Names Divine* (2005). In 1999, Professor Bloom received the prestigious American Academy of Arts and Letters Gold Medal for Criticism. He has also received the International Prize of Catalonia, the Alfonso Reyes Prize of Mexico, and the Hans Christian Andersen Bicentennial Prize of Denmark.

JAMES ROBERT SAUNDERS is professor of English at Purdue University. He is the author of *The Wayward Preacher in the Literature of African American Women* (1995) and *Urban Renewal and the End of Black Culture in Charlottesville, Virginia,* with Renae Nadine Shackelford (1998).

PIERRE A. WALKER is professor of English at Salem State College in Massachusetts. He edited *Henry James on Culture: Collected Essays on Politics and the American Social Scene* (1999) and *The Complete Letters of Henry James, 1855–1872,* with Greg W. Zacharias (2006). Prof Walker was president of the Henry James Society in 2006.

MARION M. TANGUM is an associate professor of English and the associate vice president for research and sponsored programs at Southwest Texas State University in San Marcos, Texas. She teaches and conducts research on black American women writers and Southern writers from a rhetorical perspective.

SIPHOKAZI KOYANA is manager of the Thuthuka Programme at the National Research Foundation in Pretoria, South Africa and co-director of *MiniMag,* South Africa's leading children's magazine. She has published articles on Sindiwe Magona, Maya Angelou, Elana Bregin, and Zakes Mda.

CLARA JUNCKER is associate professor of American literature at the University of Southern Denmark, where she directed the Center for American Studies from 1996 to 1999. Her books include *Through Random Doors We Wandered: Women Writing the South* (2002) and *Transnational America: Contours of Modern U.S. Culture* (2004)

MARY JANE LUPTON is professor emeritus at Morgan State University. Her books include *Maya Angelou: A Critical Companion* (1998) *James Welch: A Critical Companion* (2004), and *Lucille Clifton: Her Life and Letters* (2006).

ELEANOR W. TRAYLOR, graduate professor of English and chair of the department of English in the college of arts and sciences at Howard University.

SUZETTE A. HENKE is Thruston B. Morton Sr. Professor of English at the University of Louisville. Her books include *Women in Joyce* (1982), *James Joyce and the Politics of Desire* (1990), and *Shattered Subjects: Trauma and Testimony in Women's Life-Writing* (1998).

YASMIN Y. DeGOUT is associate professor of English at Howard University. She has published on Frederick Douglass and Harriet Jacobs, James Baldwin, and Ed Bullins in addition to Maya Angelou.

CHERRON A. BARNWELL is a member of the English department at the College of New Rochelle, School of New Resources (Brooklyn Campus). She has written on African American women activists and writers.

REMUS BEJAN is a professor and pro-dean at the University of Humanities and Theology in Bucharest, specializing in Romanian and English Language and Literature. His books include *Confession as Literature* (1998) and *Britain: Past and Present* (2000).

Bibliography

Als, Hilton. "Songbird: Maya Angelou Takes Another Look at Herself," *New Yorker*, 78:22 (2002 August 5), 72–76.

Arensberg, Liliane K. "Death as Metaphor of Self in *I Know Why the Caged Bird Sings*," *CLA Journal*, 20:2 (December 1976): 273–291.

Babb, Valerie. "Maya Angelou," *Langston Hughes Review*, 19 (Spring 2005): 1–81.

Benson, Carol. "Out of the Cage and Still Singing," *Writer's Digest* (January 1975): 18–20.

Bertolino, James. "Maya Angelou Is Three Writers: *I Know Why the Caged Bird Sings*," *Censored Books: Critical Viewpoints*. Ed. Nicholas J. Karolides, Lee Burress, and John M. Kean. Metuchen, NJ: The Scarecrow Press, 1993. pp. 299–305.

Bloom, Lynn Z. "Maya Angelou," *Dictionary of Literary Biography*, 38. Detroit: Gale, 1985. pp. 3–12.

Butterfield, Stephen. *Black Autobiography in America*. Amherst: University of Massachusetts Press, 1974.

Chrisman, Robert. "*The Black Scholar* Interviews Maya Angelou," *Black Scholar* (January–February 1977): 44–52.

Cole-Leonard, Natasha. "Maya Angelou's *Hallelujah! The Welcome Table, A Lifetime of Memories with Recipes* as Evocative Text, or, 'Ain't' Jemima's Recipes," *Langston Hughes Review*, 19 (Spring 2005): 66–69.

Cordell, Shirley J. "The Black Woman: A Focus on 'Strength of Character' in *I Know Why the Caged Bird Sings*," *Virginia English Bulletin*, 36:2 (Winter 1986): 36–39.

Demetrakopoulos, Stephanie A. "The Metaphysics of Matrilinearism in Women's Autobiography: Studies of Mead's *Blackberry Winter,* Hellman's *Pentimento,* Angelou's *I Know Why the Caged Bird Sings,* and Kingston's *The Woman Warrior,*" in *Women's Autobiography: Essays in Criticism.* Ed. Estelle Jelinek. Bloomington: Indiana University Press, 1980. pp. 180–205.

Elliott, Jeffrey M., ed. *Conversations with Maya Angelou.* Jackson: University Press of Mississippi, 1989.

Estes-Hicks, Onita. "The Way We Were: Precious Memories of the Black Segregated South," *African American Review,* 27:1 (Spring 1993): 9–18.

Foster, Frances. "Parents and Children in Autobiography by Southern Afro-American Writers," *Home Ground: Southern Autobiography.* Columbia: University of Missouri Press, 1992. pp. 98–109.

Froula, Christine. "The Daughter's Seduction: Sexual Violence and Literary History," *Signs,* 11:4 (Summer 1986): 621–644.

Fulghum, Robert. "Home Truths and Homilies," *Washington Post Book World* (September 19, 1993): 4.

Gabbin, Joanne V. "Maya Angelou: The People's Poet Laureate: An Introduction," *Langston Hughes Review,* 19 (Spring 2005): 3–7.

Georgoudaki, Ekaterini, *Race, Gender, and Class Perspectives in the Works of Maya Angelou, Gwendolyn Brooks, Rita Dove, Nikki Giovanni, and Audre Lorde.* Thessaloniki: Aristotle University of Thessaloniki, 1991.

Gilbert, Susan. "Maya Angelou's *I Know Why the Caged Bird Sings:* Paths to Escape," *Mount Olive Review,* 1:1 (Spring 1987): 39–50.

Goodman, G., Jr. "Maya Angelou's Lonely Black Chick Outlook," *The New York Times* (March 24, 1972): 28.

Gottlieb, Annie. "Growing Up and the Serious Business of Survival," *New York Times Book Review* (June 16, 1974): 16, 20.

Gruesser, John C. "Afro-American Travel Literature and Africanist Discourse," *Black American Literature Forum,* 24:1 (Spring 1990): 5–20.

Hord, Fred Lee. "Someplace to Be a Black Girl," *Reconstructing Memory: Black Literary Criticism.* Chicago: Third World Press, 1991. pp. 75–85.

Inge, Tonette Bond, ed. *Southern Women Writers: The New Generation.* Tuscaloosa: University of Alabama Press, 1990.

Kelly, Ernece B. Review of *I Know Why the Caged Bird Sings, Harvard Educational Review,* 40:4 (November 1970): 681–682.

Kent, George E. "Maya Angelou's *I Know Why the Caged Bird Sings* and Black Autobiographical Tradition," *Kansas Quarterly,* 7 (1975): 75–78. Reprinted in *African American Autobiography: A Collection of Critical Essays.* Ed. William L. Andrews. Englewood Cliffs, NJ: Prentice-Hall, 1993. pp. 162–170.

Kinnamon, Keneth. "Call and Response: Intertextuality in Two Autobiographical Works by Richard Wright and Maya Angelou," *Studies in Black American*

Literature, Vol. II: Belief vs. Theory in Black American Literary Criticism. Ed. Joe Weixlmann and Chester J. Fontenot. Greenwood, FL: Penkevill Publishing Co., 1986. pp. 121–134.

MacKethan, Lucinda H. "Mother Wit: Humor in Afro-American Women's Autobiography," *Studies in American Humor,* 4:1–2 (Spring 1985): 51–61.

Maierhofer, Roberta. "'Hold! Stop! Don't Pity Me': Age, Gender, and Ethnicity in American Studies," *Arbeiten aus Anglistik und Amerikanistik,* 25:1 (2000): 107–118.

Manora, Yolanda M. "'What You Looking at Me For? I Didn't Come to Stay': Displacement, Disruption, and Black Female Subjectivity in Maya Angelou's *I Know Why the Caged Bird Sings,*" *Women's Studies: An Interdisciplinary Journal,* 34:5 (2005 July–August): 359–375.

McMurry, Myra K. "Role-Playing as Art in Maya Angelou's *Caged Bird,*" *South Atlantic Bulletin,* 41:2 (May 1976): 106–111.

McPherson, Dolly. "Defining the Self through Place and Culture: Maya Angelou's *I Know Why the Caged Bird Sings,*" *MAWA Review,* 5:1 (June 1990): 12–14.

———. *Order Out of Chaos: The Autobiographical Works of Maya Angelou.* New York: Peter Lang, 1990.

Megna-Wallace, Joanne. "Simone de Beauvoir and Maya Angelou: Birds of a Feather," *Simone de Beauvoir Studies,* 6 (1986): 49–55.

Moore, Opal. "Learning to Live: When the Caged Bird Breaks From the Cage," *Censored Books: Critical Viewpoints.* Ed. Nicholas J. Karolides, Lee Burress, and John M. Kean. Metuchen, NJ: The Scarecrow Press, 1993. pp. 306–316.

Nero, Clarence. "A Discursive Trifecta: Community, Education, and Language in *I Know Why the Caged Bird Sings,*" *Langston Hughes Review,* 19 (Spring 2005): 61–65.

Phillips, Frank Lamont. Review of *Gather Together In My Name, Black World,* 24:9 (July 1975): 52, 61.

Premo, Cassie. "When the Difference Becomes Too Great: Images of the Self and Survival in a Postmodern World," *Genre,* 16 (1995): 183–191.

Redmond, Eugene B. "Boldness of Language and Breadth: An Interview with Maya Angelou," *Black American Literature Forum,* 22:2 (Summer 1988): 156–157.

Sample, Maxine. "Gender, Identity, and the Liminal Self: The Emerging Woman in Buchi Emecheta's *The Bride Price* and Maya Angelou's *I Know Why the Caged Bird Sings,*" in *North-South Linkages and Connections in Continental and Diaspora African Literatures,* edited by Edris Makward, Mark Lilleleht, and Ahmed Saber. (Trenton, New Jersey: Africa World, 2005): pp. 213–225.

Saunders, James Robert. "Breaking Out of the Cage: The Autobiographical Writings of Maya Angelou," *The Hollins Critic,* 28:4 (October 1991): 1–11.

Schramm, Katharina. "Imagined Pasts-Present Confrontations: Literary and Ethnographic Explorations into Explorations into Pan-African Identity

Politics," in *Africa, Europe, and (Post)Colonialism: Racism, Migration and Disapora in African Literatures,* edited by Susan Arndt and, Marek Spitczok von Brisinski (Bayreuth, Germany: Bayreuth University, 2006): pp. 243–256.

Tate, Claudia, ed. *Black Women Writers at Work.* New York: Continuum, 1983. pp. 1–11.

Tawake, Sandra Kiser. "Multi-Ethnic Literature in the Classroom: Whose Standards?" *World Englishes: Journal of English as an International and Intranational Language,* 10:3 (Winter 1991): 335–340.

Tinnie, Wallis. "Maya Angelou," in *The History of Southern Women's Literature,* edited by Carolyn Perry, Mary Louise Weaks, and Doris Betts (Baton Rouge: Louisiana State University Press, 2002): pp. 517–524.

Vermillion, Mary. "Reembodying the Self: Representations of Rape in *Incidents in the Life of a Slave Girl* and *I Know Why the Caged Bird Sings,*" *Biography,* 15:3 (Summer 1992): 243–260.

Wall, Cheryl. "Maya Angelou," *Women Writer's Talking.* Ed. Janet Todd. New York: Holmes & Meier, 1983: pp. 59–67.

Weller, Sheila. "Work in Progress/Maya Angelou," *Intellectual Digest* (June 1973).

Acknowledgments

James Robert Saunders. "Breaking Out of the Cage: The Autobiographical Writings of Maya Angelou." *The Hollins Critic*, Volume 28, Number 4 (October 1991): pp. 1–11. Copyright © 1991 The Hollins Critic. Reprinted by permission of the publisher.

Pierre A. Walker. "Racial Protest, Identity, Words, and Form in Maya Angelou's *I Know Why the Caged Bird Sings*." *College Literature*, Volume 22, Number 3 (October 1995): pp. 91–108. Copyright © 1995 *College Literature*, Westchester University. Reprinted by permission of the publisher.

Clara Juncker & Edward Sanford. "Only Necessary Baggage: Maya Angelou's Life Journeys." *Xavier Review*, Volume 16, Number 2 (1996): pp. 12–23. Copyright © 1996 Clara Juncker. Reprinted by permission of the author.

Marion M. Tangum & Marjorie Smelstor. "Hurston's and Angelou's Visual Art: The Distancing Vision and the Beckoning Gaze." *Southern Literary Journal*, Volume 31, Number 1 (Fall 1998): pp. 80–97. Copyright © University of North Carolina Press. Reprinted by permission of the publisher.

Siphokazi Koyana. "The Heart of the Matter: Motherhood and Marriage in the Autobiographies of Maya Angelou." *The Black Scholar*, Volume 32, Number 2 (Summer 2002): pp. 35–44. Copyright © 2002 *The Black Scholar*. Reprinted by permission of the publisher.

Mary Jane Lupton. "'Spinning in a Whirlwind': Sexuality in Maya Angelou's Sixth Autobiography," *MAWA Review*, Volume 18, Numbers 1–2 (June–December 2003): pp. 1–6. Copyright © 2003 Mary Jane Lupton. Reprinted by permission of the author.

Eleanor W. Traylor. "Maya Angelou Writing Life, Inventing Literary Genre," *Langston Hughes Review*, Volume 19 (Spring 2005): pp. 8–21. Copyright © 2005 Eleanor W. Traylor. Reprinted by permission of the author.

Suzette A. Henke. "Maya Angelou's *Caged Bird* as Trauma Narrative," *Langston Hughes Review*, Volume 19 (Spring 2005), pp. 22–36. Copyright © 2005 Suzette A. Henke. Reprinted by permission of the author.

Yasmin Y. DeGout. "The Poetry of Maya Angelou: Liberation Ideology and Technique," *Langston Hughes Review*, Volume 19 (Spring 2005): pp. 36–47. Copyright © 2005 *The Langston Hughes Review*. Reprinted by permission of the publisher.

Cherron A. Barnwell. "Singin' de Blues: Writing Black Female Survival in *I Know Why the Caged Bird Sings*," *Langston Hughes Review*, Volume 19 (Spring 2005): pp. 48–60. Copyright © 2005 *The Langston Hughes Review*. Reprinted by permission of the publisher.

Remus Bejan. "Nigrescence: Mapping the Journey in Maya Angelou's *I Know Why the Caged Bird Sings*," *Romanian Journal of English Studies*, Volume 4 (2007), pp. 200–207.

Index